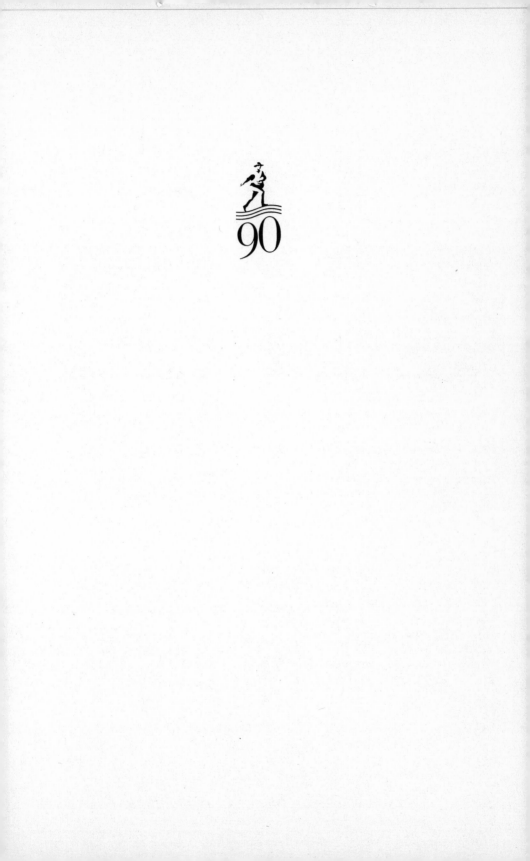

LET THE

TORNADO

COME

A MEMOIR

RITA ZOEY CHIN

SIMON & SCHUSTER
New York   London   Toronto   Sydney   New Delhi

90

Simon & Schuster
1230 Avenue of the Americas
New York, NY 10020

First Simon & Schuster hardcover edition June 2014

SIMON & SCHUSTER and colophon are registered trademarks of Simon & Schuster, Inc.

For information about special discounts for bulk purchases, please contact Simon & Schuster Special Sales at 1-866-506-1949 or business@simonandschuster.com.

The Simon & Schuster Speakers Bureau can bring authors to your live event. For more information or to book an event, contact the Simon & Schuster Speakers Bureau at 1-866-248-3049 or visit our website at www.simonspeakers.com.

Interior design by Ruth Lee-Mui
Jacket design by Rex Bonomelli
Jacket photograph © Alessandro Passerini/PhotoVogue/Art+Commerce; horse © Ken Gillespie photography/Alamy

Manufactured in the United States of America

10 9 8 7 6 5 4 3 2 1

Library of Congress Cataloging-in-Publication Data

Chin, Rita Zoey, author.
    Let the tornado come : a memoir / Rita Zoey Chin. — First Simon & Schuster hardcover edition.
        pages   cm
    1. Chin, Rita Zoey—Mental health.   2. Panic attacks—Patients—United States—Biography.   3. Authors, American—Biography.   4. Human-animal relationships.   5. Horses—Behavior.   I. Title.
    RC535.C45   2014
    616.85'2230092—dc23
    [B]   2013050803

ISBN 978-1-4767-3486-6
ISBN 978-1-4767-3488-0 (ebook)

for Larry

In a murderous time
   the heart breaks and breaks
      and lives by breaking.
It is necessary to go
   through dark and deeper dark
      and not to turn.
I am looking for the trail.

                       —Stanley Kunitz

Let the morning time
drop all its petals on me.
Life I love you
all is groovy.

                       —Simon & Garfunkel

LET THE

TORNADO

COME

In the dark, especially in the dark, against the pillow, I hear them. I hear them in the quiet and in the ruckus. I hear them when I am three and just beginning to remember, when I am eight and my mother lies on her back and stares at the ceiling and will not look at me. I hear them in steel and dirt and sidewalks, in distances and conversations. I hear them when the sky is the color of oil. I hear them in the blank sun and in the rushing of bathwater. When I run, I hear them loudest.

On the day of my birth, I'm sure they were there—thunderous, rhythmic, coming and coming: hoofbeats.

Icicles drip from the windows encircling the dressage arena, and as they melt, they grow longer. They are dazzling, glistening in the sun, but right now each one is a threat. The light would be dazzling, too—the brazen shaft of sun angling into the arena, catching the dust as if it were fog—but as we pass the sunray, Claret curves his body away from it. His horse brain is naturally wired to flee from any perceived danger, but for this horse, who has had real reasons to be afraid, anything unexpected is dangerous. He has no way of understanding why this shaft of light has suddenly appeared—why the sun's journey on the ecliptic has just aligned itself with this particular window—but I know he trusts me, so I speak to him with the insides of my calves and keep our rhythm, steady, forward, one-two, one-two, one-two. I keep circling back to the light, each time getting closer. "You're okay," I tell him, leaning forward to pat his neck. I want him to feel my determination, solid as a ball of silver. And I want him to feel that my confidence is, in part, born of him, of his strength, of the many days he carried me through my own fears, those days when I wasn't sure if he'd throw me off his back, those days when he had every reason to but didn't. Eventually, we ride right through the light, our little triumph. And then, as if by conquering it, we have forced it to surrender, and like the melting ice, it disappears.

We are alone. The only sounds in the arena are our sounds: Claret's feet hitting the ground, his breathing, my breathing, the slip of my breeches against the saddle. Outside the arena are the discordant sounds of the rest of the world: trucks rumbling by on the main road, water dripping, the barn workers speaking loudly as they drive the tractor around. I slip my outside leg back and ask Claret to canter. He steps up into the stride, and I ride the swing of him, powerful and deep. These are the moments when I feel free.

Claret and I are in constant conversation. With each gentle tap or shift of pressure, he knows what I'm asking of him. Usually he answers yes, and occasionally he answers no, but most of the time I go with him, and he goes with me. It is a kind of dance, and while we're not always graceful, we have moments when we move together as one.

I have come to know Claret's body better than I've known most bodies. I know when his back is supple or his hind legs are stiff, when he has energy or when he wants to stand still and gaze ahead dreamily. And I know when he's distracted, when he has an itch, and—sometimes before he does—when he's about to trip. I know that today he is more easily spooked than other days. I feel it under his skin, a frequency, like lightning close by. But I don't focus on his fear because it's amorphous and contagious, and because I've learned that while every flash of lightning doesn't mean a storm, I'm ready for it when it does. So for now, I focus on the three beats of the canter, on this cool air rushing over us as we go faster down the long side of the arena.

Suddenly, one of the icicles crashes down, and Claret panics. He spins, bucks, spins, bucks. Though his erratic movements are swift, time slows. I'm acutely aware of the inexorable force of him, the adrenaline zinging through his fourteen-hundred-pound body. I know his impulse to flee as well as I know anything, because for years the same impulse ruled me. There was a time when my pounding heart would have matched his, when fear would have been the only answer for us both, but right now, as the irregular beats of Claret's hooves mark an eerie uncertainty about where the next steps will land, I'm surprised to find that what would once have been fear is now a strange curiosity: will I fall? But it's a distant curiosity because mostly I'm not thinking; mostly I'm a body following a body, and there's a freedom—and even a kind of excitement—in that. As Claret jumps forward and yanks on the reins, I feel each degree of movement as if it were a snapshot, frame by frame. And between each frame and the next lives the smallest, almost imperceptible, glimmer of calm. "Whoa," I say, softly. "Whoa."

Claret stops then, and I pat his neck. We have survived the icicle. I tell him he's a good boy, and he exhales a long breath. Then I ask him to canter again. I'm not going to worry about all the other melting icicles ready to come down. This is the only moment we've got, and everything about what we're doing demands one thing from both of us: trust.

When we pass the window where the icicle fell, I can feel the pause in Claret's body, his impulse to pull away, but with my body I assure him it's safe. I can't promise him it won't happen again, only that when it does, we'll get through it. And he listens. And we are safe. When we finish, I drape myself over his long neck and breathe into his mane, as his body softens against me.

There is no single way to tell a story. For me, Claret's story begins many times; both of us hold many stories, and sometimes it's hard to imagine there ever having been a time when Claret wasn't part of mine. We've saved each other in countless ways since he entered my life, even when it didn't feel like anyone was being saved at all. Sometimes parts of our story feel so immediate when I think of them that they trump the present moment. The story of my childhood is the same: those years of loss and wandering keep happening, as if they're rewriting themselves on the inside of my body, zapping me afresh some days while I'm busy living my new life. They say memory is like that, that to the brain there is little to distinguish a memory from the actual event. So as resounding and complete as any present moment is, one side of it is always touching, even in the gentlest of ways, the past, where there is always a story inside the story, waiting to be told.

ONE

When we arrived in Massachusetts, spring's thaw had already begun to hatch the first crocuses, small bold banners breaking through the grayed dirt. We drove slowly up the driveway as I turned off the car radio and rolled the windows down. This was a big moment, and I wanted to experience it with all my senses. Birds flittered about busily, weaving a cacophony of tweeting and cawing into the air. But a quiet hovered outside their music, enclosing it the way an ocean takes on rain.

And then we were facing it: our new home. As I stepped from the car, I still couldn't completely reconcile that this sturdy colonial, with its sweeping yard and old trees and roomy bathtub, was ours, and that I was actually going to live in it. Even more astonishing was this: I'd get to do that living with a good man and our two sweet rescue dogs, Aramis and Starlet. Here in the driveway, with the bright flowers and the birds and their attendant silence and the man I married five years ago standing just outside the car in the navy pullover fleece he often wore, was, by all appearances, a manifestation of the imaginary life I'd swiped from countless L.L. Bean Christmas catalogs as a child—the imaginary life I'd cobbled during my homeless, wandering years, staring into people's houses after dark and wishing for their soft lamplight, their mazes of rooms, and the safety of their front doors, that clear demarcation of home.

Now, two decades later, I held a key to that long-imagined front door. Larry and I smiled at each other over the roof of the car.

We'd moved from a modest house in Maryland, where my family still lived, so that Larry could take a job as neurosurgery chair and work to resurrect Boston Medical Center's failing neurosurgery department. I was going to take a break from teaching and devote myself full-time to writing, while the cows lowed on the farm across the road and our dogs frolicked in the yard and the forests all around us kept thrusting upward into the sky. It was going to be a happy life—that was the plan.

My mother liked saying, "Man plans, God laughs," usually during some major disappointment or catastrophe of mine. I didn't believe in her spiteful, cackling God, yet her words wormed their way into my psyche and left me always a little on edge, as if the minute I began to put faith in the future, something would come and scramble it. "Aha!" her God would say. "So much for your plans!"

Though I'd been putting distance between my parents and me for most of my life, and had finally marked that distance in miles, her words followed me like the wind chime outside her bedroom window, that eerie clanging I never got used to and can still hear. So the revolution of thoughts in the driveway that day was swift: *Is this really my life? Yes, this is my life. Too bad I'll lose it.*

I put the key in the lock and opened the door anyway.

One of my favorite things about our new house was the generous placement of windows. As soon as I walked in the front, I could see out the back, and wherever I looked there was a haven of trees—majestic oaks and elms and maples, and a variety of conifers—the kind of woods that seemed inhabited by sprites and other fanciful creatures. And over the course of those first days, as I unpacked boxes and made our first cups of tea and set up my writing desk and hung white fluffy towels and blasted the music and danced from room to room, occasionally stopping to squeeze Larry exuberantly, a childlike wonder persisted in me.

I trotted around outside like a seven-year-old, skipping down hills with the dogs chasing behind, plucking rocks from the woods, parking myself in the fragrant shade of a pine tree and squinting up at its fans of needles. I'd left a lot behind in Maryland—my sister and her daughter, friends I loved, my favorite sushi bar, a kick-ass Sunday morning yoga class, a rewarding teaching gig, and the familiarity that can only come with time spent living in a place—but here, even in those first hours, I felt more at home than I'd ever felt anyplace else. The opening of our front door that day signified one of the clearest thresholds, literally, of my life: a beginning, a clean slate, the long quiet afternoon into which I could finally exhale.

"You make everything beautiful," Larry said to me as I opened a window. He was standing in the middle of the room, pivoting around in his blue pullover.

"You make it easy," I told him.

Once the books were arranged on the shelves, the dishes snug in their cabinets, the rugs unrolled on the floors, I parked myself at my desk and started working. As the words slowly spread into pages, the yard outside my window kept erupting into blossom—tulips, irises, peonies, lilies, lilacs, a blazing pink dogwood, rhododendrons, hydrangeas, azaleas. Someone had once loved this place, and that love still lived.

When I took breaks from writing and watching the blooming wonderland of our garden, I explored nearby towns and discovered small countryside markets, ponds shimmering up at the trees, secondhand bookstores selling rare books, strawberry fields where people filled their own baskets, unmanned flower stands with homemade bouquets in mason jars and an envelope for the honor system of paying, and a rocky beach with swings facing the ocean. In the evenings I would lead Larry around the garden and show him what new things had popped up, and he would bend down to sniff whatever I pointed out, even the flowers that had no scent. Then I would tell him what I'd found on my travels that day.

I had always been a solo wanderer. As a kid, in many ways I hadn't had a choice. But on the moody October day of my twenty-first birthday, I chose to go hiking alone in the woods, and in the years that followed, I went to festivals and museums and restaurants as my own date, slipped into the bat-encrusted mouths of caves where no one saw me enter or exit, navigated road trips to new cities and to rickety spider-run cabins in backcountry towns. And in most of my favorite dreams—the ones that send me flying over trees or swimming in a glacial sea or visiting an unexplored planet—I'm by myself.

Even my secret road-trip fantasy, the one I'd been imagining for years, was one of solitude: I'm driving a convertible, always heading south, and the sun is always on its way down, setting freckles on my face while the wind whips my hair and Dylan plays on my radio, singing about a brass bed. I drive and drive with the self-possession of a girl who knows where she's going, even when she's lost. Also, in the fantasy, I'm wearing cowboy boots.

My fantasy used to culminate in my stopping at a roadside bar and beating a stranger at a game of pool. He'd be wearing a big-buckled belt and a cowboy hat, and he'd have deep laugh-lines around his eyes and large hands. After I'd win, he'd take me back to his humble digs and undress me on his brass bed. But over time, the fantasy revised itself, by editing him out. It turned out the thrill wasn't about the man; it was about the journey, about making it alone.

Larry and I got along well because we both flourished in the vast and solitary space of our interior lives. We never demanded time from each other, and when we did converge, we appreciated the respective otherness of our different worlds. I relished what I learned about the brain—that its covering, for example, is called dura mater, which means hard mother; or that there is a kind of seizure that makes people laugh; or that you can remove a pituitary tumor through a person's nose. And Larry enjoyed being quizzed on poetic forms and rules of punctuation, having discussions about narrative arcs and character development, listening to me wax on about the importance of imagery.

And now, on the open canvas of our new life together, yes, I wanted to make something beautiful.

W hen the ambulance arrived two months later, I was hunched over on our front step, clutching at my heart. It was summer by then, the shadows long on the lawn. The trees stood full and heavy, their leaves wet with light. I was certain I was going to die—and on such a glorious morning.

Within minutes an EMT was taking my pulse. As he leaned over me, the hulk of his shoulders blocked out the sun. He might have been a football player. His fingers were gentle at my wrist, and his touch comforted me, as if his hand could mean the difference between life and the grave. "Yeah" he announced, slowly giving my arm back, "one hundred and seventy-eight is pretty fast."

He wanted to know if I had any history of heart problems. I didn't. Had I taken any medications? I hadn't. Was I on drugs? I wasn't. I'd simply been sitting at my desk when a strange vertiginous sensation jolted me, like one of those falling dreams, and my heart began stampeding. That's when I grabbed the phone and ran out the front door.

"You ran out the front door?" he repeated. A smile came slowly to one side of his mouth, as if he'd just unearthed a clue, and I took this as a sign that maybe I'd be okay. But I kept my hand on my chest anyway, and when he told me my heart was starting to slow, I could feel it was true. According to him, my blood was one hundred percent saturated with oxygen, my lungs were clear, and my heart, though fast, was beating in a normal rhythm. At the uncertainty in my voice as I declined a trip to the hospital, he told me not to worry. "We have a lady who calls all the time with panic attacks," he said, still with that smile.

Panic attacks? How could something so physical—the pounding heart, the shaking hands, the tunnel vision—have been a product of my own mind? I wanted to call Larry, but he was in the operating room, removing a tumor from a patient's brain. So after the ambulance left, I Googled my symptoms and stared at words like *hypoglycemia, thyroid disease, heart arrhythmia*. My face turned cold with recognition at the last: there was my diagnosis—a heart arrhythmia. Though the EMT had told me otherwise, my belief lived far deeper than his words could reach: these words in front of me, as bold as truth, were confirmation of a lifelong fear.

I'd first suspected something was wrong with my heart when I was eleven and noticed it thumping in my chest. My sister and stepbrother let me check their chests, but theirs were still. "Look," I said, pointing at mine, "it's moving!" Later, when the school nurse told me the reason my heartbeat was visible was simply that I was skinny, I didn't entirely trust her. I worried constantly over my defective heart, and for months after she shooed me back to class, I regularly took my pulse and the pulses of my friends. Mine was always the fastest.

Now that my childhood fear had come full circle, I didn't know whether to gloat or start planning my will. Instead, I looked up one more thing: panic attacks. There again, my symptoms matched. I was surprised to find that panic attacks can strike "out of the blue" and are often initially mistaken for heart attacks. But in reality, a panic attack is simply a fight-flight response that occurs at the wrong time—like a fire alarm going off when there's no fire.

I abandoned the sea of disorienting medical text on my computer and the sketchy websites that promised a cure in exchange for my credit card number, and spent the rest of the day feeling shaky and alone.

The hours trickled by, and when Larry came home that evening, I approached him solemnly in the foyer and told him my news. "I think something's wrong with my heart. Also, I may have had a panic attack."

Larry, being a thoughtful and steady man, and also a man who, unlike me, took his time when given information to which he was expected to respond, went about his usual habit of unloading his keys and wallet onto the front table, then walking into the kitchen to place the mail on the counter. We gave each other the standard hug and kiss, and then he asked, "What happened?"

I told him about the palpitations and the paramedics, half watching him and half watching the trees outside hold the late light like honey while the sun rested like a slingshot in a low branch. Larry exhaled audibly, and for what seemed like a long time. His scrub top was coming untucked, and his hair had lost its gelled stiffness and flopped forward onto his forehead. It had been a long day for us both. "You're fine," he decided, smiling as if there were no other choice. And we stood like that, in the kitchen, with all that light between us.

I couldn't entirely blame him for dismissing me. We each had hypcochondriacal tendencies, which I found to be a source of both intrigue and familiarity when we were first getting to know each other. In fact, it was when we discovered that we'd both taken a semester off from college after diagnosing ourselves with MS that I fell in love with him. Since then, we'd both gone the neurotic route on occasion, thinking our headaches were tumors, our stomachaches cancer, our fevers malaria.

But that night, everything seemed different, as if the earth had shifted by a degree so that nothing was quite as I'd left it. The small mosaic lamp on the bookshelf glowed cooler; I noticed creaks in the floorboards I hadn't noticed before; and when I wasn't looking, someone had altered all the angles of the trees in our yard. In bed, I threw my arm around Larry and blinked into the darkness. "I'm scared," I said.

Larry was silent again for a moment, and in that moment I wanted so many things—both reasonable and unreasonable things. I wanted him to ask me what I was afraid of, even if I didn't have the answer. I wanted him to turn on the light and look at me, and maybe touch my face. I wanted him to tell me a story about a girl who was afraid and who found magical things in the woods. But it was late, and Larry was already overwhelmed by his new job in a new city, and being afraid is such a vague affliction that all he could do was tell me it was time to go to sleep. So I went to sleep.

The next morning I woke up still terrified of being alone. "Do you have to go in today?" I asked, reaching for Larry's hand in the predawn light. "Can't you call in sick?"

"You know I can't," he said, apologetically. So I watched him through the glass as he showered. He was sloppy with the shampoo, soaping his scalp as one might wash a black Lab. The suds ran down his face, his smooth chest. When he got out, I handed him his towel, then watched him drive his electric razor over his cheeks. I watched him spit toothpaste into the sink. I watched him pull on his boxers—the red ones with the gray whales—and his socks, and his scrubs. I watched his taillights disappear into the morning, and the night slink away like a lover behind him. I watched the daylight come on, steady as a train.

I looked down at Aramis and Starlet. "Now what?" They looked back up at me, wide-eyed and silent.

TWO

If I could take one seed from childhood and propagate it, it would be what might seem like an ordinary couple of minutes outside a grocery store: I am eight, standing under an awning with my little sister, Joanne, who is five. Our mother has left us with the bags to go get the car. The world is slanted with rain, and our mother is disappearing into gray mist. Piped-in music reverberates against the clanging of metal carts, and fog spreads across the parking lot. It reaches under the awning and envelops us. I stare out into the spot where my mother vanished as if into an ocean, waiting for her to reappear. At first I don't notice that Joanne, beside me, has her pointer finger pressing down on top of her bowl-cut head and her other hand at rest on her chubby hip as she pirouettes to the grocery store version of "Music Box Dancer." She is pretending to be a ballerina. There my little sister spins and spins, for nobody but herself. There, she seems, for a minute or two, not to know the sounds of our mother's screams or our father's bellows; she seems not to know anything but a song, and the joy of moving to it.

If I could show you only one picture of my sister, it would be of her in that moment, dancing in the mist in a juice-stained shirt in her favorite color, purple. I would choose that picture because it is an allegory of how the spirit wants to thrive and how, no matter the depth and weight of a particular kind of darkness, our spirits still seek light, still attempt to nurture the truest parts of ourselves. I would show it to you because it marks the last time I remember seeing my sister completely unfettered, happy.

When it comes to everything that is tender and sacred about childhood, that moment is the purest one I've got. But it is also the most heartbreaking, because it represents a kind of loss in motion: as my sister twirled, even my eight-year-old self recognized her joy as a fragile thing, a thing that wouldn't survive the cataclysmic world in which we lived. I could see then, unmistakably, what I had already lost, and what she would lose, too. A child myself, I ached for that moment as it happened. I wanted to keep it. But it was my sister's moment—it was her seed, and it would not grow. If I could have, I would have cultivated it; I would have handed it back to her, a field of pale purple irises that smelled like candy.

Later that same year, my mother took my sister and me shopping at a department store in a strip mall, and I made my mother angry by whining for something I wasn't allowed to get. This escalated into a standoff, during which she walked through the store ignoring me while I pretended to vanish, following her from a safe distance while hiding behind racks of clothes so she couldn't see me. I didn't come to the register when she paid and left the store, and only after counting twenty Mississippis did I step outside to stand under the awning, my arms crossed in steely defiance. After loading the car, my mother pulled up and gave it to me—my one shot, her two words. "Get in." But

I wouldn't budge. So my mother rolled the window back up, and I heard the click of the gears as she slowly began to drive away. I watched her turn past a row of cars and speed up. I saw my sister swiveled around, seat belt off, her fists balled, her red face stricken and furious behind the back window as she wailed and wailed and was silenced by the closed windows of the car and the growing distance between us. Then the awareness came—the night's cool tip against my cheek, the ebb of my mother's taillights, her car steadily approaching the parking lot exit— and I started running. I chased her car with every bit of strength my scrawny legs could muster, screaming for her to stop, but it was too late. She turned onto the main road and was gone.

At first I cried the kind of cry that makes you stagger, that jars your mouth open. But then the crying mellowed to a soft whimpering, and I started counting the lamps in the parking lot, listening to the buzz of their yellow glow. I could hear traffic from the road hissing past. I could hear crickets waking up, their metallic chirp. And as I listened, the tears abated like a flash rain, and for a strange moment I felt peacefully untethered—free.

That day became the first of what would be many days that my mother would leave me in parking lots. It became a routine, each of us playing our part—my threatening to leave, and her letting me go. But in the end, she always came back for me. After ten or twenty minutes, I'd recognize our Grand Prix as it turned in off the road, and my heart would spring, and I'd watch her headlights come toward me, and the car would stop, and my sister would be looking at me through the glass, and my mother would open the door, and this time I'd get in, and none of us would say anything, but the music would be playing, and my sister would reach for me, and I would take her hand, and we would head down the road in the direction of home.

THREE

Solitude had always been the place where I went to be with my secrets, where I felt them thriving and banging in my blood, where I felt as alive as I could feel. But after that first panic attack, solitude had transformed overnight into a fate almost unbearable, and I wanted nothing to do with it. For a long time, I stood by the window and watched the driveway, the empty space Larry had left behind when he went to work. Unlike my usual strong, levelheaded self, I felt like a child abandoned again, and I had to keep resisting the urge to call and beg him to come back.

All I could think about was what would happen if another attack came. And then, probably because I was worrying about it, one did come, this time while I was peering noncommittally into the refrigerator.

Once again, my speeding heart offered no reasons for its alarm. My body trembled and my breath came short and my heart rattled against my rib cage. My sense of space warped so that with each step, as I clutched the phone and hustled outside, I thought I was falling. I tried to focus on something, but everything around me had gone fuzzy—the slate stones of the walkway, the azalea bushes primly in their row, the Caribbean blue flowerpot with its sun-crackled paint. There was only pounding, pounding, and the inescapable feeling I was going to die.

This wasn't a quiet feeling; it was a loud and jagged scream; it was the terror of drowning; it was all the terrible things I had ever known and ever feared, uncoiling into a thousand savage arms ruggedly pulling me under until I could not see or think or feel beyond my most basic hardwired need to claw through and take another breath.

I called 911, but when I heard the voice on the other end, I remembered the men who'd been here just the day before, how they'd smiled at me, and I couldn't bear the thought of facing them again. With my fingertips pressed against the side of my neck, I told the 911 operator that I'd misdialed, then hung up and hunched over on the front step, my head in my lap.

When I called Larry, I spoke into my knees. "It's happening again."

"What's happening again? I'm in the middle of seeing patients."

"My heart," I said. "Can you come home?"

"You're okay," he said. Then he repeated himself, as if there were no other thing to say.

But those words didn't help, no matter how many times he repeated them. They were both a dismissal and a directive, and I wanted neither. I wanted him to make some gesture that would magically gather me up, like a basket of fallen fruit. The phone shook in my hand, rattled against my ear. "You can't come home, can you?"

Larry sighed. "I'll be home as soon as I can." We both knew what that meant: not soon at all.

Outside, it was obnoxiously summer, things blooming all over the place. And my fear seemed to be part of the pollen, stuck in the air, collecting in my lungs. I thought of friends I could call, but somehow I couldn't bring myself to say some version of *Hi, I thought I'd give you a call between panic attacks or heart arrhythmias or whatever the hell*

is happening to me, just to let you know that I'm afraid—of everything.
Also, I may be going crazy.

I couldn't understand how I would be so afraid now, here. As a
child in my parents' custody and as a teenage runaway, I'd had countless
reasons to be afraid, but when I was nineteen, I'd walked away from that
world and given myself a fresh start. For the sixteen years that followed,
I'd found what seemed to me a stable and happy life. I'd once come
across a saying attributed to the Buddha—"How sweetly the lotus grows
in the litter of the wayside"—and I liked imagining myself as that lotus,
having emerged from the filth of my past still clean. It was nice to think
that the chaos I'd lived through not only hadn't damaged me but had
provided me with a hard-won wisdom I could offer my friends. I was
happy to be the one they came to with their love spats, their sadness,
their uncertainty. That was my role with most people in my life—a calm
presence who could show others how to move toward light—and I took
it on gratefully. I wanted to believe that I had already learned the hard
lessons of life, that the majority of my struggles—real struggles—were
behind me now. And I liked the idea that by taking charge of my life at
such a young age, by having pulled myself up out of the abyss by the
force of my own will, I'd discovered a power I probably would never
have otherwise known I had, a power that made it possible for me to
be relentless about going after what I wanted—love, safety, a happy
life—and to build it. But now, as I sat in terror, for the second time in
as many days, on the front step of the beautiful home I shared with the
beautiful man I loved, I felt utterly powerless.

When Larry came home that night, I greeted him with his old
stethoscope from medical school, which I'd found in the basement
in the equally old black doctor's bag that he'd purchased earnestly for
his first day as a doctor-to-be and never carried again after he realized
that the only doctors who had them were in 1950s movies. He looked
crumpled—not only his scrubs but also his expression—and I could see
the toll this intensely stressful new job was taking on him. Normally,
I would have pulled him toward me and tried to make him smile, but

instead, in my obsession, I thrust his stethoscope at him. "My heart," I said. "Something's wrong with it." As far as I was concerned, my diagnosis wasn't a matter of choosing between panic attacks and heart problems; it was both.

He placed an armful of papers down on the foyer table and listened to my heart. "It's bad," I said. "Isn't it?"

"Shhhh."

"It's an arrhythmia."

"It's not an arrhythmia."

"Then it's a murmur."

"Shhhh," he said, tracing the stethoscope around under my shirt. "It sounds fine." He pulled the stethoscope out of his ears and placed it on top of the table.

I picked it up and gave my heart a listen. It was fast. "I don't know," I said. "How much did you study hearts in medical school?"

"Not that much."

"Then how do you know it's normal?"

"Because I know."

"That's not very convincing." I took the stethoscope back. "Maybe I should see a cardiologist."

"I'm telling you," he said, his voice rising in exasperation, "your heart is fine." He stood silently looking at me with that wide-eyed defiant stare he gave when he had nothing more to say.

I knew what he was thinking—that this was nothing more than the worries of a hypochondriac—and I understood why he would see it that way. Maybe if I'd told him that my heart had felt out of control since I was eleven, he would have invited me to come sit with him, and we could have talked about it. But my past frightened Larry, and sometimes it frightened me to tell him about it. He knew a basic sketch of my childhood, my years of homelessness, but the details stayed tucked away. It was complicated, what to tell and what not to tell. Part of what I loved so much about Larry was his wholesomeness—his persistent boyishness (even as a chairman in his early forties, he was regularly mistaken for a student) and general lack of worldly experience—and how everything about him stood as an antidote to the darkness of the life I'd once known. In omitting the grit of my childhood, it was as if I were claiming some of Larry's innocence as my own, as if together we could create a different story.

And we did. We'd filled our first house, a small old Cape Cod, with dancing, with the scents of fresh flowers and roasting vegetables and sweet things baking, with pictures of us smiling the smiles of people in love. We held hands always—whether we were in the car, bobbing our heads to corny disco songs, or lying in bed, having random discussions about the interconnectedness of particles—even in the rare moments when we were arguing. Sometimes when Larry got called in to do trauma surgery in the middle of the night, I went with him. When I taught writing classes in the evening, he waited outside the door of my classroom just to carry my books the hundred feet to my car. We spent hours past midnight standing in our backyard and watching the sky through Larry's telescope, then talked into the morning about the universe, old dreams, what our children might look like. There's an old question meant to test your love: would you fight a bear to save this person? And with Larry, I never had any doubts. I would have braved any bear for him, and he would have done the same for me. And for a while in the beginning, as we were creating our new story, I forgot about my own. I let myself believe that ours was the only one.

But palimpsests are problematic. No matter how many stories you put on top of the first story, the first one is always there, visible. And more than innocence, I wanted intimacy, which is difficult when you give your partner only sketches of yourself, when the person who loves you doesn't want to know more. It's not that Larry didn't know me—he knew my character, my quirks, my joys; he knew who I'd become—but not who I'd been. And I wanted him to *want* to know the rest. Because what was going on inside me, most of the time, was more than what Larry was willing to see. Peeling the layers back and back, underneath it all I would always be, foremost, a runaway—a girl ruled by the tempestuousness of her heart. It would be the story that would tell itself again and again, no matter how I tried to silence it.

We didn't talk about hearts anymore that night. Instead, we ate dinner in front of the television, my hand incessantly darting to the pulse at my neck—as if by monitoring it I could somehow control it; I could be truly certain I was alive—while Larry pretended not to notice. Eventually I picked the stethoscope back up, pressed the circle to my chest, and listened to my heart. It sounded like a washing machine that gets unbalanced in the spin cycle, knocking urgently, louder and louder. I don't remember what we watched on television, only that it was narrated by the sound of my heartbeat.

Later that night, in the unfamiliar dark of our bedroom, Larry climbed on top of me, the stethoscope still around my neck like a wind-blown tie. I liked having it there, waiting to monitor the goings-on of my viscera. As we moved together, I thought it's amazing, all the different ways one can live in a body.

FOUR

My earliest memories are of my father's hands, of attachment. In my first memory, I have no words, only sensation: a tight wrap in blankets, small flecks of light flickering above in the night sky, my father's hand pressing me to his chest. He hovered godlike above me. The sky was the color of dark plums.

I was born in Queens, where we lived in a dismal apartment near Kennedy Airport. What I remember most about my four years living there was the noise: at all hours, airplanes roared overhead and rattled our apartment. When the planes came, my father would rush to me and cup the fleshy insides of his hands over my ears. Sometimes even at night he'd rise from their bed, from the darkness, and come to me in my crib, where his hands went about their steady work of muffling the sound. But sometimes he and my mother were fighting, and then he didn't come to me. Then the three of us would be screaming—my father's deep roar, my mother's high howl, my breathless wailing—and the planes would thunder, and my ears would ache, and life seemed like one big rumbling hole that wanted to swallow us.

In my earliest memories, I do not remember my mother's hands. Or rather, I remember the absence of them. During the days, when my father was at work, I reached for my mother, yearned for all the pieces of her—her hands, her lap, her smile—but she didn't reach back. Sometimes when a plane came, we would both cry. My mother cried not only because of the planes but also because she was gaining weight, because her mother-in-law told her to cut her long blond hair to the nape, and she did. She was crying because she had no friends and because *Sesame Street* was only an hour long and she didn't know what to do with me when it was over. She was crying because she was in her early twenties and could already see her life drawn out, a sketch on paper she couldn't rip up.

Sometimes she sat in the kitchen and asked, "Can you see him?" She always pointed at the same one of the three empty chairs at the table, while I stood beside her leg. "It's Jesus."

I looked at the chair and saw only a chair.

She gazed in awe. "He's beautiful. Just beautiful."

Another plane came. We cried.

At three years old, I liked the rise of questions: "Mommy, why are you sad?" She sat in the soft green chair and stared toward the window, sobbing in bursts, wiping her nose on her arm. Startled, she turned to me, blinking quickly, as if she'd forgot not only that I could speak but that I was even in the room. "You're too wise," she said, but moved her face away again, back toward the window, its delicate haze.

I didn't know what *wise* meant. I wondered if it was like eyes.

My mother's belly was growing like a moon. "You're wise," I told it, while she slept flat-backed on top of her rust-colored bedspread. She slept a lot, so I watched her a lot, waiting for her to wake up. I watched the light change with the day and move shadows around the room like puppets. I watched her jaw chew invisible bites while she dreamed. I watched her chest rise and fall. Sometimes I tried to wake her by telling her I loved her—whispering it at first, then speaking it, then kind of barking it—but once she was sleeping, she was not the kind of dreamer you could rouse.

When they brought home my new sister, Joanne, I put the back of my hand to my forehead the way I'd seen people do on TV, and fell to the floor, pretending to faint. At first, I heard my grandma giggle, "Oh, Ritala," but then no one said anything. I lay there for a while, legs akimbo, head turned to one side, eyes closed, waiting for someone to notice. When I finally stood up, everyone was on the other side of the room peering at Joanne, so I went over, too. She smiled a lot, except when the planes came. Now when they did, my father rushed to her and I covered my own ears.

In the months after Joanne was born, my mother cried more. She cried in the green chair and also in the shower. She cried on her way from the green chair to the shower. But when she talked to Jesus, she never cried. I liked hearing her talk. I liked watching her nod and offer Invisible Jesus tea.

Joanne, now sitting up in her playpen, didn't understand. She was all rattles and stuffed rabbits and plastic rings that stacked into a rainbow. My game was to make her laugh by popping up over the rim of her playpen and shouting, "Boo!" The trick was to be quick, to make each time a surprise. It almost always worked, and her gummy pink laughter was the best thing I'd ever heard.

When my father came home, he yelled at my mother. "Look at you—you don't even bother to brush your hair anymore, not to mention cook a meal. What did you feed the girls today? Tell me." He opened the refrigerator.

"Rita's too picky. All she wants is spinach. But Jesus said—"

"Fuck Jesus!" He threw a bottle of ketchup. It didn't break, but it dented the wall. My mother cried. I cried. Joanne cried, too. His voice was an explosion. "I don't want to hear another fucking 'Jesus'!" He grabbed her shoulders. "Do you understand?"

She didn't answer. Instead, her face twisted into a cry that climbed louder and louder, and she didn't stop for a long time, not even after he let go and she slumped to the floor. That day Jesus walked out of our apartment and never returned.

But the planes never stopped coming, and my mother began to tremble even in the silence in between. When my father said we were moving to Maryland, I asked if Maryland had planes.

"Maryland has peace," he told me, "peace and quiet."

Before we moved to Maryland there were two events I will never forget. The first is that for my fourth birthday, my parents gave me Legos. I wanted Legos more than anything, and these people, who were gnarled up in so much pain, had given them to me. By then I was already learning to scarf up the good thing for all it was worth. So I jumped up and down on the bed as two people: a girl who was happy to have this thing she deeply wanted, and a girl who was already self-aware, who wondered, *Am I jumping up and down hard enough? Smiling big enough? Letting them know I am grateful enough?* I was already a girl trying to patch the roaring hole that my parents' misery had made in our lives.

The second thing that happened is that, in my father's hands, I broke free. He had taken me to the zoo, and we were standing at a fence, both of our arms outstretched—his lifting me up, mine reaching forward for all that massive gray: an elephant, who with one sweep of his trunk breathed the world into motion. His ears skimmed the air like ragged kites, and all I wanted was for him to take the peanut I clutched in my small hand. And with his stupendous and dexterous trunk, he did. In a single gentle swoop, he lifted the peanut from my palm, and through his swift breeze-like touch, in that moment of give-and-take, I made contact. I was seen. I learned grace.

I was allowed to bring home a souvenir that day: a lime-green flashlight that you had to squeeze on and off. It was attached to a long chain, which I wore around my neck and took to bed with me, squeezing it on under the tent of my covers. I took that flashlight everywhere because it reminded me of the elephant, and of what would turn out to be one of the last sweet times I would share with my father.

My father and his brother, sons of World War II survivors, had also grown up in Queens. Their father, my grandfather, was already old then. His first wife and three children had been killed in Treblinka, where he, too, nearly died from a gunshot wound to the abdomen. But he'd been an obstetrician in Poland, so he knew how to tend the wound, how to survive. He was a smart and good man who, here in the States, could get little more than a janitor job. He was frail by then—arthritic and nearly deaf.

The latter might have been a blessing, because my grandmother was always yelling at him. Despite her crotchety ways, I loved her because she made excellent French toast. It was soft in the middle, crisp on the edges, and drenched with maple syrup. She kept a clean house, always bending over to remove some small speck of dirt off the floor, and she served meals at the same times each day—a habit that gleamed in sharp contrast to the volatility of our usual life. Occasionally Joanne and I spent the night with her and immediately cozied into her crisp sheets and loyally followed routine. But for all my grandmother's dedication to homeyness, she seldom had a warm or witty thing to say, so I often ended up asking her to tell me again about the concentration camps. And she always told me the same story: twice a day they were given bread and coffee, and in the evenings, instead of drinking the coffee, she washed her hair with it. She seemed so proud of this detail: that not even Hitler could make her hair dirty.

Of course she was angry. My grandfather was angry because she was angry. My father was angry, too—a young boy getting into street fights, taking odd jobs to bring money home to his parents and still never being able to please his mother. "You're an idiot," she used to tell him. "What will people think of me, having an idiot for a son?"

Who knows where all the anger of war goes? Who knows the ways brutality wedges itself into the body, into the synapses of a brain? Who knows what parts of ourselves we must consume in order to survive? What I do know is that my father's family was not a happy one. I know that he had a dream of being a lawyer, and that he dropped out of college after one semester so that he could get a job to support his parents. They went without, and he went without, and though for a short time he tried to give to us, his new family, as fathers give, in the end he couldn't. So we all went without.

My mother often told me that her father, in the midst of a diabetic temper, once yelled, "You should have choked when you were born!" She was very young when he wished this on her, but she took it into herself wholly. She grew up afraid of water, always fearful she would drown. She was born in Paris and boarded a ship to New York with her parents and her older sister when she was four. She spent the entire trip seasick in the cabin, and when they arrived in New York, she hated her first impressions of America—the way people spoke, the food they ate, her estrangement from all of it. She hated that her parents gave her and her sister one doll to share between them, and that her sister hit her over the head with a bat for touching it. My mother didn't fight back. She was shy to the point of throwing up before school each day, and if I were given only one chance to describe her, then and in all the years I knew her, it was as a person who wanted to hide.

She was sixteen when she met my father on a blind date. They fell in love, and with the love came the fighting. They fought over jealousy, over their parents, over other things I will never know. They fought in cars, in the still space of my mother's bedroom, in the din of Coney Island. They fought on their honeymoon. Yet no matter how much they fought, they couldn't change the shape of each other, of their past, of the new life they had already created. For both of my parents, I represented just one more loss of freedom, and when my mother was eight months pregnant with me, my father kicked her stomach. "You came too soon," she always told me. "Three weeks early. I wasn't ready. I wanted Chinese food that night, but then you came instead."

Though my father had promised peace, after we moved to Maryland my parents' fights grew more intense. They were staggering and swing-ing from a combination of drugs and rage. They slapped and punched and bit each other. They called each other long rashes of names. Other times they were too high to do anything. Sometimes my father would sit on the sofa in the evening and watch a blue spinning lamp with crescent moons cast shadows on the walls until his head lolled back and his eyes rolled up, leaving two gashes of white. I liked him this way, because all the menace was drained from him then. He was limp, gone from us.

My mother wasn't much of a cook, but I do remember the last big meal she made for us as a family: a roast chicken with car-rots and potatoes. Unfortunately, the potatoes were undercooked, and my father punished her for this by throwing tennis balls at her and then locking her out on the balcony until it got very dark and my sister and I could barely distinguish her profile from the darkness. So it was mostly TV dinners after that. One thing my mother still cooked, though, was soft-boiled eggs, which, to my bewilderment, everyone else seemed to enjoy. Every Sunday morning they arrived at the table, upright and wobbly in their flowery blue eggcups. And every Sunday morning, I gagged at each slimy bite before giving up and pushing my chair back. "You're not finished," my mother would say, to which I'd complain that the egg was cold. "Well, that's your problem. Next time, don't play with it, and it won't get cold." Once when I couldn't finish my egg, my father kicked me clear across the living room.

It wasn't the first time my father had struck me, and I knew it wouldn't be the last. I don't remember the first time either of my par-ents hit me, maybe because every time someone hits you, it feels like a first. But by then, part of my seven-year-old self knew that no matter what I did, I wouldn't ever make my father proud. Still, that didn't stop me from wanting to, or from trying. So the next week, as my father sat behind me watching television in the living room, I cast a glance at him over my shoulder and decided to finish my egg. It was a tricky egg. It squiggled to the back of my throat and got stuck there. Even with sips of my orange juice, I still gagged. When I spooned in my last bite, I didn't even bother to swallow. I ran straight in to tell my father.

"Guess what!" I stood in front of him. "I ate my whole egg!" A wet line dripped down my chin.

He fixed his eyes on me, and his lips pulled back in disgust. "I'd suggest you sit back down in that chair of yours and finish chewing," he warned. "You look like a pig, chewing like that, talking with your mouth full."

I went back to the table and let my tears fall silently. Then I felt a sharp pain at the back of my head. I turned around and saw a Play-Doh can rolling on the floor behind me. My father was sitting on the sofa with another in his hand, squinting one eye and cocking back his arm. I turned quickly and tried to duck, but the next can hit me in the same spot. I covered my head with my hands, and he threw two more cans until he missed and knocked a plant to the floor, its terra-cotta pot in pieces.

My mother rushed over. "Enough!" She crouched by the plant and scooped the dirt into her hands.

Joanne sat on the floor in the middle of the room and wailed. My father didn't move from the sofa.

After the table was cleared, the baby's breath repotted, the Play-Doh cans picked up, my father walked into Joanne's and my bedroom. I was lying on my bed, flipping through a picture book of roses that Grandma had given me, distracting myself from the lump that still throbbed on the back of my head. Some of the colors, especially the fuchsias, were so saturated and vibrant that I wanted to eat them. I pressed my nose into the crease to sniff the glossy pages, which smelled the way streets do after a rain.

My father appeared in the doorway, then paused for a moment before he walked over to me, his hands straight down by his sides. His eyes weren't angry anymore, and the muscles in his face had softened.

He cleared his throat. "I was wondering if you'd like to take a ride with me."

Sometimes, if my father really hurt me or my mother, he felt guilty afterward. That's how my mother got most of her jewelry. I looked down at my roses and turned a page. "Okay," I said, without lifting my eyes.

He sat on the bed beside me, and I cringed a little. "You know I love you and Joanne very much, don't you?" I nodded, still not wanting to look up. I knew what he would say next, because he'd already told me more than once, perhaps in an attempt to preserve some small morsel of my psyche, that the reason he and my mother never hit my sister was that she almost died when she was a baby. He thought it was important for me to know this, that perhaps if she'd been less fragile, they would have hit her, too.

She had been bleeding inside, and no one knew why. Though I was only five when she got sick, I always remembered those two weeks she spent in the intensive care unit, getting blood transfusions while my parents kept a crib-side vigil. I stayed with neighbors who lived on the same floor as we did and who had two daughters near my age, and it was there that I got my first real tastes of an ordinary life, one where people talked and laughed at the dinner table and the kids were happy and airy. While my sister clung to life, I clung to this otherworld, collecting flint in the woods with those two blond girls, then bringing our rocks inside and, in a manic dance of joy, banging them together until they made sparks. And though I missed my sister terribly, I didn't entirely understand how perilous her situation was. All I knew for sure then was that I would have traded almost anything to be able to always dance in the neighbors' living room like that, giggling with wonder, nearly causing a fire.

My mother must have taken my sister out to the playground that Sunday afternoon, because they weren't in the apartment anymore when my father and I left for our drive. It was an uncomfortable feeling, being offered this kindness from him, because I knew it wasn't a kindness I could trust, not even when, at the High's convenience store just outside of our apartment complex, he announced that I could get as much candy as I wanted. My mother generally didn't let Joanne and me have sugar, so this was a treat beyond all treats. But my head hurt, and the sadness in me felt almost like a sickness. Still, the candy aisle, like a secret corridor, was perennially seductive with its rainbowed wall almost overflowing and its fragrant mix of sugar, chocolate, and plastic. I eyed up the Hershey's bars and Fun Dip and Charleston Chews, which I knew Joanne would love, while my father stood eagerly at the end of the aisle. He was smiling. Somehow it seemed crucial not to let him down, so I started dropping candy into a small paper bag and nodding my head when he nodded his. Behind him was the door, which was shining in a giant rectangle of midday sun. The longer I stood there in that aisle selecting candy, the more transfixed I became by that door, its glow, the openness beyond it. I wanted to drop my candy and run through it, into light like a warm bath. I could hear the cars whirring past along the road. Here, gone, here.

I brought my half-filled bag to the counter where the cashier told me how lucky I was to have such a nice dad. "You're his little princess, aren't you?"

I looked down while my father clinked some change into her hand.

"Oh, she's a shy one," she said, nodding her head at me.

And then we were out in the silvery light, then in the small space of his hot car, heading home.

Occasionally Joanne and I shared days that seemed suspended, that rose up out of our usual lives and shone like balloons in the sun. Take this day, for example. It was spring. It was the stillest kind of day. The trees and bushes and even the hair hanging out of Joanne's blue and white Good Humor cap were in a deep sleep. She was selling ice cream—white, brown, and pink plastic ice pops she pulled from her plastic Good Humor truck. "Ten cents for ice cream!"

There was no one around. I sat on the front steps trying to feed a leaf to a caterpillar. As it crawled across my fingers, I turned my hand to keep it from falling off.

Joanne opened and reopened the lid to check her static inventory. "Get your fresh ice cream!"

The caterpillar wouldn't eat. I put him in the grass, and within seconds he was heading down the sidewalk at a steady gait, as if he had someplace very specific to go. Resisting the urge to reclaim him, I plucked a small yellow flower from the grass at the bottom of the hill. "Buttercup," I whispered.

I lay up the hill with my legs sprawled into gravity and stared at the muted sky, then turned to rest my ear against the grass. I listened, and they came: hoofbeats. They were galloping, strong, nearer and nearer. I imagined them behind the woods, a fleeting blaze across the field.

"Ice cream for sale! Ten cents!" Joanne adjusted her cap and looked around for someone she might be missing.

I walked up to her truck. "What flavors do you have?"

"I've got Chocolate Eclairs, Strawberry Shortcakes, and Toasted Almonds."

"I'll have a Toasted Almond."

"That'll be ten cents, please," she said eagerly.

I pressed the buttercup into her hand. "Here you go."

She expertly retrieved the white ice cream and handed it to me.

I sat back on the steps and pretended to eat my fifth ice cream of the afternoon.

Life is never all bad, and Joanne and I sipped up the joy we could, sometimes together, but more of the time apart. Though I typically spent a lot of time outside while Joanne tended to stay inside and play with her dolls or watch TV, what separated us most weren't the different things we did as much as the different things we knew, and how we'd come to know them. I knew the terror of how it felt to be pulled down the hall by my hair, backhanded in the face, and wished death by my mother—and of how it felt to be kicked, whipped with the buckle end of a belt, yanked from a bathtub, and thrown onto the floor by my father. Joanne knew the terror of how it felt to watch. We were each alone in our experiences, between which stretched an unapproachable gulf, but we shared what we could—an afternoon outside in the sun, the candy I brought home from High's, Saturday mornings watching *Road Runner* or playing Candy Land—when we could. And despite our differences, what we both knew—what we lived every day— was how it felt to be helpless, to wake up each morning and go to sleep each night afraid.

For as long as I can remember, I knew that my parents were out of control. I knew they were capable of anything. We lived in the hotbed of their most wretched selves, and in it they ran rampant. Yet despite the fear and sadness and shame I carried, hope kept sprouting up like weeds in the cracks, taking root inside me. I dreamed of a different world, wrote poems and short stories, read books and searched their pages—and the small pockets of our neighborhood—for the beautiful things. Like this, the months came and went, and the police came and went, and my father took a job back in New York, from which he came and went, arriving home on weekends. And on those weekends my parents continued to fight each other with a vehemence one could almost mistake for love. Except it wasn't love. It was my mother's clothes cut to shreds, my father's car keyed from one end to the other. It was my mother taking my father down with a coffeepot to the head; it was his hands around her throat. Sometimes you could hear them fighting all the way down the street.

That's how far I would go some days, pretending that the shrieks and bangs were coming from someone else's apartment. I collected rocks and dandelions, pressed my face to the cool grass, and felt the warmth of sun. I skirted the edge of the woods, and sometimes I ventured back to the small creek that wound through the trees, where I dipped my fingers into the cool water and peered out at the farm in the distance. No matter what happened inside my home, the world outside wouldn't stop being beautiful. And I was learning that there was a certain power in assigning my own direction in my small but tangible piece of that world.

FIVE

Dusk was slowly settling in as Larry and I got in the car and headed down the driveway—the sky shifting to evening pastels while clouds dusted past like sugar. The lanterns on our gateposts had just come on, and a bat shuddered overhead before swooping into the field across the road. The herd of Belted Galloways who lived there were clustered together at the roadside, grazing. In the first weeks in our new house, I'd grown fond of the cows, their languorous sounds drifting across the country road, though sometimes I imagined what it would be like if horses lived there, too. They were still just a romantic fantasy to me, but I desired them with the same fervor I had as a girl, staring out from the creek in the woods behind our apartment to the farm in the distance and envisioning the flight of my imaginary herd, their manes and tails a streak of motion.

As we turned onto the road, Larry changed the radio station from jazz to classic rock because he knew I liked to sing along. We were on our way to a dinner in Boston to commemorate Larry's new position as chairman of Boston Medical Center's neurosurgery department. One thing that came along with Larry's profession was my obligation to play the part of the charming, well-groomed wife at medical social events, and that meant dinners—interminable exercises in small talk with virtual strangers over plates of overpriced food. I had never been good at this sort of thing and so always dreaded these dinners, much like dentist appointments—somehow, my teeth always hurt after both. As we drove into the city that night, despite Larry's attempts to lighten the mood by quizzing me on rock trivia, I could already feel my anxiety—this new brand of terror—blooming like a mold.

As we exited the highway and entered Boston, I put my window down. Someone had turned the city on, the traffic lights and sidewalk lamps and car lights filling the air with a new glow. In the crosswalk in front of us, a young couple held hands, their faces swept with life and love. I envied the carefree way they moseyed across the street.

In the weeks before that night, my panic attacks had turned into daily, sometimes hourly, events, and I found myself held hostage to some amorphous yet decidedly growing body of fear. When I was a kid, the adults were always talking about this person or that person who'd had a nervous breakdown. I never knew what that meant exactly, and as I grew up, the expression fell out of favor. But it seemed mythical at the time, almost to the point of being glamorous. I'd overhear my mother on the phone sometimes, talking about it. "Did you hear? Judy's friend's uncle's stepdaughter had a *nervous breakdown*." And now, so many years later, I was beginning to wonder if this feeling was what they meant—the feeling of standing on solid ground yet watching myself, as if on a boat in a river, drifting away.

As Larry and I walked toward the restaurant, all I wanted to do was turn around and run. Instead, I gripped Larry's hand, and we entered the Chilton Club, a stodgy private social club to which two of the wives belonged. As we approached our table, my knees trembled like windup toys. Immediately I busied myself by noting where the exits were as I shook the hands of the dinner guests: the CEO, Elaine, and her husband; the executive vice president and his wife; the university dean and her husband; the former interim chair and his wife. I took a seat between Larry and the dean's husband, a portly man with only a thin horseshoe of hair on his head, and as we all trained our eyes on Elaine, I began to fidget—leaning forward, leaning back, placing my hands on the table, off the table, on the edge of the table, in my hair, on my collarbone, on my knees. I couldn't stop. After thirty-five years, I'd forgotten how to simply sit in my own skin.

Elaine was a well-coiffed woman in her late fifties, with the confidence of a race car driver and the eloquence of a politician. She wore pearls, and the hair spray in her frosty hair would have battled any wind. As a server filled our wineglasses, I thrust my wrist under the tablecloth, clocked fifteen seconds on my watch, and measured my pulse at 112, which was still reasonably in control. Then Elaine raised her glass. I followed eagerly, grateful for something to do. As she toasted Larry, a "young talent" who was on his way to "bright new beginnings" at Boston Medical Center, he caught my eye and smiled. If Elaine noticed, she didn't acknowledge me. Maybe she hadn't considered that it was my bright new beginning, too, that I had packed up my life alongside Larry. But we were already past that. We were clinking our glasses. And the dinner began.

"So what do *you* do?" asked the vice president's wife, fixing her eyes on me. Her nails looked like rubies against the glass.

I pinched a tip of the tablecloth between my fingers. "I'm a writer."

"Ooh, what do you write? Novels?"

"I'm a poet," I said, clearing my throat and shifting in my chair.

She nodded, as if she were waiting for the rest of my sentence.

"I'm writing a memoir," I added impulsively, instantly regretting it.

The former interim chair—a curmudgeonly, almost endearingly Napoleonic man—laughed. "At your age?"

I felt my cheeks blush as I sensed everyone's eyes on me. I couldn't sit there and tell them about my past, so I looked down and examined the condensation on my water glass. The table went quiet, and I poked my wrist under the tablecloth to recheck my pulse. It was fast.

As the traffic of conversation got moving again—something about the governor and health care—I thought about what else I could have said to the now less-endearing Napoleonic former interim chair. I could have told him that by the time I was six, I'd known violence the way some kids know bedtime stories. I could have told him that the first number I ever dialed was 911 during what would be one of many vicious fights between my parents; that, to save myself, I started running away when I was eleven and then spent years living between state-run institutions and the streets, where I wandered around looking for a safe place to call home but instead ended up sleeping in staircases or empty cars or, more often, the questionable beds of men and women. I could have told him I'd been a stripper, a junkie, the kind of girl who would never be welcome in an elite place like this. I might have also mentioned that I'd put myself through college and grad school summa cum laude, that I'd taught college students how to write, and that I did these things after dropping out of junior high in the eighth grade. I could have said that in my short life, I had teetered at the abyss of death more than once. But a charming doctor's wife wouldn't tell him any of that.

And that's how I lost my moment: by staring at my water glass, mute. I knew then that not only had I failed myself but I was failing Larry, too. I wanted to be the supportive wife he deserved, a first lady of sorts, one who would make Elaine think, *Everything's going to be great because Larry has this strong woman beside him.* But instead, I was the girl who kept fidgeting in her chair on the brink of a panic attack, then excusing myself to the restroom, where I hyperventilated into my hands and wished for a sudden exit, like a school fire drill.

To my good fortune, no one asked me another question all night. And then, finally, the dinner was over. Our standing up from the table marked the liveliest any of us had been all evening as we bid our farewells and Larry and I broke out into the open sounds of the city at night, where the streetlights stood as if their only role was to be beautiful.

SIX

If I could have gotten one glimpse of my future life when my struggle with panic started, this is the hour I think I would choose: 9:00 P.M. on New Year's Eve, 2009—more than two years after my first panic attack. I'm in a barn, in a horse stall, watching a man knead his hands into my horse, Claret. Sal's hands are large and rugged—one finger is slightly deformed where he had the tip reattached after a horse bit it off—and they move with an unquestionable intelligence as they work Claret's muscles. Sal's agreed to come on a holiday evening, while Larry waits at home for his midnight kiss, because he understands horses, and the people who love them, and he knows I would rather be here than at a party or watching Dick Clark on TV. I know so little about horses compared to most horse people, those who have been around horses all their lives, those who grew up speaking the unique language of horses, but I do know that Claret has been in pain, and I want him to feel better.

Outside the stall window, the night is luminous, ablaze in white.

There are several inches of snow on the ground, and it's a soft snow, the kind that parts around your feet as you sift through it. As Sal leans into Claret and we all exhale white smoke into the cold, I wonder if people go sledding at night. Surely they must, but who are they? Where do they go? And why aren't I one of them? I have never thought about this before, but suddenly it seems so obvious to me that I want to be someone who goes sledding at night—that girl who zips up her puffy jacket and pulls down her wool hat with the single pom-pom on top, and takes off down the hill. They say that every day is a day to claim our lives, and tonight, on New Year's Eve, I'm claiming night sledding. As long as we are alive, there is always the chance to begin again. *Begin again beginagainbeginagainbeginagain.* How easily the mind repeats this mantra.

I say nothing of this to Sal, who is mostly quiet, except when he occasionally comments on a particularly tight spot of Claret's body. "He's really reactive here," he says, pressing so hard that his hand disappears between the base of Claret's neck and his shoulder blade. Claret rears up in pain, and I step back, out of the way. But Sal doesn't release the pressure, no matter how hard Claret tries to twist away, and then suddenly something gives, and Claret's neck softens and his eyes soften and he starts making the slow chewing sounds horses make when they're relaxed. And Sal keeps his hand there, now palpating a little, while Claret gives in to the pressure, into the relief, into the new space Sal has made for him.

Watching this feels like a holy event. It's not just because the snow beginning to fall is the fat white dot snow of Christmas movies on TV—walls of it cascading straight down into the windless silver-blue night—or because in these next couple of hours we'll all be leaning together, with our collective hopes and disappointments and reflections and resolutions, into a new year. It's because what is unfolding here is the sacred purity of trust. Claret weighs fourteen hundred pounds, and if he wanted to, he could hurt, or even kill, one of us. But instead, despite what Claret has known in the past, despite the hands that have hurt him, he's choosing now to trust these hands; he's choosing to trust the pain. And to watch him come to the other side of it—to watch the release shine in his eyes—is a privilege of the highest order.

"Can I feel?" I ask. "I want to feel what you feel."

Sal takes my hand and presses into Claret's back. "Do you feel here how it kind of gives when you press it?"

"Yes." I nod. "It's kind of spongy."

"That's how it should be. Now keep going down his back and tell me where it's tight."

I've removed my gloves, and Claret's body is warm against my hands as I massage along the left side of his spine. "Here," I say. "Right here it won't yield."

Sal checks the spot below my hand. "See," he says. "You *can* feel it. Now make it yield."

Unsure of exactly how to do this, I press my fingers into Claret's tight spot and slowly begin to knead, using the weight of my body for strength. Claret arches his head around and presses his muzzle into my back, moving his lips firmly as I move my hands.

"He's reciprocating," Sal says. "That means you're doing it right."

Some people believe that snowflakes are magnets for words, that every word spoken in a snowstorm lands on a snowflake and is carried to rest, on a rooftop or mitten or field, as if on a magic carpet. Therefore, they believe, people must speak carefully in the snow, choosing every word as a child might choose crayons, one at a time.

I lean into the great dark head nuzzling my back. "Thank you," I say, while time inches closer to midnight.

SEVEN

I didn't see the glass when I ran through it. I saw my sister's face.

She was sitting at the kitchen table, drawing. I was outside on the patio, watching a distant uncle try to light coals on a barbecue grill. We rarely ever visited extended family, so it was an exciting day. Drizzling gently, the patting of rain against the trees sounded like a fire crackling. Someone had left the sliding glass door open, and I could see the women inside talking in the kitchen, waving their hands about. I was nine and thought it was more fun to hang around the adults than to do any of the kid activities my aunt had arranged on the table for us. And when the matches were spent and the grill still wasn't lit, I wanted to help. "I'll go get more matches!" I exclaimed, turning to run inside. I could see Joanne then, engrossed in her crayons. I ran toward her. But I hadn't seen someone close the door. And I didn't see the glass, either, before I shattered it.

For a second, no one moved. I spoke evenly: "I think I'm bleeding." Then everything exploded. Someone was shouting, "Oh my God, oh my God!" I couldn't really see. My mother pulled me toward the kitchen sink and started to throw handfuls of water at my face. "I've gotta see if it's her eyes," she was saying.

"Someone call a doctor!" my grandmother yelled.

"Call a fucking ambulance!" my mother screamed, wiping at my eyes with paper towels. "Now!"

As they leaned me back into a chair, my head felt dizzy. My mother propped my leg up on another chair, and I caught a glimpse of a gash across my knee. I quickly turned my head away and saw the floor, so much of it now covered with my blood.

Soon the wail of a siren approached. The rain came flooding down. Two men rolled a stretcher toward me, and one of them squatted down beside me.

"Hey, how ya doin'?" he asked, smiling.

"Am I going to die?" Suddenly this seemed like the only question in the world.

"Well, not today," he said, still grinning. "Not if I can help it."

At the hospital, my mother stroked my hair while we waited for the doctor. I had four deep lacerations, two on my leg and two on my face, across my forehead and nose. In my small room, loud light beamed into every corner. Though I was drowsy and nauseated from the Demerol they gave me, the comfort of my mother's hand on my head was a new discovery, and I didn't want to close my eyes and miss one second of it.

But it didn't last long. They wheeled me away from her and into a different room, where they injected my wounds with lidocaine. I kicked and punched from the pain, until they finally strapped me down and finished. But when the doctor was about to put in the first suture, my mother broke into the room. "Wait!" she said. "I want a plastic surgeon."

Four hours and a second round of lidocaine later, I was sewn up neatly with 150 stitches and ready to go home. Outside, the rain came in sheets. The darkness had been settling in for hours and was now immersed in itself, everything immersed in it, so that it was hard to imagine there ever having been a sun. For the ride home, my mother left the radio off. The swish of tires against the road and the rain pelting against the car with the beat of the windshield wipers made their own song.

Maybe because my mother had never formed into a solid enough person, one who believed in her own strength and abilities, she didn't have much in the way of coping skills. This always made me sad for her, because occasionally I caught glimpses of what she could have been. One of those glimpses had been a costume she'd made for me to wear to school for our second-grade Thanksgiving celebration. With construction paper, string, and crayons, she turned me into an impressive replica of a Native American, and I spent the whole day boasting to everybody, "My mother made this." My mother could draw, too. I often liked to pull her old boxes of papers from the closet and sift through all the things she'd drawn—mostly faces of long-haired women, beautiful and haunting. "You see the eyes?" she would say. "I like the eyes. It's as if they're looking at you." So I would stare into the eyes of the women my mother made and feel, in a way more immediate and true than most other moments, as if I were seeing her.

But it was when I ran through the plate-glass door that I had the biggest glimpse into my mother's strength. That one day, she coped. She rose. She threw the water on me, propped up my bleeding leg, insisted on the ambulance. She comforted me in the emergency room. She saved me, at the last second, from having to live the rest of my life with two big scars on my face. I think she knew this was her moment, too, because she never stopped talking about that day, how she'd taken charge from the start, how she'd thought to ask for a plastic surgeon. How she'd been a good mother.

That same year, my father stopped coming home on weekends. Some nights, instead of getting ready for bed, Joanne and I piled into the back of our mother's car, our pillows and stuffed animals dangling lazily from our hands, and on my mother's hunch, we took to searching for him. We usually pulled out of our apartment complex just as it was getting dark, when the air had a smoky quality to it, a signal to get a last good look at things before they disappeared for the night. I watched the trees' charcoal silhouettes against the deepening sky. I pressed my nose to the window and tried to find things hiding in the branches. Then night snapped down like a dome and filled the car with its damp green grasshopper smell.

I was mesmerized by the wispy night clouds, striated like rills in sand, and the flashes of streetlights and the steady thump of the road. Joanne always fell asleep holding her little blue doll with the string in the back that, when you pulled it, made her say *I luuuv you.* My mother sang along with Eric Clapton: *I don't care if you never come home . . .*

We drove and drove, circling restaurants and hotels, getting lost in neighborhoods and turning around while song after song kept the car beating. And then one night, we found it: my father's Cadillac, unabashedly parked under the drop of a streetlamp—a four-thousand-pound revelation shining in its massiveness.

We pulled in beside it, and Joanne popped up awake, but nobody said anything. We just sat there and gaped. Our windows were down, but the street was quiet, the row of town houses dark inside. There were no crickets, no buzz of the streetlamp, no movement. It was a still life, and it could never be part of our world.

"Bastard," my mother finally said, putting the car in reverse. As we pulled away, the street's silence seeped into our car.

We spent weeks repeating our adventure. It turned into a kind of game, all of us on a mission to find my father's car—scoping out restaurants and hotels when we didn't find it in front of his mistress's house.

Joanne and I helped by peering intently into parking lots and at other cars passing on the road. "Is that it?" we'd exclaim excitedly. I don't think Joanne understood why we were searching for his car, but that didn't stop her from wanting to find it.

We never did anything once we found my father's car except turn around and go home, but I think my mother just liked knowing she could find it. "I should be a private eye," she'd say.

My parents finally divorced that same year, viciously, bitterly. Kramer vs. Kramer had nothing on them. My father prepared me for the divorce by keeping me up late when I stayed with him at his girl-friend's town house, the same one my mother had discovered months earlier. "I know things have been rough for you the past few years. I know your mother and I fought a lot, and we both hurt you." He wrapped his fingers into gentle fists, as if he were holding bouquets of flowers. "And I'm sorry for that." His eyes seemed to moisten a little as he scanned my face. He was searching for something.

I clenched my teeth to keep the tears back. I felt like a grown-up sitting there with him, and I didn't want to ruin it by crying.

"I want you to know that what your mother and I had—our marriage—it was poison. It made me do things I shouldn't have done. But I also want you to know that things can be different now, here. We could be a real family. We could even get a dog. You like dogs, don't you?"

I nodded exuberantly, not wanting him to stop talking.

"Okay, picture this: a big house, maybe a swimming pool, nice backyard for tossin' a ball around or having a barbecue, a puppy chasing a Frisbee, and all the love you could ever imagine. That's what I'd like to give you—a normal, happy life. No more fighting, no more craziness."

The thought of a normal life, the kind my friends had, the kind I'd always dreamed of, pushed through me and broke the dam. As I wiped at my eyes, I let his movie play on in my mind. I saw picnics and laughter and dinners together. I saw the shimmering burst of blue water in our very own pool. I saw a yard filled with kickball games and snow igloos and a sweet dog panting in the sun.

My father's voice brought me back. "There's just one thing. I'm gonna need your help."

By help, he meant that I'd have to convince a judge that Joanne and I should live with him and not our mother. We were making a deal—a happy life in exchange for a long list on his yellow pad of everything bad my mother had ever done to me: the bruises and the horrible names and the days she didn't let me in after school—and we stayed up for hours at the table while everyone else slept and the sky got as black as it could get.

"So there were all the times she slapped you in the face when you wouldn't finish your dinner, right? And made your lips bleed?"

I nodded, remembering the sharpness of her diamond when she used the back of her hand. "But it wasn't dinner," I corrected. "It was the raw eggs and milk she made me drink with my vitamins before bed."

"And she gave you those vitamins because she didn't cook for you, right? Because she neglected you."

I watched his pen darken the page. "I guess."

He paused then, put his pen down on the pad. "You can't be wishy-washy about this, Rita. Yes or no?"

I felt my stomach tense. "Yes."

He nodded smugly. "So, 'fucking bitch,' 'piece of shit'—what other names did she call you, besides the usual?" My father's fists tightened. "You know it made me sick when I heard her call you—I can hardly stand to say it now—Rita Retard. Just sick."

I was surprised by my father's sudden protectiveness, but I relished it all the same. I would have taken almost anything he would have given me. And it was true: she'd called me that, and other names. She reminded me almost daily, in one way or another, that I disgusted her—I was too skinny, too pigeon-toed, too hyper—that I would never be as pretty as my friend Kimberly and that, next to her, I would always just be "Creeperly." That was her most used name for me, and it alone held all of her loathing, and all of my shame.

Still, I knew what we were doing was unfair—we were telling only half of the story. But I could almost feel it drawing me toward my new life—that particular sun, that particular joy, that particular love. So I sat in the judge's chambers in an enormous leather chair, and I told him that I didn't want to live with my mother. I can't remember what he looked like, probably because my sight bore right through him, through the walls of that courthouse, and into the future my father was promising. "I hate her," I told the judge. And as I spoke those words, I felt them turn back on me, as if they would devour me. But none of that mattered, because what I was doing there, in front of that man whose face I don't remember, was fighting for my life. And then I told him the rest. I told him the truth. I just didn't tell him everything.

During that time, I stopped visiting my mother on weekends, and Joanne started going alone. The last time I'd seen my mother, she'd broken down sobbing. "He's turning you against me!" she cried. "You think he loves you, that he wants you? He doesn't. He wants to win. He wants to hurt me. And he doesn't want to pay child support. That's why he's doing all this—for the money."

"That's not true," I protested, feeling doubt rise up like a fever.

"Oh, it's true all right. It's all for money," she kept saying. "Mark my words. He cares about his wallet way more than he'll ever care about you."

During their divorce trial, Joanne stayed with friends of my mother, and I spent those summer days sitting on a bench outside the courtroom, filling my notebook with more poems and stories, waiting to see how the judge would decide our lives. I tried not to look at my mother when she walked by—I looked down at my shoes, out the window, anywhere but in her direction—because I didn't know how to face her. And then one afternoon she tore through those courtroom doors in a bleary-eyed fury and ran right past me, wailing uncontrollably as she disappeared down the corridor. As I watched her go, I felt the same gut-lurching urge I'd felt running after her car when she drove off without me in parking lots. Except now there was nothing left for me to chase. Our fate was in the hands of a stranger, whose face I will never remember.

In the end, my father won. Joanne and I moved to Long Island to live with him and his new wife, Janice, and her son, Bobby. Janice was grand—tall and big-breasted and wafting Halston perfume in every direction. She cooked beef briskets and made a mean Texas sheet cake, and was, from all angles, the opposite of my mother. We all agreed she was beautiful, with her flashy smile and bouncy hair and meticulously applied eye makeup. In the beginning, I followed her around a lot, asking her questions and staring at her pretty red lipstick, but in the way of many mixed families, we never bonded. She wanted my father, and she tolerated Joanne and me.

Bobby split the difference between Joanne's and my ages. He was a dark-haired, long-lashed beauty of a boy, who was quiet, asthmatic, and slow at math. I liked him for all of these things and felt, very quickly, the same older-sister protectiveness I felt toward Joanne. My father, however, was less enamored of Bobby. He took his shakiness and failure to make eye contact as a weakness, and often berated him for it at the dinner table. "You're a putz," my father would say. "Don't you know how to hold a fork?" The more my father spoke to him, the more Bobby stared into the abyss of his food, his hands trembling, until eventually all of us, except my father, lost our appetites. Janice just rested her knife and fork on her plate without ever saying a word.

Janice also didn't say a word the first time she saw my father hit me. I'd gotten caught attempting to swipe a few quarters from the large watercooler jug my father filled with coins, and was sent to my room. When my father appeared in my doorway a couple of hours later, I knew instantly by the wild look in his eyes that everything I'd dreamed of and fought for was about to come crashing down. Then I saw the gleam of my sister's twirling baton. He was holding it in his hand. Zapped by a streak of cold fear, I called out for Janice, but was quickly silenced by the first strike of the baton against my head. I let out a howl, and my father raised the baton again. This time, he stopped short of my arm, laughing as I jerked away. After that, he made it a game: sometimes he'd bring the baton up as if he were going to hit me, only to stop midway and watch me flinch. Then he'd mimic the way I was crying by stretching his mouth into a contorted O and making taunting sounds in a horrid falsetto. And on the few times he let the baton connect, I remember feeling grateful that he hadn't hit me harder, as if that little bit of restraint was still a kind of love. My father ended my punishment by wrecking my room with the baton, then ordering me to clean it up.

True to my father's word, we had a pool and a barbecue grill and a German shepherd named Lady, whom I loved. But that's where his promises ended. And life went back to how it had been before, with my father cornering me in various rooms in the house while I begged him to stop. What was different now was that, unlike the way my parents fought when they were married, my father didn't hit Janice. And he must have known that his cruelty toward Bobby could go no farther than the dinner table, because he never hit him, either. And Joanne, of course, had always been off-limits. So I was the only one; my mistakes (the usual mistakes kids make, like continuing to jump off a ladder after I was told not to, or being mean to my sister, or sneaking cookies before breakfast) were the ones he fixated on. Through it all, Janice said nothing, and if she objected, she never showed it. But sometimes when the air changed and it was clear that my father was getting ready to deliver another round, she sent Joanne and Bobby outside to play, presumably so that they wouldn't have to watch. Those were the worst of the days, the ones when I felt most alone, the ones when I wondered if my father would finally kill me.

But when it seemed that death had finally come, it wasn't mine: it was my father's. He and Janice had been arguing that day, so she took us three kids and Lady for a walk. We meandered for miles, into neighborhoods entirely new to us. Down streets and sidewalks Joanne and I skipped, and Bobby and I raced, and Lady sniffed and sniffed, and Janice walked steadily, her shoulders squared, her steps long.

When we arrived back home hours later, I was first in the door. A bright spot on the floor caught my eye—a drop of blood. "Dad?" I called. I stepped forward, toward the spot. Why blood? Why the next drop, near it? Once when a kid in our Maryland apartment complex got hit in the nose, he bled a long trail as he walked home, and I followed it, those perfect coin-shaped drops, all the way to the steps in front of his building. I felt queasy the entire time, but the intimacy of it lured me to the end. These drops on the tiles inside our house were bigger, and I followed them, too. "Dad?"

The trail ended at their bedroom doorway. I peered in and found my father in his usual place on the bed. But this time, he wasn't watching television. He was very still. The blinds were closed. Lying across his chest like a seat belt was a shotgun. A comet of blood trailed across his forehead. The lamp on his night table was on. The TV flickered but was silent. He wasn't moving. His eyes were closed.

The sound in my head was a million airplanes at once. I spun around to run back out but couldn't move. I needed desperately to erase my last fifteen steps, to erase my father's blood, which felt like my own blood, from the floor. "Help!" I called. It came out a whisper. "Help!" Now my voice was behind it; now my legs were moving; now I was running straight into Janice. "Dad killed himself, Dad killed himself!" I cried, running past her to the door. Joanne and Bobby were just coming in. "Dad killed himself!"

Outside I pitched myself onto the lawn. All the fury of my entire life was right there in my fists as I pulled up clumps of grass and screamed and stared accusingly at the sky.

But my father was not dead. Janice explained this to me after she wrestled me from the ground and slapped my face: it had been a joke, a fake; she had gone to him to feel for a pulse, and as she turned to call an ambulance, she heard him move. When she turned back around to face him, his eyes were open, and he was pointing the gun at her.

We left him that night, stayed with friends of theirs I'd never met before. And as I lay in this unfamiliar bed in this unfamiliar house and watched cobwebs float from the ceiling, I was strangely happy. My father had finally done it: he'd crossed the line of crazy, and now everyone would know it, and Joanne and I could return to our mother's house, and everything would be the way it ought to have been. My father had lost us now. He couldn't hurt us anymore. We would never have to go back.

Except we did. The next day, my stepmother drove us home, and no one ever spoke of my father's pretend suicide again.

EIGHT

Here is a story about my mother: for a year and a half, she loved me. After I told the judge to let me live with my father and he did, and my mother tore out of the courtroom in a blur, away from me, and my father's promises soon began to splinter and implode, and enough time had passed to allow my mother to rise from her grief and find that her new single life was one big party, which often left its guests passed out in various rooms of her apartment, my father began following his end of the visitation order by driving Joanne and me back down to Baltimore to stay with our mother one weekend each month. By then I knew I'd misspent my single moment of power, and I was paying for it. My mother knew it, too. When I called her, she heard the tremor in my voice as I crouched in a far corner of my father's house and bit my lip so I wouldn't cry when she asked me how my great new life was. And when we saw her, she felt the lumps on my head. She saw the sadness in

Joanne's eyes. She'd shake her head and look down at the floor. "What is he doing to you up there?" she'd ask, as if there were an answer.

But then Joanne and I would pull our duffel bags back to our old room, and my mother would play Supertramp on the record player, and we'd dance around the living room on the faded pink carpet as if that were our only life. In the evenings, after my sister went to sleep, I'd stay up late and listen to my mother's tales of friendship, betrayal, and romance. We'd pull out astrology books and leaf through urgently, looking up the sun signs of her various crushes. "We're both Libras," she'd say, "so Geminis are balancing for us." On those nights, she'd sometimes tell me stories about her childhood, how she still dreamed of the French chocolate-filled pastries of her young life in Paris. Other times, she'd stand in front of her bedroom mirror and try on different outfits to see which one I liked best. "But which is sexier?" she'd ask, and I'd point at various red and black and silky things. And my mother, with her new giggle and new barrettes and new cast of friends, became a heroine of light and laughter, became the moon outside the window of my bedroom in my father's house, when I lay there dreaming up at it, longing for things I didn't know how to name and the one thing I did: *mother*. In the weeks between our visits, I wrote her letters, and sometimes she wrote back. And each loop of her handwriting was proof that she loved me. I had a red purse then, adorned with puppy key chains and a small koala bear that clutched onto the strap, and I carried her letters in it so that they would always be with me.

NINE

Just after Larry's first birthday, his parents, Chinese immigrants struggling to earn their graduate degrees in the United States, sent him to Taiwan to live with his maternal grandparents for three years. His childhood picture albums show the gap. It begins with a fuzzy-haired baby smiling in a high chair: before him burns a single candle on a small white cake. He hasn't massacred it with his fingers or pressed his dimpled face into it the way so many babies do; instead, he's looking at his mother, who must be smiling back at him from behind the camera. But his mother is missing from the following pages, a few square black-and-white photographs, each not much larger than a stamp. In them, Larry grins in his po-po's arms or holds hands with his tall and regal-looking grandfather, Gong-Gong. And the next photographs, colorized again, show a four-year-old boy standing obediently beside his parents. Now the boy looks careful, smiling perfunctorily to complete the portrait that says, *This is my family.*

On the plane back from Taiwan, Larry's grandparents helped him practice his introduction speech to his parents. He had virtually no memory of these people he would soon be calling Mama and Baba. He spoke no English, and he missed his dog—a Pekinese who'd surprised everyone when he ended up killing the family monkey.

At the terminal gate, Larry's parents waited eagerly, like a couple about to adopt their first child. While Larry was away, his parents had missed him, but having to navigate their rigorous studies in a new language, they hadn't had much time to think about it.

Larry and his grandparents were among the first people to get off the plane. His grandmother had combed his straight hair neatly to one side and fitted his neck with a red bow tie, which he tugged at during the long flight. His parents stood immobile as they watched the baby they'd sent away now walking toward them, a young boy. Behind him, his grandmother was prodding, pushing him forward. "Go, go!" she urged. Larry acquiesced, walking steadily across the great plain between the generations. In Taiwan he'd seen pictures, and so he recognized his parents instantly; they were leaning over now, holding out their arms. But Larry stopped short, looked up squarely into each of their faces, and recited what he'd practiced: "Respectful greetings, honorable Mother and Father." Then, as people kept scurrying past him, he bowed.

I have always loved this story of Larry as a four-year-old boy about to meet his parents, in part because every time I think about it, it breaks my heart. I imagine Larry in his bow tie, wanting so desperately to be a good boy, a boy his parents would want to keep. And as he grew up, he never lost the awareness that parents can put you on a plane and send you away, so he fashioned himself into a boy whose indisputable goodness would prevent that from happening again. He never got into trouble, never missed a day of school, and skipped two grades in the process. There was never a temper tantrum, never a stolen pack of gum, never a cigarette smoked. There was never dirt tracked into the house or a harsh word spoken or a grade less than an A. Still, his mother was quick to point out when another boy got higher accolades on a science project or when another boy was more adoring of his mother. So for Larry, love was a constant negotiation based on merit. And the formality he'd first experienced when he was reunited with his parents lasted. His parents shared it, too: his father, when he became enraged at his mother, would lock himself in a closet and mutter under his breath. In their home, this was how you dealt with emotion: you quite literally locked it in a closet. Part of what I found comforting about Larry when we started dating was his emotional steadfastness: he didn't like things that were messy and unpredictable, and after years with parents so violent that the police were regular guests at our apartment, that was fine by me. But the panic attacks happening to me now were exactly that: messy and unpredictable. And they threatened everything that Larry had grown up believing; they threatened the white-picket parcel of his life.

In the weeks following my first encounter with the ambulance staff, my panic attacks had proliferated like mice. I simply woke up one day, infested. I began to fear things I didn't know were possible to fear: the shower, the grocery store checkout line, open spaces, small spaces, heat, crossing a street, driving, any form of exertion—even climbing a flight of stairs filled me with dread, because most of all, I feared my heart: despite what the paramedics said, despite what Larry said, I was convinced my heart was a time bomb. I didn't trust it. So I tiptoed around it carefully, as if it were a sleeping monster. And I began to avoid anything that might disrupt it. If I just sat very still, maybe my heart and I could coexist.

But of course, I had to get up. I had to pee, wash my hair, buy eggs. And when I did those things, I panicked. I panicked in the shower, in the car, in the grocery store. I panicked slicing avocados, running a brush through my hair. I panicked for no apparent reason, over and over again, each time feeling slightly more battered than the last. Most of the time I ran outside to the front step, as if it were the magical place of safety, the cusp, the line between out and in, the place where both options were possible.

When I wasn't panicking, I worried about panicking and about all the grizzly calamities that can befall a person. I began to narrate everything as if it were a scene in a horror movie. As I got dressed, I'd think, *You're going to fall down the stairs and break your neck.* No matter what I did or where I went, there were the thoughts: *A plane will crash into the living room. A tree branch will fall on your head. You will choke on a bite of sandwich. A mosquito will infect you with eastern equine encephalitis.* There was no end or escape. Everything seemed fraught with danger, even the most benign things, even the most absurd.

Sometimes I couldn't make it through the checkout line at the grocery store. I'd drop my basket and run from the store trying to catch my breath, my body trembling. Even in the safety of my own home, the most basic tasks, like going upstairs to make the bed or taking a shower by myself, soon became insurmountable. So I planned my showers for times when Larry was home. I avoided the stairs as much as possible. I stopped driving on the highway. Worst of all, I stopped writing.

My life was overrun. So I panicked my way to the bookstore, because I knew one thing: the only way I was ever going to have a chance of getting my life back was to understand what was taking it away.

But even the bookstore I'd always loved had morphed into a terrifying place since the last time I'd visited. There was its cavernous size, the milling people, the lights that bleached the air. There was the weight of so many words, the finiteness of time they suggested, the importance of choice. And there were so many things to account for: where were the exits, where were the bathrooms, what were obstacles between those things and me? And why was that man with the rapidly blinking eyes wearing an oversize coat?

Okay, I thought, sizing up the second half of the store. *I can make it back to the anxiety books. I can choose one, I can buy it, and I can leave.* As I walked past the racks, I tried to ignore the thoughts, which were like a bully's finger poking me on the shoulder. *You're gonna die.*

You're going to suffer a fatal arrhythmia, and they'll find you on the floor beside the anxiety books. Screw you, I thought, trying on bravado like a costume. But then I thought, *My last thought will have been "Screw you,"* and then I thought, *No, my last thought will be a thought about my last thought being "Screw you,"* and then I started furiously pulling books from the shelves, anything with *panic* or *anxiety* in the title. *If I can just make it out with these books . . .* I thought, as I scurried to the nearest register. *If I can just make it to the car . . .* And once I was back in the glassy still of my house, the conversation continued. *If I can just make it until Larry gets home . . .*

Until then, I would read. I learned that at least forty million Americans are affected by some kind of anxiety disorder, and that there's a distinction between anxiety and panic: anxiety is like a sky full of brooding cumulonimbus clouds, ominously dark and amorphous, while panic is the lightning crack that sends you running for cover. I would learn that when a person is in fight-flight mode, the body undergoes an awe-inspiring transformation as several physiological events occur at once: the nervous system sends out a shot of adrenaline, like a war call to the troops; this gets the heart pumping vigorously, filling the major muscles with blood, while blood is directed away from less essential places, like the stomach and the skin, which is why people go pale with fright; respiration increases, pulling needed oxygen into the body; pupils dilate to let in more light, and certain muscles in the eyes relax so that even the farthest predator can be seen; hearing becomes sharper; glycogen stored in the liver is turned to glucose, which gives us the sugar rush needed for energy and endurance; our sweat glands go to work to cool us and to scare off predators with our scent—all of this makes the body strong and fast, in preparation for a life-saving fight or a hightailing chase.

It's a handy survival mechanism, one that's been with us throughout our evolution, but when it happens without an actual threat, the symptoms themselves—rapid heart rate, shortness of breath, shakiness, tunnel vision, tingling hands, cold sweats, nausea, a strong urge to flee, an overwhelming sense that one is going crazy or about to die—are terrifying, and soon become, themselves, the thing we fear. *Fear of fear,* the books call it—that self-feeding beast that can quickly metastasize through a person's entire life.

Panic disorder can sometimes be triggered by major life events (death of a loved one, divorce, a move, et cetera) but can also appear without any provocation at all. Whatever the cause, once a person starts panicking, it's hard to stop. On the checklist of panic, I filled every box: my symptoms fit the description of a panic attack like snaps on a coat. Still, the voice in my head taunted: *You have panic disorder* and *a heart disorder.*

"There is no passion so contagious as that of fear," said Montaigne, while Emerson knew that "fear defeats more people than any other one thing in the world." But reading about panic didn't seem to allay my fear any more than throwing a book at a tornado would have changed its funnel shape. Still, I kept reading, and the books offered some practical suggestions.

I started with deep abdominal breathing. Lying back on the sofa, I concentrated on my lower belly and tried to slowly pull a breath in, but I couldn't seem to get the air past my diaphragm. I tried again, fidgeting around to find a more comfortable position, but I couldn't fill my lungs. Each time I tried, my breath got caught high in my chest, until finally I started wrestling with my windpipe, desperately sucking in air. *Great,* I thought. *Now I've forgotten how to breathe.* I might have felt humiliated had I not started hyperventilating, which led my heart to begin its mad race.

"Why are you doing this to me?" I cried. And then, as if to answer, my heart punched me in the chest. Once, and then a second time, like the kick of a rabbit's hind legs. I leapt off the couch, grabbed the phone, ran out the front door, perched myself back on the front step, and called Larry.

"It's happening again," I told him, gasping for air. "My heart just jumped in my chest. It *moved.*"

Though I yearned for my former independent self, the self that was logical and strong, Larry was the most unshakable person I'd ever known, and I'd come to depend on it. "It probably just skipped a beat," he assured me. "You're having a little anxiety. That's all."

"I think you should come home."

"It was just a palpitation. You're okay."

"Do you promise?"

"I promise. You're my sweet girl, and you're fine, and I love you."

I let myself be momentarily soothed, but then couldn't help myself. "I still think you should come home."

When I hung up the phone I rocked myself like a pendulum, as if the motion itself would be the one thing to move me from one minute to the next. I stayed like that for a vast span of the afternoon, swaying on the front step with one hand on the phone and two fingers against the pulse in my neck, while birds tossed their voices and the blunt strokes of a hammer reverberated in the distance and the bees skimmed the tops of the pink spirea, while the trees fluttered, tossing the light around.

TEN

The neighborhood is buzzing in electric green while kids my sister's age scrape their BigWheels along the sidewalks and newly hatched insects take to the air. I rip through it, fast as fever. It's spring, and everything is vibrating. As I run, I turn to look over my shoulder and can almost see my father as a flickering apparition behind me, growing smaller, plumes of gray smoke rising from his messy head. I can't see his fists, but I know they're flailing. The key is that he's getting smaller, that I have crossed a threshold.

Out of the neighborhood and out of breath, I walk up Rockville Pike. Sometimes a car honks; sometimes guys call out something indiscernible, which I answer with an extra swing to my hips. Last summer when I was twelve, my friend Dawn and I learned that if we shook our asses when we walked, we could get cars to honk at us. Each time we went to the Hawaiian snowball stand on Liberty Road, we'd count how many honks we got.

My father moved us here to Rockville, Maryland, last year, right in the middle of seventh grade. He was in some kind of trouble with his job—I could hear him yelling, sometimes pleading, on the phone, then playing back the conversations he'd taped on his phone recorder and telling my stepmother how he was going to sue everybody (and also how he would have made an excellent lawyer)—so in a hurry we packed up our stuff and moved here. But the moving truck couldn't fit all of our stuff, so the kids' things got left behind. I lost my beloved rock collection, my prized Barbie doll collection, the Snoopy that I'd slept with since I was a baby, and the Legos my parents gave me for my fourth birthday—the few things that had made me happy during all those hours I spent hiding away in my room. Luckily, I'd thought to bring my sticker collection in the car with me, and wedged in next to my sister and stepbrother, I kept peeking at them as we headed south—the sparkly stars and shiny ice cream cones and butterflies in every color.

But now that I've escaped, I've left even those behind. When I finally make it the few miles to the high-rise apartment building where my friend Cindy lives, I call her from the lobby. No one answers, so I sit on the small bench by the phone and watch people get their mail.

The first time I ran away, I flung the front door open with a fury and bolted straight out of the neighborhood. My father had just ransacked my room, and as he sat with Janice on their bed, my red purse emptied on the duvet, my diary splayed, my mother's letters shelled from their envelopes, I knew I couldn't spend one more minute in that house, given what would come next. I didn't stop running until I reached a grocery store a couple of miles away. I had no plan—just a small lifetime of running built up in my legs and a knowledge that out there, somewhere, was something better for me. When I called my mother collect from the pay phone and begged her to help me, she told me she wished she could help me, but she couldn't. "I'm sorry, but you should have thought about all this before you told the judge you wanted to live with your father." It didn't matter that I begged, that I promised to be the best daughter anyone could ever be. She was done with courts, she said. Her hands were tied.

Defeated and unsure what to do next, I poked around the grocery store parking lot until the police picked me up three hours later. I begged them not to take me back, but they took me back anyway.

That night, my father didn't beat me; he didn't even yell. He simply stepped aside and let me go to bed. And when I got to my room, I found that my red purse had been returned to me intact. I will never know what prompted this momentary softness from him—had I shaken him up? given him a brief sense of my latent power?—but pretty soon life went back to its tumultuous norm, and my father didn't change, and my stepmother didn't change, and my mother didn't change. But I did. Feeling the wind rush over me as I ran, I got a sense of the distance I could put between them and me: I'd found my way out.

I ran away several more times after that, but as I wait in Cindy's lobby, this time feels different. All the other times, I asked the wrong people for help. Once I spent the day at a pay phone calling runaway hotlines. But all the hotline operators did was try to get me to say where I was. "I'm not telling you where I am," I kept saying. "I just want you to help me. Aren't you supposed to help runaways?" Finally, the last one I called told me to go home. I guess he thought it was better to get beat up by your own parents than by strangers on the street. But the difference is a stranger isn't supposed to love you.

Another time I stole a few twenties from my father's wallet and took a train to my mother's parents in New York, but they said they were too old to take care of more children. "But I'm not a child," I said. "I could do all of the dishes. I could go to school and get good grades and make you proud." My grandmother shook her head while dragging on a cigarette, and the next day they put me on the train back to my father. It was a good night though, sleeping there with the window open and the familiar scent of my grandparents' apartment.

I don't know how I know it, but as soon as I see him stick his key into his mailbox, I know I'm looking at Mr. Malekzadeh—Cindy's Mr. Malekzadeh, the rich older man who liked to bend her over the washing machine in the mezzanine laundry room. She told me all about it once during recess at our junior high, but when I asked her if she actually enjoyed having sex, she just looked down and kicked at the grass. I think about that sometimes, how she kicked at nothing.

He takes his time with the key and the door and the mail, watching me all the while. "Hi," he says, in an accent that makes it sound more like *hoi*.

A minute later, I'm standing beside him in the elevator. As we rise in silence, his cologne screams. I try to ignore it and pretend I'm a glamorous and sophisticated woman on her way to someplace important.

Mr. Malekzadeh's apartment is small but plush, replete with mirrored walls, leather furniture, and a bar full of bottles. I've never been alone with a man like this before.

"Why don't you sit down, have a drink?" His words move slowly under the weight of his accent. In this forbidden territory, I don't know what else to do but awkwardly insert my thumbs into the two front pockets of my jeans, until he hands me my wine, which he pronounces *vine*.

I've never had wine before, and it burns my throat. We make small talk, while our reflections mimic us across the room. Then he produces a small pipe and asks if I smoke pot.

"Yeah," I lie, starting to feel warm from the wine. "Well, once."

He lights the pipe and pulls on it three times. The pot glows orange as he inhales, reminds me of jack-o'-lanterns.

When it's my turn, I inhale deeply and cough. Seeing myself coughing in the mirror somehow makes me cough harder. Meanwhile, Mr. Malekzadeh has put the pipe on the coffee table and is leaning close to me. "You're a pretty girl," he says.

Suddenly he is all face. It's kind of a turtle face, and I expect some turtley voice to come out, slightly squashed and nasal. "A very pretty girl," he says. And I start laughing because the face and voice are too much.

The push of his tongue into my mouth stops me cold. I have kissed a boy only once—a single shy peck on the lips at a birthday party—and this feels nothing like that.

I pull back sharply. "I have to go." My voice bounds unfamiliarly in my head, and I wobble on my feet as I stand up.

"C'mon," he says. "You just got here."

I tell him that Cindy's expecting me, so he puts the pipe down on the table beside his wineglass and grabs a piece of paper. "Call me any-time," he says, pressing his phone number into my hand. On my way out the door, he runs his fingers down my spine. Even after he's closed the door, I can still feel his hand there.

ELEVEN

Larry wasn't coming home anytime soon, and I couldn't stay on the front step forever. So I gathered myself and went back inside to my panic and anxiety books. Deep breathing clearly wasn't for me, but there was still a long list of exercises left to try, including one that would make my "tension melt away": progressive muscle relaxation. To do this, I lay supine on our blue flowered rug and started with my feet. The idea is that by clenching different muscles in the body and then releasing them, we also release all of the body's stored-up tension. I curled my toes downward and held the pose for ten tense seconds before moving up to my calves.

Though the book recommended tensing one muscle group at a time, my whole body wanted to participate. When I tensed my quads, all the muscles in my neck joined in. And my glutes were very clearly connected to my biceps. Soon all my muscles were jumping in like crazed teens in a mosh pit, and that's how I had my next panic attack. The phone, the front door, the step. The rocking. By the time I came back in again, my body felt at once fatigued and on high alert, like a sleepy watchman at a hideout.

It was getting late, and Larry still wasn't home, so I decided to do something that left the majority of my body alone: affirmations. I sat up on the edge of the couch with my hands on my knees, my spine straight; I was going to kick some panic ass. "When anxious thoughts come up," I said aloud, "I can slow down, breathe, and let them go." The second time, to really concentrate, I squeezed my eyes shut. "When anxious thoughts come up, I can slow down, breathe, and let them go."

My voice in the room was a strange sound. But I ignored that and tried the affirmation a third time: "When anxious thoughts come up, I can slow down, breathe, and let them go." It was futile. Worse than not liking the sound of my voice was that I didn't trust it.

I decided maybe visualization would be easier. According to the book, I was supposed to visualize someplace peaceful. So I closed my eyes and started with the author's example: the beach—the salty air of the Atlantic, the lull of waves, the moist sand molding into the arches of my feet. As I walked the surf in my mind, I remembered how I'd once read that in the calm before a tidal wave, the ocean pulls back on itself, receding toward the horizon so far that a person could walk out for miles where the ocean had been. I kept thinking about that person, the one who would walk out onto the bare sand, about that giant wall of water.

So I left the beach and headed to the forest, the air a collage of cool bursts and ripples of warmth. I sat under the pines, gazed up at their shagged canopies. I spied deer gliding along the rock lines in the distance. My wooded trail was shaping into a lovely reverie, until suddenly every grim news report I'd ever heard about a woman being abducted in the woods—or found in the woods—began blaring in my mind at once. Forget the air, the trees, the deer—all I could think about was some menacing figure hiding in the brush.

I left the forest and closed the book. There was no safe place.

So I lay on the couch. I monitored my pulse. I sighed audibly. I watched the trees through the window. I thought about the ways people give up and wondered if this was how it would end for me: a fixture on a sofa.

Between the ages of four and nine, I spent a lot of time on my parents' sofa, sick. But when I turned ten—after I moved to New York with my father, ready for the new life he'd promised me—I stopped getting sick. It was the one year of my childhood that my body and I coexisted peacefully, the year before I began to worry about my heart. It was also the year I made friends with a girl named Jennifer, who lived on my street. She rode horses, slept on a frilled white canopy bed, and had the best sticker collection in our neighborhood. Together we pierced the woods with sticks, dove down to the deepest parts of our pools, divulged secret crushes. Her life was the opposite of mine—a safe and cherished life—and I peered into it hungrily.

One day Jennifer invited me to come to the barn and visit her horse with her, and the night before I went to the stable, I was too excited to sleep. I kicked the covers around, looked for stars outside my window, and listened. And I could hear them—so many of them—galloping, galloping . . .

When we got to the barn, I knew by smell alone that I was in a different world. The combined scent of hay and manure and sweat was at once exotic and familiar. It registered someplace deep in me—that place where you know things before you know them—yet in those first seconds that I breathed it all in, even as my heart leapt, I began to sink inside. I understood too quickly that all of this belonged to Jennifer—it was *her* beautiful bay horse whinnying for her at the fence, *her* special riding pants and black velvet helmet, *her* mother cheering for her when she and her horse cleared the jumps—and it could never be mine. And on that day, our differences became a chasm I could no longer traverse. As it turned out, I was simply too jealous to be her friend.

But oh, those horses. How I pined for them. For days and weeks and years after, I imagined what it would be like to feel a horse move beneath me, to be able to trust a creature so large and so powerful.

TWELVE

Before Claret's bright eyes and hourglass-shaped blaze changed my life the first time I saw him, there were other horses. The first was a sweet gray named Applesauce, whom I met after pulling up at a roadside barn one day on the way home from a session with a therapist, many months into my panic attacks. I rode Applesauce only once, but he opened the door to the world that would ultimately save me. And in the year that followed, the year before my search ended with a chestnut horse named Claret, I would ride ravenously, if inexpertly— geldings and mares at various barns with various riding instructors. And before those horses, there were the six months I spent at the end of a long rope, riding Shaddad, a small gray Arabian who lived a life of questionably shaped circles based on the shaky communication aids of the small children bouncing around on his back. At thirty-six, I would be one of those children.

Panic was still nearby then, the way a mountain can loom in the rearview mirror as you drive away from it, but after impulsively stopping at Applesauce's roadside barn that day, I knew that my childhood desire for horses was greater than my fear of them. By then I'd already hit the nadir of panic, had lost myself in its depths, had tried therapies and chants and healings of all kinds, had questioned more than once if I would ever get my life back. And though, slowly, I was learning the lifesaving strokes that would lead me eventually to resurface, it wasn't until I followed the hoofbeats of my earliest memories that I would fully find my way free. So while Larry was doing the serious work of medicine, I was getting indoctrinated into a children's equine lesson program.

My riding instructor, Tommy, was a middle-aged woman who, as far as I could tell, sought the approval of no one. If anything, she sought to make people understand that most likely, she could, and would, kick your ass. This was underscored by a part of her daily attire that I'd never seen before: sharp silver Chinese nail guards that looked like daggers pressed onto the tips of all of her fingers.

My first meeting with Tommy was instantly humbling. As I walked into the indoor arena, she yelled at me. "Stop!"

I stopped.

She was sitting in the corner of the arena, and there were a few people and two dogs looking on. "Whenever you enter an arena, you always yell 'door' before opening the door. That way you don't startle the horses, and you don't get run over."

"Door," I said, though the way I said it made it sound like a question.

"No. Go back outside, close the door, and try it again. And say it louder. You want to be heard, don't you?"

I nodded as I backed out, closed the door, yelled "Door!," and opened it again.

As I began to walk in, she yelled at me again. "Stop!"

So I stopped.

"Always look both ways when you enter. You don't want to get trampled, do you?"

I shook my head and looked both ways—there were no horses in the arena—then stood frozen, unsure if I should continue walking in or if she was going to make me go back out and start over again.

"Close the door behind you," she said. So, a little wobbly from my first lesson in Things You Have to Do Around Horses That You Never Heard of Before, I closed the door, took a deep breath, smiled, and headed toward the corner.

"I'm Rita," I said, holding out my hand.

"Your half chaps are on backwards," said Tommy, extending a palm full of silver.

They say when you're young, it's much easier to learn new languages. It's also easier for the body to learn new skills. I was acutely aware of both of these facts as Tommy brought Shaddad out of his stall and attached him to the crossties. All I wanted to do was look at his long white eyelashes and keep touching the soft down of his nose, but Tommy was busy talking about nosebands and throatlatches and leg wraps and girths and billet straps, and suddenly there was a huge chasm between us made up of all I did not know. Worse still was that I had to manipulate these items by placing them on Shaddad, who stood by imperviously, periodically blinking those long white lashes while I fumbled against him.

When, after a lot of struggle and nearly losing a finger, I managed to get the bit into Shaddad's mouth, Tommy, who was holding the other side of the bridle, told me to buckle the noseband. But when I buckled it, she was clearly irritated. "That's the flash," she said. "This"—she grabbed hold of another leather strap—"is the noseband." I spent the next half hour putting on all of Shaddad's clothes.

"It's called 'tacking up,'" Tommy said, and I added that to the long list of new words I was promptly forgetting.

When it was time to tighten the girth, Tommy warned that sometimes Shaddad gets a little girthy.

"Girthy?"

"Basically, if he tries to bite you when you tighten the girth, smack him in the face."

I could take a lot of yelling and a fair amount of humiliation, but one thing I knew I wouldn't be able to do was smack a horse in the face. "I can't do that," I told her.

"You have to."

"Well, I can't."

"Look at the size of him, and look at the size of you. You think that little hand of yours is going to hurt him? If he tries to bite you, you have to let him know that you're the one in charge. If you don't establish that at the beginning, he'll take advantage of you."

I looked at Shaddad's face, ignored Tommy, and attempted to tighten the girth while leaning as far from the range of his teeth as possible.

"You can't cower away from him like that. Use your body language to let him know you're not afraid."

"But I am afraid."

In three quick steps, Tommy stormed over to me and stood facing me, inches from my face. Her shoulders were pitched forward, and instinctively I stepped back, away from her.

"See. That's what you have to do."

So I forced myself to stand as if I weren't afraid even though I was afraid, and not only didn't I panic, but I finished tightening Shaddad's girth without him biting me. But by the time we were all finished tacking him up, I didn't know whether to cry or to run out the door. Instead, I took hold of Shaddad's lead rope the way Tommy showed me and walked him into the arena, making sure to yell "door" and to look both ways.

THIRTEEN

Having fled Cindy's apartment building and headed back to Rockville Pike, I don't know where else to head but in the direction I came from. Cindy never answered her phone, and all I see now is this long road, these headlights coming at me through the bruised dusk.

When I get back to my father's neighborhood, I prowl past people's windows. Occasionally someone is eating or walking into a room or just watching TV, its blue light strobing into the street, but mostly the rooms are empty, like dioramas into which you could put anything. You could put a girl there. You could give her real parents.

I think about Joanne. I wonder what she's doing, if she's downstairs in the basement watching television as usual, and how she feels being the only kid left in our father's house. Our stepbrother left months ago. After three years of my father's torment, Bobby finally broke down and cried three years' worth of crying, howling and screaming inconsolably, and he wouldn't stop until my stepmother carried him and his suitcase to the car and drove him to his father's house, where he stayed. I envied him that night, how easily he could leave.

I know it's risky, but I can't help sidling up to my father's house and unlatching the gate to his small backyard. I just want a glimpse of Joanne. I've been gone for only a few hours, but I still want to know she's all right. I tiptoe down the steps and sneak over to the patio door, and suddenly I'm looking at her: my little sister sitting alone in the middle of the couch, her hands clasped in her lap. She's watching television, and her face is sad. It's surreal to be spying on her like this, to find this sheet of glass marking the line between our worlds. I want to run and I want never to leave her, both at once. I want whatever she's watching to make her smile. If I could just see her smile—

I wait, and her face is so still, and the longer I stand there, the greater the heaviness that presses on me. For a second, the clock winds back, and I remember her standing behind the balcony door of our parents' apartment, waiting for me to come home from school. I can see her dark hair. I can see the shape of her, the roundness. I was in second grade then, and she was still too young for school. She was also too young to pronounce my name properly, so she called me Bee, and though I couldn't hear her as I made my way toward our building from the bus stop, I knew that's what she was saying as she pointed her chubby finger excitedly and pressed herself against the glass. From the moment Joanne was born, she was the light I came home to.

But now I've left her, and she is sitting alone watching television, and the basement lights are spilling out onto the patio, and behind me it's getting dark, and I don't know if I should sneak away or stay here watching her. Overhead, birds are making their final trails of the evening across the sky. It's time to do something.

I knock gently. Joanne doesn't hear me over the television, so I knock a little louder and whisper her name, and this time she looks. She sees me, and a moment of recognition, deep and visceral, passes between us. As she comes to let me in, I put my finger to my lips to ask her to be quiet, but as soon as she slides the door open, she starts speaking normally, almost authoritatively. "Where have you been? Dad called the police and said you ran away."

"Shhh," I whisper. "Please."

I try to hug her, but she folds her arms against her ribs. She whispers back, "Why do I have to shush? Why can't you just come home already?"

I crouch down to hide behind the love seat. "Because I can't."

"Why not, Rita? Why not?"

I don't know how to answer, so I ask her to bring me something to eat instead.

"Why should I bring you something to eat if you're not coming home?" She's on the edge of tears, I can tell, but holding firm, her arms locked across her.

"Because I'm hungry," I say, looking up at her.

"Fine," she says, dropping her hands to her sides, and as she goes up to the kitchen, I start regretting how easily she gave in.

She returns with an ice cream sandwich. "Thank you," I say, unwrapping it quickly. Sweet cold fills my mouth. "What's Dad doing?"

"I don't know. He's up in his room." She crouches down next to me. "Is it good?"

I nod. Joanne has always loved food—not only eating it but watching others eat it, and in this regard, she and I have been great partners. When it came to French fries, I ate the soggy ones, and she ate the crisp ones. I sucked the chocolate off peanut M&M's, and she ate my spit-out peanuts. I licked the cream out of the Oreos, and she ate the cookies. Anyone else would think this was gross, but not Joanne. She watched me wide-eyed and hungry, and whatever I discarded, she ate with gusto—pizza crusts, meat, empty ice cream cones.

I offer her a bite of my ice cream, but she shakes her head no. I sense the wrongness then, not only of this moment when, for the first time, she's refusing something I'm giving her, but also of our lives, and how neither of us has the power to fix it. "I'm sorry—" I start, but just then I hear the heavy plodding of my father's footsteps overhead.

Startled, I jump up and drop my ice cream on the floor. Joanne and I look at each other, not sure what will happen next, but then my father's footsteps are coming closer, and I panic, and I bolt. I slip back out onto the patio, but before I take off, I look over my shoulder. Joanne is standing behind the glass, crying.

I love you, I mouth to her, and then I'm gone.

As I pound through the neighborhood at top speed, I'm aware that I can't possibly get far enough fast enough. Still, my sneakers mark their quick and steady rhythm on the pavement, and I think that maybe if I run hard enough, the air will catch me, and I will fly.

But eventually I get tired of running. Then I get tired of walking. I settle onto a back staircase of an apartment building and close my eyes. But I can't shake that last image of my sister; I can't stop seeing her face.

Once, when I was in the sixth grade, my gifted and talented group went to a library, where we were told to think of any question in the world we wanted the answer to. We all wrote our questions down on little slips of paper, and when I brought mine up to the teacher, she stopped and looked at me as if I'd offended her somehow. My question was *Why do parents hit their children?* She folded my paper up and handed it back to me, then told me I should think of a different question. My questions now are no easier to answer: How could I leave my sister like that? How could I stay? So I change the question: How can I sleep here tonight? I curl up on one side, just below the top step, and rest my head on my arm. The night is cool, the concrete steps like a vacuum sucking the heat from my body. I briefly consider trying to sneak back into my father's house and grab a jacket. No going back, I tell myself.

But the night is rough. No matter how I turn my body, the stairs dig into my ribs. Every so often I'm jolted by late-nighters coming home. "I'm just waiting for a friend," I mutter, sitting up straight and trying to look awake, though they don't seem to care.

In the morning, I find a church and go inside because I've seen in movies how people get saved in churches. Though they're too far away,

I want to touch the stained glass windows, the glowing colors. One of my favorite toys ever was the Lite-Brite my grandmother gave me for my fifth birthday, because you could push into the black and find light, and because you could actually touch the light—those jeweled pegs—as opposed to the one time I touched a lightbulb and blistered my finger.

So I sit on the wooden bench watching the light change on the windows and waiting for someone to come and tell me about God. But no one comes.

Eventually I walk back up Rockville Pike. I call Cindy from the lobby again, and this time she answers the phone. I ride the elevator up, and she sneaks me into her room, and we spend the night giggling in her bed, and while she's in school the next day, I hide in her closet. For eight hours I sit beneath her dresses and whisper songs into the darkness—*sweet dreams are made of this*—until she comes home and we eat hot dogs and call boys and pluck our eyebrows in the mirror.

But that evening, the police find me in her room, and this time instead of taking me home, they take me to a group home called Open Door, where I spend two weeks with girls who tease me for being a virgin and who make my short experience as a runaway seem laughable. But we cook tortellini together in a big kitchen, and that's sort of fun. In order to be released from the group home, I have to promise I won't run away again. So I promise, and then it's summer, and Joanne and I go to stay with our mother, and Joanne and I are still in our different worlds even when we're right next to each other, and she starts spending most of her time with her best friend's family across the street, and my mother is like a giant beanstalk of anger, cracking things as it grows, and when I start wearing a bra, my mother starts saying I'm just like a hooker, especially when I'm sitting down and forget to cross my legs, and now she's raging through the house, flinging books and candles around and yelling at her boyfriend, telling him he's a dumb fuck and why does he have to be such a dumb fuck, and then at me, wanting to know why I'm such a slut and why I have to wear so much eyeliner. I don't know why my eyeliner makes her so angry. But I can't stop remembering that once, for a little while, she loved me.

"I'm going outside," I say.

She puts her hand on her hip and looks toward the window. "You better not go farther than where I can see you."

The air outside is balmy and slightly sweet. A streetlight emits a small halo into the dark, while summer lingers around everything—my bare shoulders and legs, the occasional car that whooshes by, the silver half-face of the moon. There's something exciting about this stillness, about the slow air settling on my skin. I sit on the hood of my mother's car and tilt my head back to watch the sky.

Someone has turned on music, and Roger Daltrey's gravelly voice comes surging from an open window into me. He's singing about teenage wasteland, and the force of his voice, surrounded by the power of the guitar and drums and even a violin, is like a dozen hands on my body, lifting me. After the song crescendos, I feel its last note resound inside me, and though whoever turned the music on has now turned it off again, all I can feel is the lasting vibration of it. The stillness that, a few minutes earlier, was welcoming, now seems stagnant. And suddenly I can't stop thinking about the road outside our apartment complex. All I'd need to do is cross a field to get to it.

I make my move.

Out on Liberty Road, I hitch a ride back to Rockville and check my reflection in the pay phone outside a 7-Eleven. Here there is motion, every minute a new car, a new face, the sound of tires moving over the asphalt. I waste no time calling Cindy.

"Guess what!" I practically yell. "I'm on Rockville Pike!"

"What are you doing here?" Her voice is guarded, and it crushes me instantly. "I thought you were supposed to be at your mom's for the summer."

"Yeah, but she was going psycho again, so I took off."

"Wow, girl, you're crazy! What are you gonna do now?"

A car pulls in behind me and lights up my legs. "I'm not sure."

"Well, I'd tell you to stay here, but you know what happened last time. After the whole police thing, Uncle Frank would throw a fit if he saw you."

"I guess he's home, now, huh?"

"Yeah, he's here all right. Look, Rita, I really wish I could help you, but—"

"No, I totally understand." My voice comes out too high. "Besides, the police would probably check there again anyway." I scrape at the sidewalk with the front of my sandal.

"Do you need any money? I could meet you," she says, apologetically.

I push through the makeup and scraps of paper in my purse and collect my change. "No, I'm fine. I've got money."

"Okay. Well maybe we can get together soon, meet at the mall or something." We both know this won't happen.

"Sounds good. Thanks, Cindy."

"Be careful, you."

I stand leaning into the phone booth for a minute, trying to think. Cars keep driving by and it's late and warm and I'm getting tired. I consider walking back the mile to the apartments near my father's house, but I can't bear the thought of another night on those steps. I dig through my purse again and find a phone number I'd been keeping, just in case.

Fifteen minutes later, a Rolls-Royce pulls into the 7-Eleven, and I get in. The car reeks of cologne.

"I'm so glad you called," says Mr. Malekzadeh, stretching out the last word. "I thought you probably got rid of my number."

"Why would I do that?" I ask, looking out the window at the buildings passing by. I know I should feel nervous, but I don't. I feel resigned.

We drive the rest of the way in silence, and this time in the elevator I don't pretend to be glamorous. This time, I know where I'm going.

Out comes the wine, the pot, the tongue—and now I don't resist.

Now I will know what Cindy knows, what the group home girls know. Mr. Malekzadeh unties my halter and shoves his tongue inside my mouth. But when he unzips his pants, I step back. I don't expect it to be so big, so aggressive-looking.

"Put your hand on it," he says.

But I can't. "I've never done this before."

Mr. Malekzadeh's pursed lips curve to a smile, as if he's seeing me for the first time. "You're a virgin?"

I nod.

"Then we'll go slow," he says, taking my hand and leading me into the bedroom, where he takes off the rest of my clothes and lays me down on the bed. There's a window behind me, and I tilt my head back to see the moon, a halved pearl.

Mr. Malekzadeh reaches for the bottle of Vaseline Intensive Care lotion on his nightstand and pumps it into his hand, slathering it on himself and on me. The scent reminds me of baby diapers, a thought quickly knocked out by the force of him pushing against me. But it won't go in.

He becomes relentless with the lotion, pumping, then trying to push himself in again, then pumping, then pushing. It seems as if a week goes by. And then suddenly something breaks. There is the moon. There is Mr. Malekzadeh on top of me thrusting and grunting. There is the moon. There is the pressure, the pain. There is the lumbering sound of my father's footsteps; there are my mother's glazed eyes. There is the moon. There is the screaming in my mind with every thrust: *Fuck you, Mom! Fuck you, Dad!* I can't say it enough. We are both relentless.

When it's over, there's a fire between my legs. Mr. Malekzadeh lies back sweating and lights a cigarette. I smoke one, too, and grow older. Our smoke curls toward the ceiling, swirling up to a single haze over the room. On the sheets, my blood is smeared into a sloppy star. There's a power in the destruction, a strange satisfaction in the proof.

After we press our cigarettes out, he gets up and, without a word, starts dressing, so I get dressed, too. He moves briskly, matter-of-factly, as he pulls his polo over his head. He won't look at me. I feel suddenly forgotten, almost like a trespasser. The alarm clock glows 3:37 A.M., and I'm exhausted. I want to go back to the bed and close my eyes, to travel back and back, to a Halloween sleepover with friends, to dreams about water and boats, to an early childhood carnival spinning and glittering while trees stand quietly around it in the darkness and all I have inside me is hope.

FOURTEEN

It would be many months before I would stop at a road-side barn and ride my first horse—and even longer before I would meet Tommy and Shaddad. In these early months, I was trapped within my panic and could see no way out. I couldn't write. I could barely dress myself without tumbling headlong into another panic attack. And though Larry would never say it, I could sense his disappointment. He would say you need to write; it's your job to write. And I would say I don't know how to write when I feel like I'm dying, and he would say you're not dying, and I would say nothing is logical anymore; I'm not me anymore. And he would say you're you. And I would say I'm not me if I'm not writing, and he would say that's why you should write.

But it wasn't just the writing. I knew Larry needed me—the neuro-surgery department had been in much worse shape than he'd under-stood when he took the job—and in the past, he'd always leaned on me, and I'd always been strong enough to hold him. Now I needed him to hold me, but the timing was wrong. Also, I was vaguely aware that his holding me would require him to face what was happening to me: he would have to look straight at me; he would have to admit that his wife was coming unhinged. But by then we were already five years into a marriage in which we'd both tacitly agreed that I would hide certain parts of myself, that I would let him see only what he wanted, and that somehow this pact would keep us both safe—unsullied by my past. There were moments, though, that tested this arrangement, like the time he accidentally saw a page of a manuscript I'd left open. The sentences he read were about sex I'd had as a runaway. "I don't like it," he pouted, "that you had sex with other people."

"It's not like I enjoyed it," I pointed out. "But why should that matter anyway? You're the only one I want to have sex with now."

Larry shook his head. "I still don't like it. I wish I could have met you when you were a virgin."

"Sometimes I feel like a virgin."

He shook his head again. "Sometimes I wish I could just put you away on a shelf, so nobody else can get to you."

"But I'm right here with you. I'm alive."

It took me days to console Larry after that, as if I were comforting a child who'd just woken from a bad dream. Except the dream was my life.

"Maybe if I go to work with you, I'll be able to write," I suggested, "in your office. Maybe if I'm not alone, I won't be as scared."

When we were first dating, Larry took me to work with him several times. I was a technical writer then, and I'd met him at a summer party thrown by my boss. The tipsy woman who introduced us joked that Larry was her landscaper, but I didn't know it was a joke at the time. I didn't notice at first how soft his hands were. Instead, I noticed that he had a paramecium-shaped scar on his knee that was similar to the two I had on mine. I noticed that there was a boyishness about him that belied his age. And I noticed that the fields around us were lit gold in the afternoon sun.

So for a short time, I believed this boy-man, whose hair kept flopping forward onto his forehead, and which he kept abruptly brushing away each time with the curve of his hand, was a gardener. I had never dated a man of the earth before, and as I flirted, I imagined his hands reaching into the cool soil. That's when I eyed his hands—the clean, neatly clipped nails; the unmarked, supple skin—and the truth came out. Of course, it's hard to be disappointed when you discover that the man you're flirting with is not a gardener but a brain surgeon.

Immediately, I wanted to know more. I am nothing if not curious, which is how I ended up following Larry, weeks after we met, into the operating room in a pair of loose pink scrubs that could have easily housed two of me. I didn't tell him about my squeamishness, and he didn't tell me that the patient's open skull would be only inches away from me when we entered the room. There would be no special viewing theater like in the movies—just the throbbing, bleeding brain of a human being. As we stood around the patient and the residents told Larry how the opening went, I was bombarded with thoughts, the primary being a question of math: what were the odds that if I fainted, I would fall directly onto this man's head?

But I neither fell nor fainted. I stood and watched. It was a long five hours observing Larry remove blackish pieces of tumor bit by microscopic bit while I fought back alternating waves of nausea and hunger, but I wanted to be there. I wanted to know everything about what Larry did—not only that he saved lives, but also the grit of it, the blood dripping into a clear plastic bag beneath the patient's head, the growing hole where the pinkish frontal lobe was disappearing, the acrid smell of bone dust.

Now what I wanted was simpler, yet seemingly impossible: to have one whole day free from fear. So Larry agreed to bring me, his emotionally unstable wife, to his new job. I figured if something went wrong, I was already in a hospital. Luckily, what I'd hoped turned out to be true: being there helped me feel slightly less scared than usual. But still, despite the company of my trusty notebook and laptop, I couldn't write. So I drew a picture for Larry instead. Only, two-year-olds can draw better than I can, so the elephant I sketched came out looking like George Washington. Larry put it up on the corkboard in his office anyway, and as he pushed the tack in, he smiled. This, I thought, is the family I never had.

When Larry went off to see patients, I busied myself by watching *Meet the Parents* on my laptop. I don't know what Larry's assistant thought each time she entered the room to put something on Larry's desk, but when she said hello and commented on the rain, neither of us discussed the fact that I was curled up on my side watching Ben Stiller spray-paint the tail of a cat. Normally I might have tried to snap the laptop shut or at least make some excuse for myself, but she came in each time without warning. Besides, when it's a matter of survival, it's hard to care what people think of you. And for me, that's what it felt like: survival.

What I found comforting about *Meet the Parents* was that nothing terrible happens, and the wispy blond schoolteacher's parents will always keep her childhood room as she left it, wallpapered in flowers and frilled with fluffed bedding and a delicate string-pull lamp. And I could imagine that room—that safe, unchanging place—as my own.

When I finally decided to confide my predicament to someone, I called my friend Annie, a sprightly Floridian lawyer with a toothpaste commercial smile and a Suzuki GSX motorcycle. As soon as I told her what was going on, I could feel the slap of her words across the states. "What the hell are you doing? It's been nearly two months. Two months you haven't had any control over your life. How long do you plan to suffer with this?"

"I'm just trying to figure it out. If I can start to understand—"

"What you need to understand is that sometimes you need help, and you should get it. Get two prescriptions—one for Prozac and one for Xanax—and pull yourself together."

I tried to explain that I'd made it this far in my life without medication, so why change now?

"Because you need it," she said. "That's why."

"What if I need something else? What if I'm supposed to learn something from this? Wouldn't taking drugs just mask it?"

She was silent so long that I thought she'd hung up.

"Hello?" I said.

"Suit yourself," she sighed. "If you want to suffer, then suffer."

Of course I didn't want to suffer. Who does? But a wise social worker once told me that the only way to be truly happy is to also be willing to suffer our suffering. I wasn't entirely sure what he meant at first, and I didn't like the sound of it, but what he meant was simple: each of us will endure pain in our lifetimes—there's no escaping it (there is an entire religion based upon this truth)—and we can keep trying to flee this pain, or we can abide by it. Those are our only two choices. Most of us get twitchy for relief and try to squirm away. But the social worker's point was that by moving through our suffering, instead of away from it, we learn the most about ourselves.

"I love you, Annie," I told my friend. "And I appreciate your advice, but I really think there's something here for me to learn."

"I love you, too," she said. "Learn well."

I decided to try learning something at a local Unitarian Universalist church, mostly because of the rainbow on the church sign, which suggested people who might be accepting, who wouldn't judge me for obsessively taking my pulse or for needing to stand near the door for an entire service, people who left their houses each Sunday morning because, like me, they were searching for something.

As I stood with Larry beside the door in the back of the church, I had to reconcile the difference between the churches I'd attended in the past and this one. By all appearances, they had a lot in common: the acolytes, the hymns, the announcements, the older white man at the pulpit. But that's where the similarities ended. Because this minister wasn't quoting from Mark or Luke or John; he was quoting from Vonnegut: " 'I tell you, even a half-dead man hates to be alive and not be able to see any sense to it.' " That was exactly it. I didn't understand what was happening to me, but to make it all disappear with a pill wouldn't solve the fundamental question of *why*. I wanted to make sense of my panic; I wanted the *why*.

The minister went on to espouse words from a local ornithologist, along with Whitman and Pound, all of which were enough to entice me to grab Larry's hand and, after standing for half the service, sit down in the last pew—still close enough to the door to make a quick getaway in case of a fire or collapsing roof or sudden collective ridicule from a hundred turned heads. As we settled in, I thought I saw the minister smile at us. And it felt good, that quick acknowledgment in our seat beside a woman and her young child. I realized then how lonely I'd been.

The minister gently sculpted the air with his hands as he spoke about gifts, how we should always pass them on, how one of these gifts is "to love whoever is around to be loved." *Wow,* I thought, *this is one special place.* But then, after placing our money in the tidings bowl, I gave a nod to Larry and we slipped out the back before the exodus.

FIFTEEN

Time slows. It stretches into a great vat, each second a drop falling in slow motion. Each drop explodes into liquid, changing the liquid each time. We're standing in the kitchen, lined up like kids at a bus stop. We're drinking tall glasses of many kinds of liquor from my mother's cabinet, and someone has given me these pills that are pink hearts, and now they're leaving, and I don't know why they're leaving. Wait, I want to say, but the word resists me, won't rise. One boy stays, holds his glass, and his eyes are the color of whiskey, and the whiskey is staring at me. He puts his glass on the counter, and the earth stutters. "Come here," he says, clutching the back of my head and pulling me toward him. The slimy muscle of his tongue grows, snakes its way into my throat. I'm going to throw up.

While I heave in the bathroom, he slips out. Then I am leaving, too, because a weight is pulling me down, out of the light. I stumble out of the bathroom and vomit onto the pink carpet. I'm trying to get to the phone because I feel a blackness I've never felt before, like the pressing of tires against a road. I crawl across the living room floor and pull myself up onto the old pink sofa, to the phone. I try to speak, but my voice comes out like pulp. Then everything falls, and there is nothing but impenetrable black.

In the week since my mother admitted me to this teenage psych ward, I've learned to play Spades, taught a few of the girls the perfect three-part eye shadow application, and met a cute boy named Tony. I'm partnered up with him in the middle of a Spades game when a jowly middle-aged man approaches our table. We're playing against Paul and Stacey—a pretty girl who compulsively puts on lip gloss—and Tony and I are winning.

"Hi, Dr. Kosarin," Stacy sings.

"Rita?" he asks, looking at me.

"Yes."

"I'm Dr. Kosarin, the psychiatrist here. Would you please come with me?"

"We'll pick this up later," assures Tony with a wink.

I nod back, smiling shyly, and follow Dr. Kosarin to his office.

"So, Rita, can you tell me why you're here?"

I lean back in my little metal-legged chair. "I guess because I keep running away."

The last time I ran away, that night after Mr. Malekzadeh was finished with me, I roamed through the apartment building, riding the elevator up and down, meandering down one hall and then another, until finally I went to sleep on a back staircase, which was carpeted and much warmer than the last one. When a security guard discovered me, I told him I was eighteen and just very tired, and he smiled sadly at me and told me we could call either my parents or the police. I chose my mother. The sun was up by the time she drove the hour to get me. I hugged her and thanked her and wondered, as she lightly hugged me back, if she could sense what had just happened to my body. If she could, she didn't show it.

Dr. Kosarin leans back in his plush leather chair and pulls off his glasses. "Is that all?" he asks, rubbing his hand over his eyes. He puts his glasses back on and picks up my file. "It says here that you were recently admitted to Baltimore County General Hospital for an overdose of—let's see here—a mixture of amphetamines and alcohol. Do you want to tell me about that?"

"There's not much to tell. Some friends came over, and we made these really strong drinks, and then one of them had some speed, so I tried it."

"Uh-huh, I see. And have you ever attempted suicide prior to this episode?"

"Of course not. I wasn't trying to commit suicide."

"Okay. Tell me then, have you ever had any suicidal thoughts? Ever feel like it might just be easier to end it all—you know, run away for good, that sort of thing?"

"No." I'm starting to get annoyed. "I mean, yes, I've thought about running away for good, but I've never wanted to kill myself."

"Because it's okay if you have. A lot of people do. We're here to help you, Rita."

I'm beginning to learn that many adults aren't any wiser than children, that, in fact, they can be the blindest, meanest people on earth. "Right," I say. "But I'm not suicidal." I look him defiantly in the eyes. "Why don't you ask me why I run away?"

Dr. Kosarin sighs, and I can see he's equally annoyed with me. "Today's purpose is to do an initial evaluation. We can talk more about that later. Now if you could just answer a few more questions. Tell me, how do you sleep at night?"

"Fine."

"No trouble falling asleep? No waking up in the middle of the night?"

"Like I said, fine."

"Do you ever feel like you want to hurt someone?"

I imagine knocking him off his big chair. "No."

B ack on the unit, I hear the sound first—growling, low and feral. It's coming from a girl who's squirming on the floor. Three staff members are trying to hold her down as she snarls, punches, kicks, and bites them. The counselors flinch. One is bleeding from her hand. The girl looks at nothing. She is all limbs. Her shirt has come up in the tussle, exposing her pale belly and the underside of a breast. Within seconds several men come rushing down the hall. They pin her arms and legs down as easily as if they were a doll's. One of them produces a needle, and soon the girl's eyes are rolling back in their sockets.

"They probably gave her enough Thorazine to knock her out for days," someone says.

"What happened?" I ask.

"Oh, nothing. She just goes off sometimes. They'll probably put her in seclusion for a week."

"What's wrong with her?"

"Honey, don't you know where you are?"

SIXTEEN

"Let me tell you what's wrong with the way you're sitting."

Though I'd mounted Shaddad only seconds earlier and we hadn't yet taken a single step, I was already screwing up.

"Everything." Tommy approached me and put her hand on my leg. "See how your legs are forward? We call that a 'chair seat,' but riding isn't sitting back on a sofa and letting the horse do all the work. In dressage, we're constantly engaged—we ride every stride, as they say. In terms of our position, we strive to achieve a straight line from the top of the head to the seat to the soles of the feet—mind you, I studied biomechanics, so I'm very interested in how each individual part moves in the collective whole—so for starters, move your legs back and imagine a string attached from the rafters to the top of your head. Imagine that if we took the horse away, you'd be standing, not sitting."

I did as she instructed, and for the next half an hour, Tommy adjusted my inner thighs, the angle of my hips, my back, my shoulders, my stomach, my arms, my hands, and my feet—talking at length about each body part—while Shaddad stood stoically beneath me. In the first five minutes of entering the barn, I'd felt overwhelmed, but now I was so far past information overload that I was losing track of basic English. Which was not a good time to finally start moving. But I wanted to give myself over completely to this lifelong passion, to this elegant world of horses that, though it at times seemed so inelegant it became farcical, kept inviting me to climb over fear in ways I hadn't known were possible. And if I couldn't trust that, what could I ever trust? So we started moving.

Standing in the middle of the arena, Tommy controlled Shaddad by attaching him to a long rope called a lunge line. She wiggled the whip in her other hand, and instantly, Shaddad started walking.

"You're resisting," she said after a few steps. "Can you feel how his legs move forward one at a time as he walks? Just like a person?"

The simple answer was no. It was hard for me to feel anything; I just knew that I was no longer on the ground and that I was perched on top of a large animal. "I don't know. I guess."

"Well, follow that. Let your hips move with him."

I closed my eyes and tried to feel his strides.

"Don't close your eyes. When you close your eyes, you automatically tilt your head forward, and that throws off your whole position."

And somewhere between my feeling for Shaddad's gait and having to relearn simple facts like which side was my left and which was my right, Tommy asked Shaddad to trot. I had been on a horse a total of one other time in my life—and that was a few weeks earlier, when I'd randomly stopped at a barn and walked around for a few minutes on a horse named Applesauce—so I had no way of knowing that trotting would mean getting banged in the crotch over and over by the hard pommel of the saddle. I felt a somewhat rational fear for my life as I struggled to stay on. But that wasn't all: I also had to learn to "post the trot": to rise up out of the saddle with every other beat. Never in my life had I found a physical activity so difficult or felt so uncoordinated; never had I felt more like a child, not even as a child. My legs got tired almost instantly, but if I tried to sit, Tommy yelled at me to keep posting, and as I gasped out a plea for her to make him stop, she told me this is how you learn, so I kept shakily bouncing around in and out of the saddle, and after a lot of flailing, my first riding lesson was over.

At several points during my lesson, I expected to start panicking. But those moments were fleeting; I was too caught up in my awkward physical rigor to give these deeper, more internal thoughts much airtime. And it wasn't until later that I understood a difference between panic and other kinds of fear: this haphazard floundering about on Shaddad's back presented a real concern, one based on some simple laws of physics—namely, how could I keep bumping around these circles without falling. My fear, then, of hitting the ground, had an immediate counterpoint: my fight to stay on. But in the fight-flight of panic, where the source of fear is constantly shape-shifting and shrouded in darkness, there is no obvious counterpoint, no way to fight or flee that which cannot be seen—no last rally of strength in the legs as they clutch the horse's sides, no last thoughts about how to curl the body and protect the head if the legs fail and the ground comes fast—so the panic quickly moves to consume. Could it be that by putting myself in a situation that was truly scary, I was chasing away this other fear, this phantom? Was it that simple, that one fear could fight another? Maybe it was. Because when Tommy finally asked Shaddad to stop trotting, I was already stronger.

As I slid off Shaddad and took a few steps, my whole body felt like rubber, and my legs still felt as if there were a horse between them. I reached to stroke Shaddad's neck, and he turned to look at me. In an instant, I was four again. I was reaching out my hand to the sweeping and hungry trunk of an elephant and watching the world turn on.

It had been a rough couple of hours, but I'd survived. I'd ridden a horse. I had looked into the horse's eye and found a kind of peace.

SEVENTEEN

I knew my life was shrinking. Despite the books, despite the trip to Larry's office, despite phone calls to Annie and other friends, I was still terrified of things seen and unseen, of all I could imagine and all I hadn't yet imagined, of the world at large and of the basic functioning of my own body. But somehow I had deemed safe the space between the front steps and the edge of the azalea bushes, so my daily walk consisted of a few paces of that fifteen-foot swath of flagstone—that is, until I hit the low point of low points.

As I took my ten-step stroll back and forth, phone in my hand in case of an emergency, I was thinking not about the fall air, which must have been getting cooler, or about squirrels, which must have been scampering busily, or about sentences, which I wasn't writing, but about atriums and ventricles and the heart's incessant work. It was serious thinking, much like the thinking I do on planes, when I'm reasonably certain there's no reason we shouldn't be dropping straight out of the sky: the heart, magical fist-size ticker that it is, defies my most basic logic. And as I was thinking about these things—about mitochondria and cell death and deadly rhythms, something moved beside me. I caught it in my periphery: large and dark and coming at me. I shrieked and jumped forward like a grasshopper, and my heart pitched into full speed. The culprit? My own shadow.

I was beginning to wonder if I was really going crazy. I thought about my mother's sister, Nanette, whom I saw only once or twice a year when I was a kid and we drove from Baltimore to Queens to visit my grandparents. At their house, everyone was always talking and clinking wineglasses and singing and dancing and clapping their hands, and next to Grandma, Nanette was my favorite person to dance with, her long blond hair whipping around with each dramatic turn of the tango. I loved hearing her laugh because her voice was always a bit hoarse and her laughter rolled out like a fun bumpy road. You sound like Stevie Nicks, I used to tell her. She sang, laughing, *"Women, they will come and they will go . . ."* Her blue eyes appeared huge beneath the bifocals she wore, and I thought that was magnificent.

Once, when everyone had gone out and left the two of us alone, my aunt started to drink. I was nine by then, old enough to realize, when she passed out, that the pills she took with her whiskey were what had made her lie limp, her eyes half open but not seeing. I tried shaking her awake, calling her name, shaking her harder until the bed began to scuff the wall. I was also old enough to know that the ipecac in the bathroom would make her throw up, so I forced it down her throat. I could have killed her, but I wasn't old enough to know that. Instead, she vomited, over and over, on the flowery pillows, on her own face, on my hands and arms. I held her in it, and later when we washed ourselves clean, she thanked me, that warm husk of a voice.

A decade later, on an unremarkable day, my aunt sold her condo and walked onto the streets of New York City, homeless. Schizophrenia, the doctors diagnosed—a paranoid schizophrenic. I would see it for myself once while I was visiting my grandparents. She turned up one afternoon covered in black shoe polish—not just her face, but her entire body. She wore a man's haircut and baggy jeans. She had lost her glasses and most of her teeth, and she held a magnifying glass up to one giant eye when she arrived. "Look at you," she said, running the spyglass up and down. "You're all grown up now. So pretty." She spoke to me as if she were the aunt I remembered, as if her face weren't smeared black, as if she didn't smell of sweat and urine. "It's a lovely day," she said, smiling a gummy smile. Then her eyes shifted around the room, squinting. She poked her head forward and began to sniff. "Tell me," she said, locking her gaze on me, "do you ever smell the mafia?"

I told her I didn't think I did, and she told me that she was really a black boy named Tony, that my grandparents had castrated her when she was a baby, that people kept operating on her mouth and taking all her teeth. "Do you remember when we used to dance?" I asked her. "When I was little?" She laughed—she still had her same laugh—"Of course I do." But her eyes quickly narrowed. "They're doing experiments on me," she whispered.

She had been nearly my age when the doctors diagnosed her with schizophrenia. And now I wondered if it was my turn, if this was how she'd lost those pieces of herself, quick as a fire destroys a forest. What I knew was this: each second of my life felt like a near escape from death, the way the bridge falls apart in cartoons, rung by rung, just behind the runner's feet.

I knew I needed help. And I decided it should come in the form of a mother. Though I had let my own mother go a couple of years earlier, I still hadn't let the *idea* of a mother go. I still hadn't stopped wanting that particular and important kind of love. The mother I often imagined was an amalgam of several mothers: Carol Brady from *The Brady Bunch*; several of the hefty no-nonsense brown-skinned women I'd encountered through my years in lockup; and my horse-loving friend Jennifer's mother, who once wrapped a towel around my shoulders when I'd gotten out of their pool shivering. My new mother would arrive replete with her sensible shoes and a plate of still-warm banana bread. She would say, "Hey, you silly child panicking on the sofa. You quit it now and come get yourself some banana bread." And I would.

So that was my plan. And I heard no God laughing. I was going to go out and find myself a mom, plain and simple. A calm fell over me then, and I was able to get up and let the dogs out without panicking at all.

Later that day I found a long chain in the back of a kitchen drawer, with a small white plastic device at the end of it. It was roughly two inches long, with a button in the center and the name of our alarm company printed above it. Below the button was the word PANIC. My very own panic button! I must not have noticed it when we'd moved in, but without another thought I promptly pulled the chain over my head. All I would have to do, in the event of robbers or a deteriorating arrhythmia or the accidental inhalation of a dried apricot, was press the button. It was a revelation. It was my new necklace.

EIGHTEEN

My second lesson on Shaddad was roughly a repeat of my first lesson, even down to Tommy's reprimanding me about bridle parts. But to a novice, a bridle is an evil thing, a leather contraption full of loops and buckles that you have to manage while maneuvering a metal bar, the bit, into the horse's mouth. "Look," Tommy said, holding up the bridle. "See the shape of the horse's head? Now look at the shape of the bridle and you can see how it fits."

But what I saw didn't appear to match the shape of Shaddad's head at all. "Yes." I nodded, not wanting to let on that I was failing some kind of basic IQ test.

"Then go ahead and do it by yourself this time."

Tommy handed the bridle to me, and I looked at Shaddad, and he blinked, and then he sighed. "Okay, let's see here," I said, slipping one of the loops over Shaddad's nose.

"Nope," said Tommy. "You forgot to put the reins over his head. You always, *always* have to put the reins over the horse's head first, so that if he tries to go somewhere, you have something you can stop him with."

I tossed the reins over Shaddad's head, and then attempted to reinsert his nose into the same loop as before.

"Nope," said Tommy. "That's the browband."

"Oh."

It took me several tries, but Shaddad, in his tremendous patience, stood calmly while I wrestled with the bridle, fumbling the various straps against his nostrils and cheeks. Finally Tommy, who could no longer bear the spectacle, took the bridle from my hand. "One day," she said, easily slipping the bit into Shaddad's mouth, "you'll be able to stand right beside him like I am and put the bridle on without even looking."

But I was discouraged. And for a moment I felt foolish for attempting to enter a world that I had no business entering. All the other people I encountered in the barn seemed so at ease around the horses, and I wondered if that was the kind of confidence a person could learn only as a child—if maybe it was too late for me.

But when I climbed onto Shaddad and wrapped my legs around him, I could feel that between my first lesson and this one, something had already shifted: immediately I remembered the sensation of the straight line my spine was supposed to make over his back, and I sat up tall, and Tommy said, "I see you remember something from last time," and I beamed with the learning.

And then Tommy flicked her whip and Shaddad began to trot, thumping into all the already sore parts of me, and the glowy feeling I'd been enjoying was promptly swallowed by desperate pain. After a few minutes I asked Tommy to please make him stop, but like the last time, she refused. "If a horse is bolting on you, you might not be able to make him stop. Then what do you do?" But I couldn't answer her question because every iota of my consciousness was focused on one thing: making the horse stop.

"I'm serious," I said, flailing in an endless loop around Tommy. "I need to catch my breath."

But Tommy kept the whip moving across the ground, which kept Shaddad trotting. "I once had a sixty-year-old asthmatic woman ask me to make the horse stop. And you know what?"

"I . . . really . . . mean . . . it . . . Stop!"

"I kept him going, that's what I did. She was so mad. But later she thanked me, because she learned she could push herself farther than she thought she could."

It was at that moment that I felt unadulterated terror. My life was in the hands of a virtual stranger, a stranger with obvious control issues, and my lungs and legs and crotch were burning, and Shaddad was moving along as if he would never tire, and it occurred to me again that I might panic, but I was too busy trying not to die to panic, and just when I was sure I was seconds away from collapsing, Tommy asked Shaddad to walk. And though I never would have admitted this to her, what she'd said was true: I was learning, in those many circles of torture, that I could push myself farther than I thought.

Weeks went by, then months, and in that time I came faithfully to ride Shaddad and get yelled at by Tommy. The learning process was slow and repetitive, and my inner thighs were constantly sore, and the world of horses continued to feel like an elite club to which I was undergoing a seemingly endless initiation. But I was learning. After a while, I could put on Shaddad's bridle without poking either of us in the eye, and I could post the trot without wishing I were wearing a jockstrap. Some days I wanted to cry and some days I did cry and some days I gave Tommy the evil eye when her head was turned, but what kept me coming back were the horses, plain and simple. Just being near them felt like an oasis, as if the rest of my life switched off and there was only horse smell, horse sound, horse motion, horse stillness.

NINETEEN

A few days after I resolved to find myself a mother, on a day when I was courageous enough to travel the two miles to the local grocery store, I scoped out potential mothers in the produce aisle, because the way a woman chooses her fruit and vegetables says a lot about her. I watched women delicately cradle tomatoes in their fingers and others tear them roughly off the vine. I watched women knock on watermelons, shake water off romaine, stuff their bags with fiddlehead ferns.

When I spotted a possible candidate, I'd smile at her and ask her how she planned to cook her vegetables. Most women love to talk about what they're making for dinner that night. "Oh, Brussels sprouts are easy—you just roast 'em in the oven. Cut 'em in half, drizzle with olive oil, a little salt and pepper, and you're set. Four hundred degrees. Delicious."

After a few trips to the produce aisle, I'd acquired several cooking tips but no mother. It had been more than two months since my first panic attack, and almost as long since I'd driven farther than a five-mile radius on our local country roads, and I had to face what I'd become: a woman who accessorized her outfits with medical gear and security devices. Even *Meet the Parents* was losing its charm. I needed a mother, fast. So I called a dog sitter.

My plan was simple: (1) find a sweet and nurturing older woman who loves animals; (2) invite her over for a trial visit with my two dogs; (3) charm her with my sad but eager eyes; (4) become her daughter.

When the dog sitter arrived, I was instantly disappointed. For one, she didn't smile. And she didn't acknowledge my two dogs, now in a frenzy of tail wagging at her feet. But I was willing to forgive the first impression. She had every right to be wary about entering a stranger's house at night. So I smiled at her and knelt down to introduce her to my dogs, giving them both a good scratch under their collars.

"What breed are they?" she asked, still standing.

Maybe she had a bad back, I thought. "They're a Jack Russell–dachshund mix. I rescued them from the pound when they were ten months old. Littermates. The white one is Aramis, and the black one is Starlet."

"Pound dogs are the best," she said.

I can work with this, I thought. "Come, sit down. Can I bring you a cup of tea?"

I took the opportunity to quickly check my pulse. *Don't panic, don't panic, don't panic,* I told myself while the water rushed into the kettle. Of course, I panicked. Then I sat at the other end of the couch, with the dogs between us, and shakily held my teacup.

The dog sitter looked at me. "Aren't you going to, you know, leave?"

"Oh, I thought I explained. I wanted this to be a get-to-know-you visit."

"It's just that people usually run a few errands or something, so their pets and I have a chance to get to know each other."

Was this woman kicking me out of my own house? "If it's okay with you, I'd prefer you guys get acquainted while I'm here."

As she sighed and looked up at the TV, I examined her profile, the sharp point of her nose, the kinky fair hair obscuring the side of her cheek. I wondered if she had been attractive when she was younger, if she had smiled more then. There had to be some way I could connect with her. "I'm a writer," I volunteered. "But I haven't been writing lately because I've been going through a pretty intense bout of anxiety." And that's when I learned the quickest way to get rid of a dog sitter.

Later that evening, Larry came home and took me to the grocery store. He was selecting cuts of meat for one of his stews while I lingered in the bakery, which is arguably the happiest place in any grocery store. I ordered a fruit tart laden with fresh berries and smiled at the baker. I had noticed her before, on first glance because she was taller than everyone else, but also because she seemed to carry a sadness in her eyes, as if any moment they could fill with tears. "Do you make these?" I asked, as she placed the dessert in a box.

"I make all of it," she said. Her voice matched her eyes; it held a slight quiver.

"Wow," I said. "That's a lot of sweet."

She looked very serious then, and I thought I'd somehow misunderstood something. "This is just what I do *here*," she said. "I'm a trained chef. I can make more than pie."

On a whim, I asked if she ever gave cooking lessons. Her eyes shone. "Yes. I do."

I'd never really learned to cook. After the roast chicken dinner that went so wrong when we were kids, my mother's exclusive use of the oven was to heat the foil-wrapped Swanson TV dinners of fried chicken, with the small partitions of corn, mealy mashed potatoes, and rubbery apple cobbler. I didn't complain; I loved those things. I would zealously pick the breading off the chicken before giving the meat to my sister and starting on the potatoes. Years later, in a kitchen of my own, I figured things out as best as I could. But I didn't know basic things, such as the proper way to hold a knife or cut an onion or peel a butternut squash. I wasn't exactly sure what a roux was or what it meant to deglaze something.

"Where do I sign up?" I asked.

The woman quickly wrote her name and number on a piece of paper and handed it to me. Her name was Helen. It was a good name. It was in my pocket.

That night I showered and came to bed in my new lingerie: the stethoscope. After Larry was asleep, I studied him in the dark. He was on his back, naked in the yellow glow of the hall light, covers kicked off. His left leg was bent off the bed. His left hand was reposed straight across his heart, his wedding band gleaming at his sternum—as if at any moment his voice would come through: "I pledge allegiance . . ." *I miss you,* I thought, watching him.

What I wanted from Larry seemed so simple—to have compassion for whatever this thing was that was going haywire inside me—but as I came to him with my fearful mind and turbulent heart, I realized it wasn't simple at all. He was impatient, disappointed, unsettled. I knew this from his curt reassurances, from the disdain in his eyes, from his unwillingness to ask me about my panic, about how it felt to be scared of the most basic tasks—and ultimately, about where I'd come from.

Though Larry was, in many respects, boyish, he was also a brave man. Sometimes I referred to him as my hero, not because he once received a Shock Trauma Hero Award from the University of Maryland's Shock Trauma Center, but because he had more integrity than anyone I'd ever met, and because I trusted him more than anyone

I'd ever known. Part of that trust came from his humility. On the night of our first date, he didn't try to impress me by casually mentioning all the lives he'd saved, though there had been many; instead, he told me how upset he was with himself over a patient he'd seen that day. He'd thought the patient had radiation necrosis, a side effect from radiosurgery, but it had actually been a recurrence of a metastatic tumor.

"Do they look different on a scan?" I'd asked.

"No, that's just it. They look very similar. And he was in the expected time window to have necrosis."

"So then any surgeon would have thought the same thing?"

"Maybe, but I just wish I hadn't."

That was the beginning of us—this honest moment, this confession of possible failure, this deep concern for another human being—and it warmed me through. Larry was a healer. He removed tumors, clipped aneurysms, cleared out blood clots, dislodged bulging disks in the spine, dealt daily with the aberrations of the body. And his specialty was brain tumors—all the varied masses that, if left untended, displaced the other parts of the brain, causing the most basic functions to go awry.

Larry healed brains. Yet here he was, married to a woman whose mind was out of control, and he didn't know how to touch it.

TWENTY

The music is so loud that I'm thinking some kind of nuclear fission is happening inside my ears. I'm jammed in the backseat with these guys, and the whole car smells like Polo cologne and pot. They're leaning into me, and one of them has his hand on my knee. Their teeth flash under the streetlights. They're shouting along with the Stray Cats in heavy Iranian accents and smiling expectantly—"She's sexy and seventeen!" The truth is I'm thirteen, but no guy wants to hear that—they just want to think it, keep it hidden like a present. So I give them that.

I don't know where we're going. For the moment, I'm glad to be heading somewhere. I'm hoping maybe I'll get lucky and they'll give me something to eat. I'd love pizza. I stare past the guy on my right to see the moon gleaming like a seashell on a night table, under a lamp. It disappears when the driver takes a turn onto the highway.

The guy to my left has run his hand up my leg, where it's resting on my inner thigh. The wind is pouring into the car like a fit of wings, sweeping my hair around. I keep wiping it from my eyes because I want to see. I want to see everything I can outside these windows—the passing cars swishing by, the spark and tail of every light, the trees standing like shadows in their quiet height, the bright green highway signs.

The Iranians like steak. In the supermarket, they shove them down the fronts of their pants. I met these guys earlier at the 7-Eleven near my father's house, when they pulled in with their car thumping and their windows down. They were smiling at me, and their eyes were like firecrackers. When they asked me if I wanted a ride, I got in and they floored it down the road. There are a lot of Middle Eastern people who live here in these towns outside Washington, D.C., but this one guy, Afshin, who now has a lap full of rib-eye, is the most gorgeous man I've ever seen, even more gorgeous than Andy Gibb and Shaun Cassidy, whose posters I stared at for years on my bedroom wall.

I used to keep count of how many times I ran away. I liked thinking it: *I have run away five times.* But now I've stopped counting, maybe because it's no longer so much a thing I do but more who I am. After I got out of Lutheran Hospital and went back to my father's house, I thought maybe I could stop running. But by then my stepmother had left my father—after three years of marriage, my father finally snapped and beat her until she clawed her way out of the house and ran barefoot in her nightgown into the February snow—and my sister had gone back to live with our mother, and my father walked around bereft and excoriated and mean, and most days I felt like I was living inside a sarcophagus. So I ran. That was three weeks ago.

The men take me back to their apartment and fire the steaks up on the broiler. I've never really liked meat, but I eat small bites anyway because I'm hungry. "This"—one of them holds his fork straight out—"is how you cook a steak!" Then, to me, "You're too skinny. Skinny like a pencil. You need more meat!"

One of the men echoes, "More meat," and they all laugh—all except Afshin, whose amber eyes seem to be on the verge of a question and whose face is the perfect arrangement of shadow and light.

"What do you do?" Afshin asks me, and I instantly feel myself blush.

Unsure how to answer, I busy myself with cutting my steak.

"Are you in school?" He tilts his head to look at me, and I can hardly breathe under his gaze.

"I'm trying to figure out my life," I say, because it is the truest and only thing I can think to say.

He nods thoughtfully. "College. That's what you should do with your life."

"Meat," says the one with the fork. "Meat is what she should do with her life."

"I'm in college," says Afshin, and his perfect smile damn near knocks me off my chair. "You should come with me, tomorrow! You will love it. You will fall absolutely in *love* with it!"

And I'm thinking that he doesn't realize I'm only thirteen and that there's an APB out on me. And I'm thinking that his fingers are so long and delicate. And I'm thinking that his optimism is one of ignorance, which makes it an optimism made out of glitter that will so quickly fall to the ground.

That night, I sleep on a bare mattress beside Afshin, and I smell his skin, and I smell the black waves of his hair, and every single thing about him is sweet, and I can hear, somewhere far off in my mind, my mother calling me names, and I feel wretched lying there beside this stranger, who I want with a hunger that seizes me and who I know I will never have.

In the morning, when I wake, he is gone. I shower in their bathroom, then start walking back down the road, my hair still wet.

TWENTY-ONE

One thing was clear: this panic wasn't going away on its own. So Larry made some phone calls and got me an appointment at the Center for Anxiety and Related Disorders (CARD) in Boston. As I sat in the waiting room filling out my intake questionnaire, which seemed to be asking the same few questions in slightly different ways—the gist of which was, *Is anxiety a problem for you?*—I was grateful for two things: (1) I was getting help; and (2) there was an elevator, so I didn't have to take the stairs.

I was relieved when Dr. E, a statuesque Nordic-looking woman in baggy linen pants, led me back to her office, a large, tidy space adorned with abstract paintings in dusky hues and tribal figures made out of metal and wood. She glanced over my questionnaire before asking me to confirm that I was, in fact, afraid to leave the house, afraid to be in the house alone, afraid to shower alone, afraid to exercise or even walk up stairs, afraid to go through checkout lines, afraid to drive, afraid of crossing the street, afraid of fainting, afraid of going crazy, afraid my heart was going to stop. "Yes," I said, for starters.

"I don't know how I got like this," I explained to her. "I've never really scared easily. Now I even wake up scared in the middle of the night. Every night."

She nodded. "It makes sense. You're having panic attacks in your sleep."

"A person can do that?"

"When it gets bad enough, absolutely."

I shifted in my seat.

"Are you on any medication?" Dr. E asked.

"I'm afraid of that, too."

"Great," she said. "I think we can help you."

We can help you. I sank into the bath of those words.

Dr. E folded her thin pale fingers on her desk and told me that I have a lizard brain. "We all have this primitive structure in our brains," she continued, "called the amygdala, which assesses potentially threatening situations and triggers our fight-flight response when necessary. It's designed to protect us; it's the same mechanism that enables the zebra to escape the lion."

I nodded knowingly, having read all of this in one of my books.

"But here's something you might not know." Dr. E leaned toward me, her arms stretched across her desk as if at any moment they'd move the extra few inches and touch me. "Our autonomic nervous system is composed of the sympathetic and parasympathetic nervous systems. The sympathetic nervous system controls the fight-flight response— which is what happens to all of us when, say, you suddenly swerve your car to avoid a collision. And the parasympathetic nervous system does the opposite: it relaxes us, slows us down. So here's the thing," she said, smiling as if she was about to hand me a present: "You never have to worry about a panic attack going out of control, because the parasympathetic nervous system is always there to balance it out."

I realized this information was supposed to immediately bring me noticeable relief, and I could feel her searching my face for some sign of it. I should have smiled or said, "Ah, I'm so glad I know this now and never have to worry about *that* again."

Instead I asked, "But what if something's wrong with my parasympathetic nervous system?"

She laughed. "Yes, you're definitely in the right place."

After taking a brief history of my panic, Dr. E explained the cycle of panic. "Scary thoughts lead to tension in the body, and that tension leads to more scary thoughts, which lead to more tension. So for you, you're worried about having a heart attack. When your heart rate gets elevated for any reason, this triggers your belief that a racing heart is a sign of a heart attack—which your brain interprets as danger—which makes your heart beat even faster, and so forth, until you're running out the door and calling 911. Each thing that gets associated with panic—driving, rapid heartbeat, being alone—becomes something you start to avoid, and that's how panic feeds on itself. It takes more and more of your life, until there is no safe place left, not even your own body."

It seemed so simple. Yet just thinking of panic made my body feel like a guitar in the hands of a child—plucked and smacked and thrumming.

"Thoughts are at the root of panic," said Dr. E. "And that's what we're going to work on."

The way we were going to work on my thoughts was through cognitive behavioral therapy (CBT), a popular and effective method claiming up to a 95 percent success rate in treating all sorts of anxiety disorders and phobias. The concept is simple: when people are gradually exposed to the objects they fear, their fears soon become little more than distant memories. Dr. E sent me off with a panic workbook, panic homework, and an appointment for the next day. I cradled the book against my side and thanked her. I didn't ask her the question pressing on my mind: *what if I'm the unlucky 5 percent?*

I waited outside the building for Larry to pick me up, while people milled along the sidewalks—the students strapped with knapsacks too big for their backs, the women with their briefcases bumping against their calves, the men with their open leather jackets. We were all together in the same place, but no one was really there—the people with their blank steady gazes forward were already someplace else. No one looked afraid.

It was getting cool now, which made everyone move faster. Meanwhile, I stood on the corner and wondered what would happen if I fainted right there. Then Larry pulled up.

"How'd it go?" he asked, reaching for a kiss. I could feel the now-familiar stress from his job surrounding him, the way a scent can stick to you when you brush by it.

At that moment, I wanted to say so many things. I wanted to say, *I'm sorry your job is so hard on you.* I wanted to say, *I'm sorry for crumbling like this. I don't know when the world became so terrifying. I don't know if I will survive this day. I don't know who I am anymore. I know I love you. I know what I want from you must seem impossible. I know I have homework. I know my heart is beating fast.* But the tears came faster than the words.

That evening, I did my homework, which consisted of filling out a Daily Panic Attack and Anxiety Record, along with a Worry Record. After chronicling the times and places of that day's four panic attacks, I checked off a list of symptoms that applied: "pounding heart, shortness of breath, dizziness, trembling, sweating, feeling of unreality, hot or cold flash, fear of dying, fear of going crazy, fear of losing control"—almost everything on the list. On my worry record, I wrote, "Am worried I will continue to be anxious while alone. Am worried about my heart. Am also worried that I'm hypoglycemic and will fall into a coma. Am worried that if I lose consciousness while the dogs are out, I won't be able to let them back in, and Larry will come home and accidentally run them over." That's as much as I could write before I had another panic attack. I handed Larry the stethoscope.

The next morning I was back in Dr. E's office. "Did you do your homework?" she asked, slipping her shoes off. She was wearing roughly the same earthy linen outfit as the day before.

I proudly handed her my anxiety and worry records, and she looked them over. "Good," she said. "So you know how CBT works?"

I thought about spiders and snakes and high ledges. "By exposing people to the things they're afraid of?"

"Right. And how do you think we're going to get control of your panic?"

"I'm not sure," I said. Suddenly I didn't like where this was headed.

"Let's put it this way: we've got a staircase in the building."

No. No no no. "The problem is," I started, "that something may really be wrong with my heart." I needed her to understand that this was absolutely not an option.

But Dr. E wasn't interested in that. She did, however, offer a compromise: instead of braving the stairs just yet, I could run in place in her office until my heart rate went up, while she timed me with a stopwatch. Reluctantly I got up and started to jog. Within a minute I was in the midst of a full-blown panic attack, gasping and trembling and eyeing the door like a fiend. *See,* I wanted to say, *I told you so.*

Dr. E flashed a pen and began asking questions about my symptoms—how severe, how many, how long they peaked. "Okay," she said in a voice so cheerful I was expecting pom-poms to pop out, "let's go again!"

Again? I was surely going to die.

I had three more panic attacks before she called it quits, at which point she showed me on a chart how my last panic attack was less severe than my first. I wanted to be happy about this, but I was traumatized. A feeling of tightness had settled into the center of my throat, like the seconds right before a good cry. I told Dr. E.

"So what worries you about this tightness?"

"It's not usually there, for one thing." I pulled my water bottle from my bag and tried to swallow the tightness away, but it wouldn't budge. "And I'm worried it won't go away."

"And what if it doesn't? Would you still be able to live your life?"

"Yes, I suppose. But I don't want to live my life that way."

"But you could if you had to."

"It's just that I feel really isolated," I said, changing the subject. "Everything is new, and I don't have any friends here, and I'm afraid my marriage is failing."

Dr. E looked at me wide-eyed, as if I were breaking some protocol. "These things are important, and for sure you should do things—take a class or join a club—to make yourself less isolated. That's number one. But to get you there, what we need to focus on right now is your panic."

I understood. I'd read the books. Cognitive behavioral therapy is, as its name implies, about retraining the mind. It likes things clean. It likes charts and statistics and lists. It's not interested in your emotions or your past or the dream you had last night.

At home, I couldn't shake the tightness in my throat. I walked from room to room trying to cough it away, then panicking when it wouldn't go, then filling out forms about it. But underneath the fear, I was excited about something: today was my first cooking lesson.

When Helen arrived, all six feet of her knelt down on the floor to cuddle my dogs. She was wearing her chef's coat and hat, and she brought everything we needed: the ingredients, the tools, the panache. "I thought we'd roast some nuts to snack on while we cook," she said, pulling things from her bag. Instantly she was at home in the kitchen, organizing her spices in one place and her baking ingredients in another. "I thought we'd make a banana cream pie for dessert, so once we get the nuts in the oven, we should start on that so it's ready after dinner. What do you think?"

I could hardly reconcile that this woman was in my kitchen, let alone comment intelligently on the order of food preparation. "Sounds pretty amazing to me," I said, as if Santa had just proposed the order in which he would deliver my presents. And from there we mixed olive oil, cayenne pepper, freshly chopped rosemary, local honey, and salt in a bowl. In went the raw cashews, which we tossed in the oil before placing in the oven. Within minutes they were roasted to perfection, and the two of us were happily chomping away.

After the nuts, Helen showed me how to make a piecrust. "You don't want to overknead the dough," she said, "or it can become stiff. And butter—you should always use butter."

I love you, I wanted to say. Instead, I said, "I love butter." And then she showed me how to work my fingers into the dough.

By the end of our four hours together, we'd cooked (and eaten almost the whole tray of) roasted rosemary cashews; parchment-wrapped Mediterranean halibut with olives, tomatoes, lemon juice, freshly chopped oregano and thyme, orange zest, and olive oil; sautéed baby squashes; and jasmine rice steamed with coconut. And we baked one hell of a banana cream pie.

Of course, I felt panic nipping at my back as I used a microplane to gently glide the thin layer of peel off the orange, as I watched the vegetables brown in the skillet, as I whipped the cream. And through it all, I felt the unrelenting tightness in my throat. But I was also aware of the gifts that had been given to me that night, and I wasn't going to let panic devour them before I had a chance to.

TWENTY-TWO

When I get back to the 7-Eleven, it's dark already, a slow and sticky summer night. There's nothing to do but watch some guy delivering donuts. His blond hair sweeps his shoulders each time he bends to pull a tray from his van, and when he turns around he snaps his head back to clear his sight. He's cute, and Rockville's getting old, so in exchange for a ride to Baltimore I have sex with him in the back of his truck on the floor in between all those donuts. He kisses me gently in the sugary air. Afterward, I ride around with him for a while on his route and smoke Marlboros, and when I try to flick one out the window, the wind blows it back in, right down the front of my shirt, and burns a blister between my breasts before I can get it out. "Smart cigarette," he says. He drones on about relationships and this girlfriend and that girlfriend, and all I know is that the road is like a dark cave we keep entering. When he lets me out a couple of hours later at the High's near my mother's apartment complex, he calls out, "Think of me next time you eat a donut!" I don't look back.

I walk through the field into the apartment complex and head to Donny and Matt's apartment. I haven't seen them since Matt played bartender with my mother's liquor bottles three months ago and I ended up in the hospital, but I'm hoping they'll let me stay with them for a night or two. It feels strange to be so near my mother and hiding at the same time.

Outside Donny and Matt's building I hear the vague bass of music. Their door is slightly open, so I walk in. They're having a party—people parked everywhere under a thick haze of smoke. Black Sabbath pounds the room: *Happiness I cannot feel, and love to me is so unreal.* I see Matt rolling a joint at the dining room table and am relieved. "Hey, Matt!" I yell over the music. He stares back at me flatly. His older brother, Donny, walks over. "Hi, Donny!" I wave. But he isn't smiling. He takes another step toward me, and I step back instinctively.

"You need to get out of here," he says.

My face tingles hot. I'm not sure I've heard him right, so I stand there trying to understand. Someone turns the music down.

He takes another step toward me. "Well, what are you waiting for? I said get the fuck out of here." A spray of his spit lands on my face.

The party falls to a hush, and everyone is watching. My throat burns. "I don't understand."

"There's nothing to understand. You're a runaway and a slut, and I don't want you around here."

Someone laughs. I feel gutted. I'm running out the door.

Outside I sit at the top of the long stairway across the street from my mother's apartment building. A soft honeyed glow pours from her windows. Against the steps, a few leaves stir in the breeze. Above me, stars turn on in their big blue-black bowl. I notice that I'm shaking.

From the corner of my eye I catch my mother move quickly past a window, and it feels at once as if something has moved across the span of my chest. I know the distinct bounce of her gait, like the beat of a familiar song. I used to listen for it at night, always wondering if she might come into our room. I spent a lot of time listening for her, sometimes after school, when I was locked out and I'd press my ear to the door. By then I'd already knocked and knocked, pressed my mouth against the door and called her name, but sometimes she forgot I was coming home. I always worried about her—was she asleep? In the bath? Breathing?—because I sensed her fragility, knew that she was stitched together with the weakest thread. But sometimes when she laughed, she invited me in, and I laughed, too, and in those moments I could almost touch her.

I spent years roaming the hills and fields and woods of this apartment complex. I knew where to find flint in the woods; I knew the best doors to knock on for candy at Halloween; I knew the distinct pitch of each slope. But now this place is my past, and I feel like a ghost coming back to haunt it.

At the end of eighth grade, my school guidance counselor told me I could be anything I wanted to be. By then I'd been running away for most of the year, and when I wasn't running, I was skipping school. "I've seen your test scores, Rita," he said, "and with a mind like that, this world could be yours." I knew he was doing something nice for me— passing me through to high school even though I should have failed eighth grade—but I didn't care much about my test scores or any of that, so I sat quietly in his office and looked at his black and gray beard. After that, I never went back.

The truth is I never wanted the world to be mine. I just wanted some small piece of it. I wanted what my friends had. I wanted not to be afraid. Now it's hard to know what to want. But suddenly, sharply, I know what I don't want: I don't want to keep having sex with strangers. I don't want someone to yell *slut* at my face again. I don't want to spend the night in another empty car or staircase. I don't want Mr. Malekzadeh.

I look up at my mother's windows, and they seem like the only warm spot on earth. I wonder what will happen if I knock on her door. And I wonder what will happen if I don't.

"Who is it?" she calls. I know she's pressing her eye to the peephole.

"It's me," I say to her one eye.

She swings the door open and stands there looking at me. "Where have you been?"

"Can I come in?"

"You can't stay here," she blurts out, stepping aside and opening the door the rest of the way.

I walk in and look around. It's as if I'm seeing her apartment for the first time—the walls cluttered with mirrors and prints of things that have nothing to do with our life: sailboats on a sea, Chinese landscapes, a Parisian cityscape, a smiling needlepoint tiger; the tables strewn with books and ashtrays and knickknacks; the stacks of record albums leaned up against the cabinet.

"Where's Joanne?" I ask.

"She's at a sleepover."

"I miss her."

"You should have thought about that before you ran away."

"Oh, because I got to see her so much when you put me in that psych ward, right? You never even came to visit me once."

"Sure, blame me. It's all my fault."

"I'm sorry," I say.

She lights a cigarette. "You should count your lucky stars that you were only in a hospital and not someplace worse." The smoke curls from her nostrils as she talks.

"Someplace worse?"

She shakes her head as if she's disagreeing with something. "I tried to have you put in detention. I told the police you were in too much danger on the streets, but they said they couldn't lock you up because running away isn't a crime."

I look at this woman who is my mother. She pulls hard on her cigarette, her mouth tight, then taps the cigarette roughly over the ashtray. The kitchen lights emphasize the sheen of her skin. I remember how once a long time ago I brought her a bunch of dandelions from the hill outside, and when I handed them to her, she held them to her nose, then to her heart. I remember thinking that I had fixed her, that maybe all she ever needed was this bright yellow slightly wilting gift. She put them in water in a small cup, but later that day I saw them in the trash.

"I was thinking that maybe I could stop running away. Maybe I could start high school like I'm supposed to."

"I already told you, you can't stay here."

Again I feel my throat burn. "Why do you hate me so much?"

"Because I'm a terrible mother, remember? Just like you told the judge."

"You're right," I say. "I was wrong. I didn't tell the judge about the bad things that Dad did, and I should have. But it was because I thought that was the only way I could have a happy life."

"And you see how far that got you."

"I was only nine. You're going to have to forgive me sometime, you know."

She doesn't answer, but her expression softens. "Are you hungry?"

She boils some spaghetti and serves it with butter and salt. I eat ravenously and get full long before my plate is clear. "Thank you," I say. "That was delicious."

"One night," she says. "You can stay here one night, but I want you gone before Joanne gets back in the morning."

Suddenly, the morning fills me with dread. Where will I go then?

After I wash the dishes, I go into the living room, lie back on the worn pink couch, and call my father. When he answers, I blurt into the phone, "I want to go back to school."

"Rita?"

I'm not sure which of us is more surprised by the suddenness of this statement. "Yeah, it's me."

"Where are you? Are you okay?"

"I'm at Mom's. She doesn't want me to stay here past tonight, but I was hoping I could come back and live with you."

"Wow, Rita. I don't know. Are you serious?"

I think for a minute. I imagine going to the store to buy school supplies—fresh pencils and new pads of paper and soft pink erasers. "Yes," I say, "I am."

He takes a long breath into the phone, followed by another. "Then I think maybe it's time you come home."

And in that moment, I feel more hope than I can remember feeling. It's as if the curtains to my future are finally opening. "Thank you."

I thank my mother, too, for letting me stay the night, but when I try to hug her, she stands stiffly. "I guess your father's the big hero now."

"No," I say. "It's just that you said I couldn't stay here."

"Big fucking hero he is."

"No, Mom, he's far from a hero."

"Well, I'm glad you're all lovey-dovey with each other now. Maybe you could ask him where my child support is."

"I'm sorry. I know it isn't fair. I'm just tired of running."

I reach to put my hand on her shoulder, but she backs away, and I give up. "I'm going to bed."

I leave her and slip back into my old room, into my old bed, and fall into a dreamless sleep. When I wake up, it's still dark, and the apartment is quiet. I can't sleep, so I tiptoe into the living room, where the records are. On the table opposite the stereo are Joanne's schoolbooks. She has a big loose-leaf binder now, the kind she's wanted since the first time she saw mine. On the front, she's drawn a single smiley-face, dead-center and perfectly round. I open the binder and look at the new block of paper, which she'll slowly fill with all the things she'll learn. I flip to a page in the middle, grab a pen, and start writing. *I love you, Joanne! And I miss you. Love, Rita.* I add a smiling dog and a postscript: *P.S. Be happy.*

I put on my mother's headphones, decide on Led Zeppelin's *In Through the Out Door,* and lean back on the carpet with my eyes closed. And as the music goes, I go with it. But in the middle of "Carouselambra," there is suddenly a hand yanking the headphone jack out of the receiver. My mother startles us both, and now the music is blasting through the apartment.

"Why aren't you in bed?" she shouts.

I turn the volume down. "I couldn't sleep."

"Why are you listening to druggie music? Are you on drugs? Did a little coke? Is that what you did?"

"I'm not on drugs, and this is *your* album."

She squints down into my face. "How did you get coke anyway? Who'd you fuck to get it?"

"I told you, I'm not high." I can see there's no use in my staying any longer, so I head back to the bedroom to get my bag.

She follows me. "It's not my fault you turned out to be a slut daughter. I never taught you that. You know, your father beat me black and blue because he wasn't my first. One lousy guy before him." Her voice bounds erratically up and down.

I turn around and brush past her. "I'm leaving."

"Where do you think you're going?"

"I'm calling Pat to see if I can stay there." Pat is my favorite of my mother's friends. She's a tall and beautiful force of a woman who lives across the street and who once made me memorize her number in case I was ever in a bind. Her daughter is Joanne's best friend, and though my mother won't tell me where Joanne is, I'm pretty sure she's there. I reach for the phone, but my mother beats me to it and snatches it off the cradle. "Please!" I beg. "Let me call her."

She sits down on the chair and clutches the phone to her chest. "Pat doesn't want any druggies over there, either," she chides.

"Give me the phone!" I lean in and try to grab it from her hands, but she kicks at me. Reflexively, I swat her leg away, and she falls backwards in her chair. Then, silence.

"Mom? Are you okay?"

She starts squirming around, and when I hold out my hand to help her up, she smacks it away. "You fucking bitch!"

"I didn't mean it! I'm sorry!"

I try again to help her up.

"Get the fuck off of me, I'm calling the police!"

"It was an accident! You know it was an accident!"

She dials the phone. "Yes, can you please send the police to 3449 Carriage Hill Circle, Apartment 104? I'd like to press charges against my daughter for assaulting me."

"What are you doing!" I shriek. "Why are you doing this?"

"You've had this coming for a long time," she says.

At that moment I realize there's only one thing for me to do. Run.

I tear out of the apartment, down the steps, and start running up the hill—just in time to meet the red swirl of police lights.

As they cuff my hands behind my back, I listen to my Miranda rights. I say nothing. The tears are warm on my cheeks.

At the station, I sit in a chair facing an officer's desk. He asks me questions in a monotone. "Have you ever been convicted of a crime?"

"No."

"Do you have any tattoos?"

"No."

"Any scars?"

"Two on my leg."

"Which leg?"

"My left."

"Eye color?" he asks, aiming his bark-colored eyes at mine. "Hazel? Green?"

"Yes."

Then it's my turn to ask him a question. "What's going to happen to me?"

He picks up a can of Coke and swigs hard. His Adam's apple bobs up and down in his neck. "Well, if your mother doesn't drop the charges, you'll have to go to court. And while you wait for a hearing, you'll probably go to Montrose."

I don't mean to start crying again, but I can't help it. I know what Montrose is: it's the nastiest detention center around.

"Can't I call my father? Can't he come get me?"

"Not unless your mother drops the charges."

I wipe at my eyes. "Okay. What if she drops the charges?"

"Then she comes to get you, and ya'll go home and make up."

I call my mother, and when I hear her voice, I immediately start begging for her to drop the charges, but she tells me there's nothing to discuss, that she's trying to sleep, that I shouldn't call her again. The phone clicks and is silent.

The officer apologizes as he shuts me into one of the station cells. "I hate to have to do this to you," he says, turning his key from the outside.

I stand behind the bars. "I didn't do it," I tell him. "I didn't assault my mother."

"You just tell the judge that, okay. Now try to get some sleep."

There's a skinny cot on one side of my cell and a silver sink paired with a matching toilet on the other. Though it's dark, the brightness from the station oozes in, along with an irregular rhythm of sounds— phones, voices, footsteps, coughing, laughing. I get into the cot, but the blanket is thin and won't warm me. I can feel the cold starting to spread below my skin, working its way deep into my body.

Rows and rows of corn line a long narrow road that leads to an out-cropping of stone buildings. They will always be cold, in any season—you can see that. You don't expect to see bars on the windows of stone buildings out in the middle of nowhere, but they're there. You don't expect the corn, or the corn beyond the corn. You don't expect to reach the corn-edged end of the world, and get dropped behind it. You don't expect to be strip-searched by a sun-wrinkled lady who tells you she ain't got all goddamned day for you to take your clothes off. And you don't expect her to watch you shower, making sure you use the whole handful of green antilice shampoo she's globbed into your palm. You don't expect the sky, before you enter one of these buildings, so ridicu-lously, painfully blue.

TWENTY-THREE

I spent six months at the end of Tommy's lunge line before I realized that, though in many respects I felt like a child around her and around the horses (though it should be noted that most of the children who rode Shaddad were better riders than I was), I was an adult, and I didn't have to accept being yelled at by someone I was paying to teach me. On a sunny afternoon, I told Tommy this. I stood in front of her with my spine straight and my head up, and this woman, whose modus operandi was to intimidate, took a step back, away from me. And after that, she never yelled at me again.

But I'd realized something else, too: there were other horses out there, and other instructors, and though Tommy had taught me a lot, I was ready to move on. So I traveled from barn to barn, and I rode.

There were warmbloods and Thoroughbreds and ponies. There were days that were cool and breezy and days that were stifling and days when the rain didn't want to stop. There were official barns and backyard barns and overgrown paddocks and open fields. There were riders of all ages and backgrounds and demographics, but in the barn, none of that mattered: we were all there for the horses—for that meditation in motion that's unlike any other thing. There were instructors who barked and ones who cooed, and there were those who taught me to feel, and to observe. *See there, how when you put your leg on gently, the horse moves away from it? Do you see how when you look in the direction you want to go, the horse goes in that direction? Do you see how a light tug on reins slows you, how a light tap with your heels makes the horse go forward? Do you see how you can control the tempo based on your posting speed? Do you see how when you slouch, the horse drops his head? Do you see that you're sitting straighter than you were the last time? Do you see how when you praise the horse, the horse's ears perk up? Do you see how the horse's spirit is a mirror? Do you see?*

And there was an instructor who taught me what I'd most wanted to learn, and also what I'd been most scared to learn: to canter. By nature, the canter is an unbalanced gait because it's a three-beat gait: a swing-like movement as the horse rises up and then comes down, each time kicking off anew. Closely related to the gallop, the canter is often a more powerful gait than the trot, and in order to ride the canter, one should be able to hinge fluidly at the hips while keeping the torso still and maintaining firm but flexible contact with the reins and keeping the legs relatively quiet—neither gripping too hard nor flopping around. In other words, a beginner rider is rarely any good at it.

But it was a crisp, sunny November afternoon, and I had been riding for over six months, and I'd heard from several people that six months was a long time to ride without cantering, and now, in the middle of an old indoor arena at the edge of a farm, on a bay horse named Rascal, under the tutelage of a warm and somewhat cherubic-looking instructor named Patricia, I was going to canter.

Patricia had me start by sitting in the saddle a few beats of the trot. "Just to get your seat used to staying in the saddle," she explained.

I did as she instructed and was reminded of how much I still had to learn: after finally becoming adept at posting the trot, I had reverted to getting jostled around in the saddle as I had when I first learned to ride Shaddad. "Ouch," I said after a few strides, rising up to free my crotch and post again.

"It takes time," she said. "Go ahead and ask him to walk, and this time when you ask him to trot, try to relax your seat a little. Let it be elastic, so it can move with Rascal and absorb the impact of each stride."

So I willed my backside to be like rubber, and for maybe thirty seconds or so I was able to stay reasonably quiet in the saddle while Rascal trotted.

"Good job!" Patricia cheered. "Now go ahead and slide your outside leg back, give him a tap, and canter!"

"Wait? What? Now?" I could feel the adrenaline shooting through my veins. "Canter now?"

"Canter! Now!"

I took a breath and slid my leg back and gave Rascal the gentlest tap. And he rose up then and leapt forward, and there was this tremendous power suddenly beneath me. His back was like a swing, was like a wave, was like flying, was like all the air and all the dreams and all the sounds of all the horses that had galloped across the flatlands of my mind, the ghost-years of my life expanding, like a soft, beautiful explosion.

TWENTY-FOUR

Not far from where we lived was a house with a sign in front: CLAY CLASSES. The sign stood perched on the road's edge, sometimes glossed with rain, sometimes splattered with mud, sometimes windblown on its back. But it was always there. It seems life is always presenting us with signs. Some of us don't notice them at all. Some of us see them and keep driving. And some of us finally stop in the rain to write down the phone number, thereby getting splashed in the face through the open car window by a passing truck.

When I arrived at my first clay class—where a group of three older women and their teacher, a tall white-haired goddess, sat quietly doting on their bowls-in-progress at a small table crammed in the middle of a small room, which was once a small garage—my first instinct was to turn around.

"Welcome," said the white-haired goddess. Her name was Phyllis, and before I could say, "Oops, sorry, wrong clay class," she'd wedged me in at the table, introduced me to the ladies, presented me with a slab of clay, and asked me what I wanted to make. Despite the ladies' warm nods and easy smiles, I still had the urge to hightail it out of that tiny crowded space. But part of the reason I was there that day was that I was looking to feel less alone. So I pulled my chair forward and looked around at the others. "A bowl maybe?"

Apparently, the way a novice potter learns to make a bowl is by placing her wet clay inside another bowl, then gently peeling it out. I learned this in twenty-minute installments punctuated by dashes from the table, when, on the verge of panic, I fled to my car and breathed and willed myself to go back inside.

At the table with the ladies I couldn't resist pressing my clay-covered fingers to the side of my neck to check my pulse. I tried to be surreptitious about it, which isn't easy when you're crammed into a tiny space. The women, though, were nothing but smiles and words of encouragement, as if everyone gets up from the table three times an hour. "Your bowl is really coming along," they'd say, as I sponged it with water the way Phyllis showed me, to keep it from drying out. And despite my anxiety, I liked the clay, its flesh-like yield to my fingers. And I liked the women, their oversize sweaters, their collective calm and quiet industriousness. Any one of them, I thought, could be a mother.

Back in Dr. E's office, things pretty much stayed the same: I left traumatized every time. We never graduated to the stairs because my panic was intense enough from simply running in place. I'd run until the alarms started resounding in my head, then sit on her couch and catch my breath while being interrogated about the severity of my tunnel vision.

"I think I'm getting worse," I told her.

"It can take time," she said, blinking her nearly invisible eyelashes.

"But I still have that tightness in my throat, like I'm about to cry."

"And have you cried?"

"Yes," I said. "But it doesn't help."

Dr. E ran her finger back and forth across her pen and gazed at me. I was waiting for her to say something, but she was intently examining my face, the way therapists sometimes do.

"I had a cooking lesson, though," I told her, "and I went to a clay class. Maybe that's helping a little."

"That's wonderful," she said. "Keep doing those things. Now let's get back to running."

I decided to call the UU church. I needed to talk to someone, and I thought maybe a minister who quotes Vonnegut and speaks about love might have some interesting advice for me. But the minister who showed up at my door the next afternoon wasn't the minister I was expecting. It turns out there were two ministers at the church, and this one was a blue-eyed, quick-witted woman named Erin. "Nice place you got here," she said. "I'm pretty sure your garage is bigger than my house."

"Come in," I said, smiling, liking her immediately. "Can I offer you some banana cream pie? It's homemade."

"Can a seal clap?"

I cut an extra large piece for Erin, and we sat in the living room with our plates in our laps.

I looked across the room at her and thanked her for coming.

"Anytime you make a pie like this," Erin said, "I'll be over."

When I was nineteen and recovering from a nasty cocaine addiction, a Baptist minister came to my apartment. I wanted him to pray for me because I didn't want to die. I wanted to believe that somehow I could be forgiven—mostly for the damage I had done to my body, but also for pushing a girl in the mud when I was a kid—because if I could be forgiven, maybe I could heal. The minister told me that first I would have to rid myself of all traces of Satan. "Do you have any Dungeons and Dragons games?" he'd asked me. "Because they're the devil's games." I explained that I was sick, that I was sorry, that I'd never played a game of Dungeons and Dragons in my life. "What about yoga?" he'd asked, accusingly. The minister and I were having two different conversations, which as it turned out, was actually a blessing. Because it was then that I realized his forgiveness would do me no good unless I learned to forgive myself.

Erin was different from the Baptist minister, mostly because we were having the same conversation, and we were both listening. And because we took turns naming our favorite Mary Oliver poems. And because I could tell Erin about my heart and about the terrifying inner sanctum of my shower and the nightmarish portal of the grocery store checkout line and the disabling oppression of the highway, while she gave me the full sphere of her gaze, along with just the right amount of commiseration—"Of course you feel that way on the highway. It's Boston! Who *doesn't* feel that way?"—and just the right amount of advice: "I'm thinking it would probably be a good idea for you to talk to a therapist who doesn't make you do calisthenics during the session."

Three things happened that afternoon that I will always remember. The first is that for the entire hour I sat with Erin, I didn't check my pulse once. But this victory probably had something to do with the second thing that happened: by the hour's end, I was in the throes of a burgeoning crush. It might have been simply because I laughed more that day than I had in a long calendar of days, but I could feel the stem of something new winding up the lattice of my fluttery little heart.

"Thanks again!" I called, waving wildly after Erin as she walked to her car. "I'll see you in church!"

It must have been the endorphins that enabled me to leave the house that day without the usual rampant monologue in my head—some version of how the world was big and scary and was, in one way or another, going to kill me. So I drove. I passed the farm across the street and the cows. I drove past the lake and watched the trees' reflections sketched onto its surface. It was November, the sky muted, the light as palpable as pages in a book. Small bodies of wind stopped short, resurrected pockets of leaves, twirled them up.

But when I crossed over into the next town, I started to panic. I was suddenly too far from my house, too far from the nearest hospital, too alone. At once my heart skipped a beat and the world grew loud. My ears were ringing with the volume. And the light, even on that cloud-heavy day, grew instantly sharp. All I could see were the hardest things—the speeding cars, the asphalt, the metal guardrail, the unforgiving mass of it all. Everything was coming at me too fast, and I wanted to close my eyes and make it all disappear. I pulled over on the shoulder and tried to focus on one single tree. I thought I should call Larry or 911 or maybe just put my window down and randomly scream for help, but I didn't take my eyes off the ribbed bark. And the panic passed.

I turned around and started heading back. By then the schoolkids were on their way home. A yellow bus stopped in front of me, and I watched a young girl step down and hitch up the backpack that was slipping from her shoulder. She was probably seven. And she was braver than I, this child who took the bus to school each day and had adventures and came home to descend the big black steps with such certainty, as if the world were there to hold her.

The girl crossed the street, where her mother was waiting to hug her. As I watched them—a mother leaning down to pull her daughter's coat closed, a daughter reaching up to take her mother's hand—a part of me turned so quiet that I thought maybe it had died. And then I realized that was the sound of emptiness.

That was the third thing that happened that afternoon.

Back at home, I eased my panic button over my head and collapsed onto the couch. I had a panic attack, filled out my panic and anxiety records, and panicked some more. It seemed the more I focused on my scary thoughts, the more scary thoughts I had, until I had no choice but to anesthetize myself with sitcoms again while lying very, very still. Larry came home late each night, and I gave him the stethoscope, and he listened to my heartbeat, and I could see in his face that he was lost, that we were lost in different places. "I miss you," I said.

"I'm right here." He held my hand, and I leaned my head against his shoulder.

"What's my heart doing?"

"Beating."

"I know that. But I mean, how does it sound?"

Larry pressed the stethoscope to the center of my chest and closed his eyes. "Strong."

"Then why do I feel so weak?"

I had to face it: I was the 5 percent. I was failing CBT.

I decided to take Erin's advice and find another therapist, which meant scrolling through therapists' pictures online until I settled on a silver-haired motherly type. By the time I got an appointment, it had been days since I'd left the house. I'd missed a clay class and never made it to church. But as I stood outside my front door, terrified to leave my front step, I was faced with a decision: turn back and sign my life over to panic, or go get myself some help.

So I drove and panicked and pulled over suddenly several times to the chagrin of horn-happy drivers gesticulating past, but I made it there, and the silver-haired lady, in her worn shoes and silk blouse buttoned at the neck, appeared right on time. She led me through her house to a small parlor lined with psychology books, and we sat facing each other in two upholstered flowered chairs. "Tell me," she said, gently removing her bifocals, "what brings you here today?"

In three breaths I'd managed to tell her about the panic, about my heart, about my marriage, my loneliness. I told her about the tightness in my throat that wouldn't go away. "It feels like that feeling right before you cry, only I don't cry. But even crying doesn't help it."

She smiled knowingly. "You know what's often behind panic, don't you?"

I shook my head no.

"Sadness."

Yes, I wanted to say. *Sadness. Let me be sad, right here, in your parlor, with the rain just starting to tap against the windows. Let me tell you about the girl who got off the bus, about her mother, about how sometimes our mothers hate us.* "I don't want to be scared," I finally said.

"Of course you don't," she said. "That's why you're here. Now tell me, have you done anything to treat your panic disorder so far?"

"I've been doing some CBT work with a doctor at the Center for Anxiety and Related Disorders, but I think it's making things worse somehow. I think what I need is just to be able to talk to someone."

She leaned forward and looked at me quizzically. "So you already have a psychiatrist?"

"No, no, she's not my psychiatrist. We're focusing on a particular program that will only last a few more weeks. But part of that program is that we don't actually talk much. So I thought this would be a good addition to what I'm already doing." I smiled, ready to talk sadness.

The silver-haired lady put her glasses back on and scratched some notes on a pad. "Let me explain my policy to you. I would need to talk with your psychiatrist before you and I could start any kind of therapy."

"I just explained to you, she's not my psychiatrist. I'm seeing her for one specific thing, but I don't have a *psychiatrist* per se."

"Still," she said, "I would need to talk with her first so that we could work as a team. I would need to know what she's doing in her therapy with you."

"Why couldn't I tell you that?"

"It's just my policy."

"Okay, here's the thing." My voice started to waver. "I don't need a team. I'm fully capable of making my own decisions about what type of therapy I want."

"That's your opinion." Again with the glasses. On the table, off the table.

I couldn't believe what was happening. How did my sweet silver-haired motherapist end up being this rigid, controlling woman? "No," I said, "it's the truth."

She finally retired her glasses to the table, alongside her pad. "I don't think this is going to work for us."

The nerve! She was dismissing *me*. "You can say that again," I said, pulling out my checkbook. My hands shook noticeably as I wrote the check, and against all that is holy and good about anger, my eyes started to fill.

On my way back to my car, I cursed her. "Fuck you," I said, backing out of her driveway, wiping the tears off my cheeks. "Fucking waste of my time. Fucking idiot." Down the road I went, incanting my new favorite word. "You don't know what the fuck I need! *I* know what I need!"

I once read that if you put a variety of foods in front of a baby, she will instinctively eat the things her body most needs. I don't know if that's true, but I suspect that we all have that power to unequivocally determine what we need, and to declare it so. "I don't need you, stupid lady, or your fucking OCD glasses habit!" I shouted. Sometimes, in interpreting what we need, it's helpful to start with what we don't.

"I don't need to be talked to as if I'm powerless! I don't need Dr. E and her stopwatch! I don't need this tightness in my throat! And I don't need a mother!"

What a revelation it was, after thirty-six years, to suddenly understand this fundamental difference between the past and present tense. I once needed a mother, that was true. I had needed her for years, needed her with the grist of my being, with the stake of my feet on the earth. I had needed her to put Band-Aids on my scrapes, to ask me questions about my days, to pull my coat closed when the cold air got in. But she didn't. And I grew up.

TWENTY-FIVE

The security guards take me to a building called Putts, which, translated phonetically in Yiddish, means idiot. "Welcome to Montrose," they say and laugh, locking the door behind them. Inside there are about twenty girls in a large room with old fluorescent lights that drown out the daylight, as if the sun stops just outside the bars on the windows. A few girls look up at me from their Spades games. Other girls shuffle ruggedly across the room, on their way to nowhere. Nobody speaks to me. I sit on an empty bench in the corner and watch until it's time for lunch.

Some of these girls have really stabbed people, have dropped their babies into Dumpsters. I can hear them talking about each other. One of them is talking about how she woke up in the infirmary to the sound of a girl crying. "It was weird," she says, "but her cries seemed to be coming from all directions at once." It was a ghost, someone at the infirmary had told her—the ghost of a girl who'd hanged herself there years before.

We walk single file in silence to the dining hall, manned by security guards and their buzzing walkie-talkies. The stone buildings are the color of thunderheads. Lunch is a plate of noodles under a sloppy brown sauce. We eat with plastic spoons so that we don't stab each other, and we have fifteen minutes to do it. Before our meal we have to say a prayer: *Our father, God, gives us this food. We bow our heads in gratitude. And from our thankful hearts we pray that we will do God's will today.*

My cell has a window with bars on it, an army-green metal cot, and a matching metal cabinet to keep exactly two changes of clothes, one pair of pajamas, a few basic toiletries, and writing paper. Each night, we have to put our day's clothes out in the hall to be laundered and returned the next morning. "To keep away the crabs," I hear one girl say.

There is one large bathroom that we can use at allotted times, and it has no mirrors. Instead, there are two rectangles of steel bolted to the wall, pretending to be mirrors. We're given only five minutes to wash, and there are at least twice as many girls as there are sinks, which means a fight for water. They quickly jam in together, reaching over each other, taking turns spitting into the sink. And I am now a part of them, these strangers elbowing each other to get clean.

Each evening, after we wash and go into our cells, a staff member comes to each door with a box of pencils, a stack of paper, and envelopes. When I ask why we have to give the pencils back, Miss Smith winks at me. "Because they can be used as weapons." So I write. I write about cornfields and about roads and about loneliness. I write letters to my mother and letters to my father, and I never send them because all they do is beg for things I know they'll never give me.

I turn fourteen, and the leaves come down. In the mornings we wake at 5:00, scrub floors with steel wool pads, pour ammonia into toilets, shine the metal mirrors while our warped reflections search back at us. Mice scurry by from one shadow to another, while girls get into fistfights and get hauled away. Winter blows in, wraps its claws around our gray building and won't let go. I think of the girl who hanged herself, wonder if it was cold then, too, as she pulled the sheet off her bed for the last time. It gets colder, and then it snows. We get donated presents of large cotton underwear, and I flip through magazines and stare at pictures of pie, and I lust for the pie, for everything that lives outside these bars.

Three months later, my arraignment date arrives. I'm handcuffed and taken to court inside a paddy wagon, then led to a holding cell to await my hearing. The cell is empty and locked inside another small room. There isn't even a toilet like in the police station. The walls, the floors, and the ceiling are all beige. I wrap my fingers around the cool metal bars and wonder who's been here before me. I remember the long day I'd spent hiding out inside Cindy's closet, singing to myself under my breath—but here is not a place to sing. Instead I pace for two hours.

Things happen fast in the courtroom. My mother won't look at me. My heart rattles like a wagon speeding downhill. My hands tremble. So do my knees. When they call me to the witness stand, I raise my hand and swear on a Bible and tell the judge the truth. The judge listens without expression. Her hair is gray and stiffened by hair spray.

When it's my mother's turn, she testifies that I pushed her, that I am a violent, drug-abusing, promiscuous runaway. She brings my diary and reads passages out loud to the entire courtroom: *I wonder if having sex will ever stop hurting. I want to like it. Maybe I just need to practice.*

No! I want to shout. *That's mine!*

My mother licks her lips and speaks surely. "Your Honor, you can see that if Rita is not supervised constantly, she is a danger not only to me but to herself."

And the judge agrees. "In the hope that you might learn a lesson from this and right your ways before it's too late, I'm going to detain you at the Montrose detention center until a bed becomes available for you at the Good Shepherd Center, where you will have plenty of time to think about what you've done, and what you're going to do differently in the future."

The gavel comes down.

TWENTY-SIX

I wish panic were fragile enough to crumble under the heft of a heart-bending epiphany experienced from the driver's seat of one's car, or that a magical number of conjugations of the word *fuck*, if exclaimed loudly enough, could annihilate it. But panic is far more tenacious than that, which might explain why anxiety disorders are the most common form of psychiatric illness.

So I didn't skip through my front door that day I drove home from the silver-haired lady, revelation in hand like a lasso that would once and for all take down the charging bull of panic. But I had taken a step toward the bull, and I found strength in that. Besides, I was beginning to suspect that the way to approach panic might be gentler than a rope at the throat; instead of a lasso, I imagined carrying a tender tuft of grass in my open hand.

In a strange way, I was grateful to the silver-haired lady because she let go one gleaming pearl: sometimes below the panic is sadness. I could feel it there, like the hidden body of something you brush against in the dark. I was grateful also for the anger, which can be a useful and motivating emotion, one that's hard to feel when you're afraid. So she gave me that, and somewhere in my rant about the things I needed and the things I didn't, the tightness in my throat disappeared.

Though the silver-haired lady insisted on treating me as if I were helpless, I wasn't helpless, and perhaps I needed to be reminded of that. I also needed to be reminded that saying no is sometimes where power is born, and that what we truly need might be the opposite of what people are telling us we need. In my case, it was knowing that CBT—despite the statistics and testimonials—was the wrong choice for me at that time, even if a psychiatrist thought it was right. So I stopped seeing Dr. E and made an appointment with a renowned author on anxiety who happened to live only a few miles from my house. He'd even landed an appearance on *Oprah,* so I figured he had to be good. Unfortunately, I would have to wait several weeks before he could see me.

Meanwhile, when Larry told me about another upcoming work-related dinner, my immediate response was "There is absolutely no way in the world I can go."

"It's not a big one," he said, sorting through the day's mail. "I don't understand why we get so many catalogs." He chucked a stack in the trash.

"Just say I'm sick."

"Okay," Larry said, not looking up, sorting through the mail a second time in a way that made me think he didn't want me to know he was hurt.

I immediately felt guilty. "Who's going?" I asked.

He kept flipping through the mail. "Steve, the chair of rehabilitative medicine, and his partner, Mike, an internist at BMC. I talked to Steve in the elevator—he seems friendly."

"Just them?"

"Just them."

"Okay," I said. "I'll go."

Larry looked up and smiled.

We met in the city. A light rain had slicked everything shiny. Even the sounds of car horns had a certain gleam to them. Mike and Steve stepped out of their building and onto the sidewalk like a couple of movie stars. To put it simply, they were gorgeous. Primped to the nines in Prada and Gucci, they were a combined festival of black—black pants, black leather, black patent shoes, black glasses. Mike wore a flashy rhinestone skull belt that extended down over his fly. "Wow," Mike said, eyeing me up, "you're beautiful."

"And I love your boots," added Steve.

"I love *your* boots," I said, and the four of us spent the next minute on the street corner admiring each other.

The rain had left a charge in the air, and the city was alive with it. People were laughing, calling to each other, waving from across streets. Their voices kept rising, collecting in the windows' light and mingling at the rooftops. As we walked to a nearby French restaurant, I squeezed Larry's hand and watched Mike and Steve stroll confidently ahead of us. Mike leaned over and kissed Steve's cheek, and for a moment I envied the intimacy I sensed between them.

When we entered the restaurant, the first thing I was confronted with was a tall wooden flight of stairs. And to get to our table, I would have to climb them. They looked so steep. So hard. An ordinary person would have followed the curvy hostess in the red wrap dress with plunging neckline straight up those stairs without a thought. But for me, those stairs might as well have been Everest. I considered making a run for it—*Well, boys, it's been a blast. Let's do this again soon!*—but Mike and Steve were already heading up, and Larry was looking at me as if to say, *Well, are you going to do this or not?* and I decided not, and then I walked up the stairs anyway. By the time I got to the top, my heart and I were a rattling mess.

We sat down at our table, and these two sweet strangers were looking at us expectantly, and I was doing my usual chair dance of angst, and I wanted to flee more than anything, and I was pretty sure I was going to collapse right there with my unbitten roll on my bread plate, and it made me sad to think I would never get to be friends with the fancy new doctors, but just then Mike leaned over and said, "I hear you're a writer. What do you write?" And I took a breath.

"I'm working on a memoir."

"Ooh," he said. "Tell me more."

Some small distant part of my brain was celebrating what looked like the first real conversation Larry and I would have at a dinner with doctors, but then there was my killjoy and devoted stalker, Panic, hovering nearby. I tried for another breath but settled for a short, sharp inhalation instead. "It's about my childhood as a runaway."

Mike turned his chair toward me and leaned forward, elbows on his knees. "You were a runaway? That's *amazing*. For how long? How old were you? Where were you? How did you survive? I have so many questions!"

These were the questions I'd always wanted Larry to ask—about this part of my life I kept secret from everyone else—and now a stranger was asking them, and I wanted to answer, but I couldn't. I could hardly even breathe. But he was being so nice to me, and I felt I owed him something more than an inexplicable bolt from the table. "Listen, Mike, this might sound strange, but I've been struggling with panic attacks for the past few months, so if I get up suddenly and leave the table, that's why."

He didn't miss a beat. "Okay. Should I follow you?"

"You know," I told him, "that's the best question anyone's asked me in a long time."

I didn't run from the table that night. But I also didn't stop teetering at the edge. Panic stayed close, skulking through the room's shadows, crouching by the stairs, waiting for me—though on this night there was an understood distance between us. As long as I was at the table eating my black truffle and wild mushroom cavatelli with these charming men, I was off-limits. It was as if by simply being able to name Panic to another person, I had temporarily weakened its power.

If only we could always say our truths—if we could name the things that haunt us—maybe they would float up from us like a kind of helium that the birds would sip in the treetops. Then they would make us laugh and laugh.

TWENTY-SEVEN

After I cantered with Rascal, all I wanted to do was canter. When I wasn't cantering, I was often talking about cantering. "It's amazing," I kept telling Larry. "It's like this great rush. It's better than any drug. Maybe even better than sex."

"Hmmm," said Larry, furrowing his forehead.

"It's so free—it's like the opposite of panic. It's powerful and graceful and even a bit clumsy all at once. It's like—"

"It's like you," he said.

And it was sweet, what he said, but not entirely true, because panic was also like me—it was built into me as it was into the horses, built into me the way being a runaway was—and I had the sense that it was, in part, my relationship with panic—along with the residue of my young life—that enabled me to fully submerge myself in the freedom and joy of riding: it was only by holding on so tightly that I could begin learning how to let go. And cantering was like a great pendulum: this wonderful swing between the two extremes, between the past and the future. The present, then, was right there, on that single point on top of the horse.

So I kept riding. I began taking dressage lessons with a German woman named Gerta, who seemed to hold the dictionary to the language I was just beginning to learn, and I began half leasing a Thoroughbred mare named Danielle, who was a bit aloof but who relished the Pink Lady apples I gave her. And as much as I loved riding—as much as I waxed lyrical about it to anyone who would listen—there was rarely a ride during which I didn't feel scared at least once. Gerta's answer to that was to teach me how to go over small jumps made up of wooden rails, also known as cavaletti. The trick was to time my communication—whether through my contact in the reins or the speed of my posting or the pressure of my legs—to control Danielle's pace so that we could get over the cavaletti without toppling the rails. "If you look at the rails, you're going to hit them," Gerta warned. Of course, all I thought about was knocking down the rails. But after knocking them down three times, I knew she was right. "Look past them," she said. "Look where you want to go, and go there."

The next time I came toward the caveletti, I took Gerta's advice and looked at the window at the end of the arena. *We'll go through the window,* I thought. *We'll fly right through the window.* And that lift in my vision translated to Danielle's lift over the cavaletti. From then on, we cleared them every time. And with each pass, I became more confident. When I submitted myself to this intense external focus—which is at once an endeavor of will and one of faith—there was nothing left of me to give to the internal world of fear.

TWENTY-EIGHT

At the Good Shepherd Center nuns are everywhere. They whiz around on motorized yellow scooters, right through the sunlight with their pale faces and impenetrable layers of black. Compared to Montrose, Good Shepherd is a utopia: cigarettes anytime, makeup, long showers, pens, pencils, forks, knives. Each unit is the size of a large apartment, with a living room, a kitchenette, a smoking lounge, a large bright bathroom and a separate vanity room, both with real mirrors. And the windows don't have bars on them.

The girls are here for all sorts of reasons. Some have criminal records like me, while others have run away or smoked pot or gotten into fistfights or were considered "troubled" by their parents because they skipped school or had sex or wrote disturbing things in their diaries. I take a shine to a girl named Melissa. She's got a purple Mohawk and honest eyes like those of a lemur—some dark beauty with night vision.

As far as I can tell, she's here mainly because of her Mohawk. Her father, a prominent D.C. judge, worried that because she was a punk and skipped the occasional day of school, she was destined to end up like Sid Vicious. I also like the redheaded self-proclaimed biker chick who floods each room she enters with the heady scent of Tatiana perfume. Nobody ever mentions her left eye, which is bigger than the right, crowned by a scar, and slow to close. Maria, an intolerant and intimidating girl who talks to none of us, plays records and dances by herself, better than anyone I've ever seen.

At virtually any time of day, a lineup of girls can be found either smoking in the lounge or primping in the vanity room, which is just large enough for the chairs behind the long counter. Staring into the large mirror, we wrap our hair around curling irons, sponge on eye shadow with small black applicators, and talk to each other while looking into our own eyes. We touch each other, push our fingers through each other's hair. Being pretty is one of our only pastimes.

Sister Maryanne is the nun who works on our unit, and I like imagining her with her habit off, her luscious dark hair falling around her. "Do you ever wish you could get married?" I ask her. With a finger, she pushes my bangs to one side and says, "Oh, but I am married. I'm married to God."

After several months of good behavior, I finally earn my first overnight visit with my mother. While I was in Montrose, she'd filed for an order of emergency temporary custody of Joanne and me, and won. "You can't go crying to Daddy anymore," she'd gloated. "And his big fancy lawyer can't save him now."

I know she doesn't want me to come home, not even for a night, but she also doesn't want to appear uncooperative to the counselor handling my case. So on a sunny afternoon, she comes with Joanne to pick me up.

It's surreal to walk freely through the parking lot to her car, and then to merge onto the highway. I've been fantasizing about this day for what seems like a lifetime—the first day in almost a year that I've been outside of an institution. But as I ride in the car with my mother and my eleven-year-old sister, I find myself estranged. I feel like an animal, some exotic thing being cautiously gauged by humans. I can almost hear their questions: *Does she bite? Will she run? What exactly is she?* But the animal itself doesn't know the answers.

We spend the day being careful with each other. Joanne makes a paper fortune-teller that predicts she will marry a boy named Joe. "Jo and Joe," I say. Her face is so serious, even when she smiles. My mother busies herself, fluttering around the house as if she's looking for something. We all know that this is temporary, that in a matter of hours I'll be back to my life at Good Shepherd, a life distinctly separate from theirs.

That night I'm a guest in my old bedroom. Our matching twin beds are still beside each other, and as we lie silently with the lights out, I hear my mother's quick steps up and down the hall. I remember how we used to listen for our parents' footsteps when we were younger, and how my stomach clenched when I heard them coming, and also when I didn't. "Rita?" Joanne whispers into the darkness.

"Yeah?"

"I got your note."

"What note?"

"The note you wrote in my loose-leaf a long time ago. The one that said to be happy."

I don't want the tears, but they come anyway. I push my face into my pillow for a minute before I can speak. "Did you like it?"

"Yeah."

"I'm glad you got it."

She turns over in her bed. "So am I."

On a rare day trip to a park, I persuade one of my favorite staff members—a slender brown-skinned woman with a dazzling smile and a husband I've never met but refer to as Mr. Dad because I like to pretend that one day I'll get out of Good Shepherd and go home to live with them—to let Melissa and me ride in the back of her pickup instead of on the bus with the rest of the girls. Melissa and I have been planning this for days, and all afternoon, while hot dogs sizzle in their skins and we dip our feet into the cool stony lake, I keep feeling like a dog on a leash, yearning for the field.

In the truck bed on our way back to the center, the wind diving through my hair is euphoric. "Now?" Melissa asks at a red light. But I keep wanting a little bit more of that wind. "Not yet," I say, waiting for the truck to accelerate again, closing my eyes again, tilting my head back, gulping up the rush. *If I could just have this,* I think. But it is a wind I can only borrow. And we are quickly heading back to the breezeless corridors, the long mirror with only our faces in it.

At the next red light, I nod, "Now!" and Melissa and I spring out into the road. We run like fugitives through a maze of cars and into the woods. Twigs snap under our feet as we bolt between the trees as if we're being chased. Our legs burn, our hearts pound. We run and run, until finally we make it to another road, our breath coming in short gasps. I stick out my thumb to hitchhike.

Almost instantly a blue pickup stops. I get in first. Melissa pulls the door shut, and the driver, a graying black man, steps on the gas.

"Where are you lovely ladies off to?" His breath smells like stale cigarettes.

"That depends on where you're going," I say.

"I'm actually headed to Virginia."

"Funny," I say, nudging Melissa, "so are we."

He turns his head and gives me a once-over. "I think we can probably work something out."

"Just keep your eyes on the road," Melissa says.

The man chuckles deep in his chest, and it sounds like a cough. "I like a girl with spunk."

"Can I turn on the radio?" I ask.

"Sure thing, sweetheart. You can turn any knob you like."

Melissa rolls her eyes, and I give her a half smile. Then Sting sings to the three of us about the "King of Pain."

TWENTY-NINE

One night after a half hour of sleep, I bolted up with my heart clattering, as I'd been doing every night for months, but this time I was crying. I'd dreamed that I was trying to call Larry, but he'd changed his number, and I kept calling his office, and his assistant kept telling me he was operating, and I knew he wasn't operating, and that he didn't want to talk to me.

I woke Larry. "I dreamed you didn't love me anymore." My voice was loud in the dark.

He switched on his bedside lamp and blinked a few times to get used to the light. Then he turned to me, squinting, all sleepy and puzzled. "I'll always love you."

"No matter what?"

"No matter what."

"You'll never leave me, no matter what I do?"

"Never."

"What if I stole a whole bunch of stuff?"

"I'd never leave you."

"What if I cheated on you?"

"I wouldn't leave you, but I'd be really mad."

"What if I got really ugly?"

"You could never be ugly."

"Do you promise you won't change your number?"

"Of course not." He laughed. "We have the same number."

I inserted myself deep into the crook of Larry's arm. "Here," I said, wrapping his arm around me like a shawl, cupping his hand against my chest, "keep me." And I fell asleep.

Larry was a particularly good sport about accompanying me to the location of the next panic remedy on my list: a Tong Ren healing class. Tong Ren was developed by an acupuncturist named Tom Tam, who claimed that by tapping different meridian points on a rubber doll—or voodoo doll, as he called it—roughly the size of Barbie, he could heal people of everything from a common cold to pancreatic cancer. The idea is based on energy healing through tapping into the collective unconscious with a magnetic hammer directed at different energy points, or "ouch points" on the doll, which correspond to a person's illness.

The room was full when we arrived, so we sat down in the back row. There were about sixty people there, some in wheelchairs, some clutching tightly the arms of loved ones, some with no apparent malady. In the center of the room stood Tom Tam, a slight man with graying hair and a youthful glint in his eye. He wore glasses and a mischievous smile, and he scanned the room shrewdly—noticing us right away—the way a comedian takes stock of an audience.

But this was no comedy. People were sick, some dying, and we were all there for one reason: to feel better. The room had an air of excitement about it—our collective hope buzzing around the windows, the backs of chairs, the tops of heads. Tom started by congratulating the Patriots on a good game. People smiled and nodded, the way New Englanders do when you compliment their sports teams. And then Tom began at the end of the first row. "How can we help you today?" he asked. The woman, who couldn't have been any older than I was, announced that she had just been diagnosed with breast cancer, and she didn't know yet if it had spread. Tom and his crew—a group of eight men and women standing behind him—went to work, tapping on their dolls according to a meridian number Tom announced. The tapping noise was like rain pattering against the side of a house. Some of the tappers were smiling blissful smiles that seemed to be made of the same kind of excitement the room was made of. Others tapped more seriously.

Tom went around the room this way, stopping at each person, giving everyone a chance to be healed. He seemed to be able to recognize anyone who had been there before, even if it was only once. "How's the cancer?" he asked one woman. She said, "My doctor just told me I'm in remission," and everyone clapped, and the room got even brighter, "but now I just have this headache," so Tom Tam treated her for a headache, all of them whacking away at their dolls' heads with their metal hammers. "How do you feel now? Warm?" he asked when they finished tapping. She answered yes.

He did this each time, asking everyone how he or she felt after the tapping—"Warm? Tingly?"—and they all said yes. And in this way he moved through the rows, treating people for things as varied as arthritis, liver tumors, strokes, allergies, and even hemorrhoids. "How do you feel now?" he asked. "Warm? More good? More nice?" Yes, everyone said. More nice.

When he got to me I had an immediate surge of regret. What if all that tapping actually worked? Was I ready, just like that, to have my panic hammered out of me? Suddenly, inexplicably, I wasn't so sure.

I once had a dream in which a man broke into my house. When he got to the threshold of my bedroom, I shot him. The bullet had mortally wounded him, so I laid him on my bed to die. Then I lay down beside him, and he began to speak to me. He told me about his life—about his secrets, his memories, his desires—and I said, "We are so alike." We smiled at each other with the delight of recognition, and all I wanted to do was keep talking. But he was dying. And I wished I'd never pulled the trigger.

"This your first time here?" Tom Tam said, looking at me.

"Yes."

"How can I help you today?"

"Actually," I said, rubbing my palms on the tops of my thighs, "I'm just here to observe today."

"Oh," he said, "you're learning."

"Yes."

Larry shot me a bewildered look. But when I smiled at him and took his hand, and he smiled back at me, I knew he understood.

I don't know firsthand if Tong Ren works, but on that day I saw a woman with severe arthritis lift her arm straight out in front of her. "This is as far as it goes," she said, straining. Tom Tam called out his formula of numbers, and he and his helpers eagerly got busy with their dolls. The room was quiet except for the tapping. When they were finished he asked the lady, "How you feel? Warm?" She answered yes, and he asked her to try lifting her arm again. This time she was able to lift it to her chin. The crowd gasped, then began clapping. Tom Tam clapped, too, looking very satisfied. *It's in her mind,* I thought. *She was able to lift it with the power of her mind.*

Though I believed in the healing force of energy, I also knew well the powers of the mind. And maybe because I believed in this power, I didn't want to abruptly depart from my panic like a passenger waving manically from the deck of a cruise ship to the one they left standing on the docks—because, as Tom Tam said, I was learning. And it seemed panic really had something to teach me. So I was going to try to listen, instead of simply bidding it a bon voyage and saying, *That was weird. Now what's for dinner?*

The question was, What was I supposed to learn? I realized then that I had been asking the wrong questions—questions like *How can I get rid of this troublesome panic? Where can I find a good mother who bakes banana bread? How can I be guaranteed that nothing bad will happen to me, ever?* But the question was simple: *What can panic teach me?* It seems to me that so much unhappiness in life comes not from a lack of answers, but from a lack of knowing the right questions to ask.

On the phone with my friend Meg, a poet I met at a reading, I told her I thought panic might be a bird.

"Write it to me," she said.

I hadn't written in months, but I opened my notebook anyway.

The bird is wet black, the size of a half-open fist. Sometimes it flutters in fits. Sometimes it leaps in fast explosions from low branches. Sometimes it sits out of sight, as high as the hawks will let it, watching. When it flies it slices the sky into triangles. Panes of glass. It is a smart bird, its sight like a heartbeat. There are days it watches me through my kitchen window and I can feel its feathers in my chest, its blood in my legs. Sometimes when the music's on, I don't notice the bird, which is a nonmusical bird, a bird that doesn't glide, that doesn't sing, but that is faithful, and that is, frankly, only trying to help.

I still panicked—not that day, but the next. But to have a day free from it—one whole long splendid day—was a message of its own: I was heading in the right direction. Sometimes we don't trust ourselves, so it's easy to believe that the power to healing lies in someone else's hands, just as the woman who couldn't lift her arm perhaps thought, *I didn't lift my arm—Tom Tam and his group with the dolls and hammers did!* But ultimately it doesn't matter. Whether by the supernatural or by our own inner wisdom, our own vibrant wills, we can get better. For me, the act of searching for answers, of trying one thing and then another and then another, was more empowering than any other single thing, because I was taking control of my life, and that action stood in direct opposition to the helplessness of panic.

Simply, we change by trying to change; we heal by trying to heal; we are strong when we stay faithful to those few words: *I know what I need.*

THIRTY

In addition to my cavaletti lessons with Gerta, I rode
other horses with other instructors whenever I got the chance. There
were jumping lessons that taught me to rise up out of the saddle and
give the horse the reins and let myself get carried through the air. And
there were trail rides into the mountains that taught me the many different sounds horse hooves can make against the earth—and that in
the sport of riding, there should always be time to relax and meander
through the trees.

I was learning so much, and the more I learned, the more I kept
coming back to dressage. The first time I heard the word *dressage,* I
was in college, rehearsing lines for an acting class with a girl who lived
in Belmont, the wealthy horse country of Maryland. She was a lovely
girl—articulate and upbeat—and when she told me she "did dressage"
with her horse, I didn't want to admit I had no idea what that meant,
though it sounded fancy, like the kind of thing a girl like me would

never do. But as I stumbled somewhat accidentally into it as I learned to ride, I discovered that the history of dressage (derived from the French: *to train*) belies what one might think when watching the prancing of upper-level horses in competitive dressage: those dance-like movements are arguably more athletically demanding than any other equestrian sport, and their earliest uses were actually to prepare horses for war, through fostering obedience, strength, and agility. Dressage replicates movements horses make naturally in the wild—whether at play, under threat, or while courting. Ultimately, so much of dressage is based on balance: on the equilibrium and strength of both the horse and the rider to carry themselves separately and to work together as a team. And none of this can happen without the willingness of the horse, which is based on his trust of the rider.

The earliest surviving documents on dressage come from the Greek master Xenophon, who advocated sympathetic training based on kindness and reward, a bedrock for an ideal practice: to combine what is best in the horse and best in the rider and cultivate this powerful harmony, this beautiful and unassailable force. Unfortunately, the reality of modern dressage is often quite different. But as I traveled around meeting horses and horse people, I didn't fully understand this yet. I was still naïve, but full of verve and hope, and after six months of lessons on Danielle, I knew it was time: I was ready to find a horse of my own.

I had planned to meet lots of horses before I made my choice, but it turned out there was only one, and he chose me: this spark-eyed chestnut looked at me—peered intently into my eyes—until I felt my world shift underneath me as if I were standing on the edge of a mountain. The first time I saw Claret, I fell in love. His face was marked by a white blaze shaped like an hourglass, and his sweeping back rose into high withers and a long neck. Not only was he beautiful but he was absolutely engaged in the world: he would paw the ground the minute you stopped paying attention to him and wasn't shy about frisking a stranger's pockets for treats. In those first few minutes he burned himself into me the way the shape of a light stays on the retina after you've closed your eyes. "Hi there," I said, running my hand along his blaze. As if to answer, he pressed his nose into my hands, then resumed his frisking. When he found the pocket with the jelly beans, he rubbed at it with his lips. "You win," I said, reaching in for the jelly beans, which he lifted gently, one at a time, from my hand.

When I rode him for the first time, I knew he was special. Bigger than most of the other horses I'd ridden so far, he trotted smoothly. His canter was comfortable and deep—a fluid power—and even though we were moving in circles, to me it felt as if we were going somewhere.

I already knew I wanted to bring him home. Gerta and I went out to his barn in New Hampshire to watch the vet conduct the prepurchase exam: a thorough physical examination that assesses a horse's soundness and seeks to uncover any underlying conditions. "He's a big boy," the vet noted, as he put Claret on a lunge line to examine his trot and canter. When he asked him to canter, Claret gave a little squeal, then bucked high into the air. "Feeling good today, huh?" The vet laughed, and I was thrilled to see Claret's spirit, right there—flashes of it igniting in the air above him. Throughout the exam, I kept noticing Claret's eye on me, and I couldn't help wondering if he was checking to see what I thought. But it wasn't until the end of the exam, when the vet tranquilized him in order to take X-rays, that I understood how deeply this horse had gotten into me. Within seconds, Claret's inquisitive eyes went sleepy, and his head drooped down into my arms. And as I held the weight of him, I felt the ache of responsibility you feel only for those you love, and I knew right then that I already belonged to Claret. I was his.

A few weeks later, I officially made him mine and brought him home to a barn ten minutes from my house. Soon even those ten minutes seemed like too much distance between this magnificent creature and me.

Despite all the lessons I'd taken over the last year, as it turned out, I still knew so little about horses. For starters, on the day I tried to bring Claret home, I realized I had no idea how to load a horse onto a trailer. I figured he'd simply waltz on, perhaps lured by a carrot or two, but even with Gerta attempting to wrangle him, he went in every direction except the trailer. It was only after a lot of angle calculation and strategic coaxing that he walked in. As I handed him the carrot, he looked around nervously, and I stroked his forehead.

Once we arrived at the barn, I walked Claret outside and led him to the paddocks, then to the indoor arena, and he followed eagerly. As we explored, he put his nose on each new thing, sometimes pausing for a couple of seconds as he inhaled deeply before turning back to me to see where I'd lead him next. "That is your mounting block," I told him. "That is your radio. That is your plastic chair." I walked him back into the barn. "This is your stall," I said, leading him in. He pressed a nostril between the bars separating the stalls and touched the nostril of the horse next door, and they breathed into each other for several seconds before Claret dismissed him and put his eyes back on me. Perhaps I should have felt fear, to stand in this small space with this relatively unknown and sizable animal, but I didn't: instead, I felt longing. So I pressed my nose to Claret's nostril like he'd done to the horse next door and I exhaled into it. Claret exhaled back, and his breath was warm and grassy and sweet, and we cycled through many breaths like this, unmoving except for the susurrus of these small waves between us. I could have spent the rest of the evening breathing into that velvety muzzle.

Eventually, he began to eat his hay, but after each time he dove down to take a bite, he lifted his head and touched his nose to my palm before diving back for another bite. We played this game until it was dark, and it was clear that he wanted me there as badly as I wanted to stay. He was calm then, and happy, and even after I left him to go home, my mind kept tracing the white hourglass on his face, until everything—the moon, the porch light spilling onto the walk, the sheets on our bed—became a reflection of his face, of this horse who, although I didn't know it yet, would change my life.

THIRTY-ONE

Our driver stops in Fairfax and parks his truck behind a building. Without fanfare, he climbs on top of me in the cramped front seat while Melissa sits motionless at my side. It doesn't take long, and then we're standing with our bags on a street in Virginia.

"Are you okay?" Melissa asks. We start walking.

"Yeah, I'm fine. You do what you gotta do," I tell her, trying to sound tough and worldly. I look at her and realize I've never really noticed how pretty she is, probably because her Mohawk gets most of the attention. On her forehead, a single curl hangs down and curves to the right, and a purple feather dangles from her left ear.

We walk and walk. As we pass a cacophony of catcalls from a construction crew, one of the workers leaves his pride to approach us. He pulls off his hard hat, and a wavy blond mane falls to his shoulders.

"Excuse me, but I just had to come over and say that you are the sexiest woman I've ever seen with a Mohawk—in fact, the only sexy woman I've seen with a Mohawk."

"You got a razor? I'd be happy to give you one of your own," Melissa says.

I hold out my hand. "I'm Roxanne, and this is my friend Anastasia."

His hand is callused and dusty. "I'm Rick, and this is your lucky day."

As we walk the streets waiting for Rick to finish his work, Melissa looks at me crossly. "Anastasia?"

"What's wrong with Anastasia?"

"Well, for one, it's like twenty-seven syllables long. Why couldn't you have given me a normal name?"

Rick brings us to his two-bedroom apartment, where he lives with his wife, Lynn, and a girl named Gina, a spunky twenty-year-old with a tan and frosty golden hair. "Just until I can get my shit together," she tells us. Her eyes are small but gleaming, her smile wide and eager.

She invites Melissa and me to freshen up in her room, where there's a small bathroom. The only furniture is a mattress with the sheets crumpled half off. Beside it towers a purple bong, and beside that is an empty container of butter pecan ice cream tipped on its side. There are piles of clothes and a few opened duffel bags strewn around.

"So Rick and his wife just let you stay here?" I ask.

"Yeah, but I have to fuck them." Gina pulls off her T-shirt and starts washing her face at the sink.

"Both?"

"Yep, and his stupid 'associates.' " She pulls on a lavender lace camisole, which glows against her tan. "But, like I said, it's just until I can get my shit together."

Melissa is by the window, looking out. I realize I've made a mistake to take her with me.

That night, Rick takes us to the house of his friend Rob, a tall, blunt-faced fellow with a puffy wheat-colored mustache and a space between his two front teeth. He pulls out five bottles of beer from his refrigerator and hands one to each of us, then looks us over. "You're all right, Rick, you know that? You are aaall riiight, my man."

Rick nods his head. "Hey, look, Gina and Ana here will party with you tonight. How's that?"

"What about this one here?" Rob asks, pointing at me.

"She's not on the menu this evening."

"Not on the menu, huh?"

"Nope," Rick says unapologetically. He's cleaned up nicely from his day job: his hair looks swept off the set of a Pert commercial, and his tight jeans, cowboy boots, and height remind me of the Marlboro Man. Before we left his apartment, he'd pulled out some black-and-white head shots of himself and presented them to us. "I'm an actor," he announced. And though he admitted to never having actually landed a part, he told us, "Man, I'm acting all day, every day. And when they call me, I'll be ready."

"Okay, ladies, it looks like just the three of us then," Rob says, putting his arms around Gina and Melissa. "Let's go on back and have some fun." Gina looks at me and winks, then rolls her eyes, so I roll mine in solidarity. Melissa doesn't look at me at all.

And the three of them disappear behind a dark wood door.

Rick knocks back his second beer. I finish mine, too, and turn on the stereo. I start to dance. Nothing can ever be wrong, I think, if you're dancing. So I keep dancing, while Rick watches.

When the bedroom door opens an hour later and the girls walk out, I go to them. Gina's hair has lost its volume, Melissa's black eyeliner is smudged, and their lipstick has been rubbed away. Rob follows them out, wearing only a pair of jeans. His hairy chest is flabby, his belly button deep. As I follow Gina and Melissa into the bathroom, I catch Rob slipping money into Rick's hand. I close the bathroom door behind us.

"Are you guys okay?" I feel as if they've traveled to the moon and back without me.

Gina sits on the toilet while Melissa hunches over the sink and swishes water in her mouth, spitting out forcefully each time.

"Sure, we're fine. Right, babe?" Gina looks up at Melissa.

Melissa spits again. "Yeah, we're fine."

Gina stands up and zips her jeans. In the toilet, a stream of blood swirls down, bright red.

The next day, Rick pulls me outside. "Ana's gotta go."

"What do you mean?"

"She's gonna drag you down," he says, flicking his cigarette ash into the grass.

"If you want us to leave, that's fine. But we came together, and we'll leave together."

"Listen, what do you think? I'm stupid? You guys have the word *runaway* written all over you. I could go to jail for having you here. And everywhere you go, she'll be sticking out like a sore thumb. I can't take that kind of risk." He hands me a cigarette, and I lean into the flame.

"And if you were smart, you wouldn't take that risk, either. You have a chance without her, but with her, you've got nothing."

The image of her spitting into the sink the night before is burned into my mind. "How much *nothing*, then, did she make you last night for fucking your friend?"

"That's not the point. The point is that she's gonna get you both caught. Besides, you'd be doing her a favor. She's not cut out for this—and you know it. If you were really her friend, you'd let her go."

I know he's right. I know that when we jumped out of the back of that truck, this wasn't what Melissa was envisioning.

I come in and sit beside her. She looks pale. "Too much beer last night?" I ask.

"No, I'm fine. Just a little tired."

I poke at the bottom of my shoe with my finger. "I don't know how to say this."

"You think we should split up."

Her impassive delivery surprises me. "It's just that they're going to be looking for the two of us together, you know?"

"I know."

"And besides, I don't think this is good for you. You shouldn't have had to do what you did last night."

"I did what I wanted to do," Melissa says flatly.

"I know, but you're probably making a big mistake. I mean, you don't *have* to run. You've got this great dad who loves you. Sure, he's insanely overprotective, but all you have to do is put in a little more time at Good Shepherd and then you'll be free. It's different for me. I belong to the courts now, and my dad's in jail, and my mother hates me. But if I had what you have, I wouldn't be here right now."

Melissa's toughness crumbles and she begins to cry. "I'm ready to go home." She presses her face into her hands. "I want to go home."

So Rick takes her home, and when he comes back, he tells me to take my pants off. He does the same, then climbs on top of me on Gina's mattress, while his wife sleeps in the next room.

With Melissa gone, the four of us establish a rhythm. Rick goes off to his construction job during the day, while his wife spends most mornings and afternoons napping. Gina and I share the mattress, sleep late, smoke weed, and peer into the refrigerator, which is usually empty. Sometimes we go to the gym at the center of the apartment complex and sit stoned in the hot tub for hours. When she isn't home, I write. I write on spare scraps of paper, torn pieces of grocery bags, the soles of my shoes, the insides of my arms. I write poems about longing and numbness and the sky. I write about trees. I write letters to my sister and ask her how school is and if she likes any boys. I write to my father, who's in Rikers Island prison for embezzling money from the newspaper he worked for as an advertising manager, and I ask him when he's getting out, even though I don't have his address. I mail nothing. My red purse fills with scraps.

I've just smoked greens. Parsley dipped in PCP. Sweetly chemical, smoother than pot, it's making the world turn to cotton. Walking is a moon-bounce. My sight is as if through the cardboard tube inside wrapping paper. A Dire Straits song is on the radio, and the radio isn't here because space keeps pushing it back and back until it's a small sound cowering in the corner of the room, in the corner of the cottony universe. Air is too heavy, my head is too big, the ground is too soft. Pushing me down like a thumbtack. I'm forgetting who I am. Gina, I'm scared. Help me, please. "You're okay." No, I think I'm dying. Gina, I'm dying. And I don't even know who I am anymore. "You're Roxanne, and you're just high." No I'm not. You don't even know my name. "It's okay, I don't need to know your name. I see your spirit, girl." But I can't breathe. Please, someone call an ambulance. "You better shut her the fuck up, Gina—I'm not messing around." "Why don't you shut up, Rick? You're only making it worse. She needs peace." "I'll give her a piece all right." Gina, I'm dying. "You're going to be fine. Just breathe." But my heart is beating too fast. Feel it, feel it. It's beating too fast. A hand like a blanket on my chest. "Your heart is fine." No, it's out of control. It's going to explode. "Just breathe. You're just high. You're gonna come down, I promise." I'm losing my mind. "No, it's all here. Just breathe. You're safe." Her voice is another song. Her hand is stroking my hair. Once my mother stroked my hair in a hospital. The scars on my leg. Do you see the scars? "Yes, and I like your scars." The hand stays at my head. Please don't ever leave me. Let me stay here with my head in your lap.

When I close my eyes, the faces are hideous, monsters morphing into monsters. Jagged teeth, fat foreheads, eyes stretching long-ways, dripping into chattering mouths, jagged teeth. This world is so scary. Please tell me you love me.

"I love you."

THIRTY-TWO

On those first days I rode Claret after I brought him home, those bright October afternoons when the scent of burning wood traced the air and shadows turned to labyrinths, it seemed like nothing could go wrong. Gerta stood in the corner of the arena and called out instructions—"ask more with your leg, tighten up your reins, pull your right shoulder back"—which I followed. She taught me, and Claret taught me, and the two of us trotted and cantered and made figure eights and serpentines and were clumsy and occasionally graceful, and with each day, we were learning the way each other's body moved. Claret was a generous but exacting teacher: he did what I asked, but if I asked incorrectly, he let me know. For instance, if, from a halt, I asked him to walk forward while I was leaning forward in the saddle, he'd take a few steps backwards until I sat up straight. If I squeezed too hard with my thighs in the canter, he stopped cantering. If I didn't use my inside leg to mark the curves of a circle, our circle turned into something of a parallelogram. But when I asked correctly—when in those brief moments I managed to get the orchestra of all my body parts in harmony—Claret became a virtuoso. What an honor it was to learn from him, to receive, each day, the gift of his back.

Outside of work, Claret quickly revealed the full sass of his mischievous nature. For instance, he clearly found it amusing to unzip my jacket with his lips while I curried his neck. He rarely missed an opportunity to snap the elastic band of my riding pants against my back while I bent over to pick his feet, or to generally pick up anything he could reach and drop it dramatically to the ground—hoof picks, riding gloves, brushes, girths, saddle pads, buckets, you name it. He once managed to extract my keys from my pocket, then stretched his neck way up as I attempted to reach for them and shook them like a tambourine over my head. In the paddock, he dug holes, dismantled the fencing so that he could play with the mare in the next paddock, and one afternoon, after Gerta had carefully walked through the paddocks to clear them of rocks, Claret entertained himself by reaching his head through the fence railings and pulling every last rock out of the bucket she'd left them in. He was a silly boy. He made me laugh, and he also exasperated me. But when I looked at him to try to read that mind of his, he was often looking back at me, almost as if I were the one he was studying instead of the other way around.

We were students of each other, Claret and I. And he was teaching me more than I'd ever expected to learn—not only about riding, but about love.

And then there were the beginnings that marked a time when things would start to fall apart—those days that would test my limited understanding of horses and the mettle of my commitment to Claret. One of those days was meant to be bucolic: a trail ride with a fellow rider at the barn, Beth, and her semiretired Thoroughbred. After all that indoor dressage work, I was excited to be doing something fun.

But a few minutes into the trail, Claret started shaking his head rapidly up and down, which made it difficult for me to keep hold of the reins. I didn't know why he was doing this, though if I'd had to guess, I would have said he was staging a protest. Against what, I didn't know. But as he flicked his head about, I could feel his back stiffening beneath the saddle, and then, in an instant, we both noticed a white drainage pipe jutting out from some rocks. Before I could gather the reins, he spooked at it and began backing up. And in his panic, he wasn't thinking about the steep ditch I knew was right behind us. "Stop!" I ordered ineffectually, not being an experienced enough rider to know how to command this with my body. He took another step back, and I could feel his hind legs starting to slip. "Kick him!" Beth yelled. "Hard!"

With both legs I kicked him forward, out of the ditch. At that point, neither of us was happy. My hands were trembling, and Claret was shaking his head up and down again, and I told Beth that I wanted to turn around and go back to the barn.

"Don't be silly," she said. "You're going to be fine."

"I really don't think he wants to do this," I said. "And I don't think I'm ready to handle him out in the woods by myself."

"Why don't we switch?" she suggested. You take my horse, and I'll ride Claret."

Beth was a far more experienced rider than I was, and her horse was a calm fellow, so I agreed. But as soon as she got on Claret, I could tell he was even less happy. He began to shake his head more violently, stopping only to swish his tail. "Really, Beth, I think we should go back."

"He's going to be fine, you'll see. He just needs a minute to adjust to a new person on his back."

But as each minute piled onto the next, Claret's displeasure became indisputable. Frustrated, Beth gave him a smack with her whip. "I'm not your mommy," she said. "You can't get away with this with me!" And in an eruptive response, Claret spun around. He backed her forcefully into a tree, then spun around again.

"Oh my God, are you okay?" I asked.

"I'm fine," she said, but she didn't look fine. Her face was pale and glistening with sweat, her eyes wide with fear.

I had the sense that I should get back on Claret, but I didn't have the courage, so instead I led the way back to the barn on her horse, while she and Claret followed. Back in his stall, I stood beside him and watched him eat hay as if nothing had happened. But I felt defeated. "What *was* that out there?" I asked. Claret chewed imperviously. "I just don't know what I'm doing," I said. "I don't know what you need." He didn't stop chewing, but he lifted his head and put his nose on my shoulder, and he held it there, and I could feel his chewing in my ear, as if it were happening inside my own head.

THIRTY-THREE

Determined to learn whatever panic had to teach me, I started carrying around a book by Rilke called *Letters to a Young Poet.* Since I had written my first poem, a third-grade ode to the stars, I had wanted to be a poet. I had always been drawn to the way poems can hold the world in a few lines, the way poetry can change the existence of things simply by looking at them, the way it can change the heart. As I read Rilke's letters, it was as if I could feel Rilke speaking to me. Of all the volumes of psychology books and cure-your-panic-now books, this turned out to be the book I took with me wherever I went. I underlined my favorite passages and reread them over and over. "Perhaps all the dragons in our lives are princesses who are only waiting to see us act, just once, with beauty and courage. Perhaps everything that frightens us is, in its deepest essence, something helpless that wants our love." I could feel Rilke's words taking root inside me. And in the moments when I felt the most despair, those lines made me feel like I could be brave.

Larry and I started going to the UU church fairly regularly. Sometimes I would start laughing when we had to sing hymns—the kind of inappropriate laughter that can only happen in a church or in the middle of a college lecture or some other holy place, that silent laughter that ravages your body and sucks your breath away so that you're shaking and red with it—because I was a very bad singer, and because I was singing badly about such joyous things, and because the women behind me were singing in their joyous falsettos. So I kind of lost it when it was time to sing, as in I came undone, as in I could not stop laughing. Larry would sometimes laugh, too, though always a little uncomfortably—and who can blame him?—but other times he'd keep on singing imperviously, almost as off-key as I was, which only made me laugh harder.

But on Christmas Eve that year, when the town was cuffed in snow and the sky was the color of bathwater and the cathedral candles flickered in the muted light, we sang a song called "Would You Harbor Me?" It began, *Would you harbor me? Would I harbor you? Would you harbor a Christian, a Muslim, a Jew?* I held the program in my hand and felt the power of those questions, of what it means to harbor someone. And then a line I wasn't prepared for came—*Would you harbor a runaway woman, or child, a poet, a prophet . . . ?*—and before I could get control of the maelstrom of emotion blossoming like a hydrogen bomb inside me, I was sobbing. A runaway. Every day of my life, since I'd first run out of my parents' house, no matter where I was, no matter what I had or didn't have, I was always that girl first, underneath it all, that unsure child looking for home. So I cried the kind of sobbing that racks the bones, deep and visceral, the kind that could go on for a very long time if you let it.

And that was only the beginning of the service. Luckily, I managed to pull myself together, though not before people noticed. They were probably thinking, *That girl has a laughing* and *crying problem.* It wasn't Erin's turn to preach, so I watched the back of her head as she sat in the front pew. The minister began to deliver his sermon, which was about harboring each other in a sometimes cruel and unsafe world, and about how no one had harbored Mary and Joseph when Mary was in labor with Jesus, and I was thinking that *harbor* must be one of the most beautiful words of all, that to be harbored must be all a panicking person wants—or what anyone wants.

Helen came bearing gifts that night—a small bottle of mandarin-flavored olive oil adorned with a red ribbon at its neck, and a collection of her favorite recipes printed on paper with little snowmen at the bottom. I gave her an assortment of rare teas and a book of poems. And it was warm and cozy, and the tree was lit with colored lights, and Larry was sitting in the next room reading a book, and I knew how lucky we were to be harbored there, in those glowing winter snapshots: people moving through rooms in a house in the soft light in a small town surrounded by hundreds of miles of snow. The picture was like one I imagined when I was on the streets, walking the neighborhoods at night, peering into people's windows to see how they lived.

Helen and I baked salmon with olive oil, lemon juice, and tarragon, topped with a shallot and caper crème fraîche. We sautéed whole young carrots in butter and honey, roasted sliced red peppers until they turned sweet, and whipped up a pot of good old-fashioned mashed potatoes. For dessert we caramelized pears with fresh maple yogurt. All my life I had been eating food, but now I was experiencing it—the fragrance of tarragon, the brightness of carrots with their tops still on, the sound of things bubbling in the pan.

Later that night, as Larry and I headed up to bed, he stopped me in the foyer and gestured toward the long wood frame with three pictures of us from his fortieth birthday party. He pointed to the first one and said, "Do you see this?"

"Yes."

"And this?" He pointed to the next one.

"Yes."

"And this?"

"Yes."

"That's us," he said, smiling.

Then he gave me a long kiss on my cheek and asked, "You know what this is?"

"A kiss?"

"It's all the love in my heart, traveling up"—he ran his hand up his chest—"through my mouth, onto your skin, and down into your heart forever."

So many days we were lost to each other. So many days I felt closest to him in the mornings, just before I watched him drive away. But in that moment, I was harbored there, in his love.

THIRTY-FOUR

I have never seen lightning like this before. It's as if the sky is raining lightning, bolt after violet bolt of it zagging down to the horizon. Sometimes there are several bolts at once, and they make a thin buzzing sound. I can feel them; they raise the hairs on my arms. I walked to this wooden split-rail fence on the edge of this country road from one of Rick's friends' houses. We're somewhere in the middle of Reston, Virginia, which means nothing to me. But I can tell you about the air here, which is warm and very still. It smells of grass and gravel. Back at Rick's friend's house, they're smoking PCP. I decided not to smoke today because every time I do I spend hours wondering if I will ever get my mind back. So I left them—Rick, who was rumbling about the difference between good beer and elephant piss; his friend Rob, who had gone mute and bug-eyed from the drugs; and Gina, who was casually smoking a cigarette and who never seems to lose her cool under any circumstance—and now there is this curtain of lightning at the edge of the field. And there are horses in the field. They keep erupting into frantic bursts, bolting as a herd, then halting and standing very close to each other. When they gallop, their manes and tails fly, and their hooves are thunder. But the sky is not thundering. And it's not raining. It's all lightning—these surges spilling from the ether like veins. I reach my hand out, over the fence, toward the horses, toward the lightning. I know I should take cover, but I can't move—maybe because this is one of the most beautiful things I've ever seen.

⁓

Though Rick never tells us how much money he gets for Gina and me, I overhear him on the phone one night referring to us as "a ticket to the Virgin Islands." He laughs. "Did you hear that? *Virgin.*"

I remind myself that the sex is better than any institution, that at least now I can have fresh air whenever I want. Only, I never get outside much. Gina works lunch shifts as a waitress, and I spend most days on the mattress doing bong hits and writing on my body. On Gina's off days, we usually get high, and even if we go outside then, the trees and sky and birds are too far away for me to feel. Soon everything begins to blur together—the drugs, the sex, the bedroom window and its sharp light gathering at the edge of our mattress, the radio feeding me music—and I feel trapped in that blur, indistinct, shrinking.

I decide to leave. I ask Gina for a ride, and she puts her arm around me. "Sure, I'll give you a lift."

When Gina asks me where I want to go, I say Rockville because I don't know where else to go. We drive most of the way in silence.

It starts to rain. I turn to look at Gina. Her profile—her strong Greek nose, her smooth skin and deep dimple—is lovely and familiar. "I'm going to miss you," I say. "And I really appreciate all you've done for me."

"I'm going to miss you, too." She glances at me, then back to the road. "But this isn't goodbye forever. I'm going to give you my mom's number, so you always know how to find me."

I try to find comfort in this, but I know the odds: I'll probably never see her again, just as I'll probably never see my friend Cindy or my old friend Dawn or Afshin or the donut guy or so many people, each one eclipsed by the next. So we drive in the rain, and I write *I love you* on a small scrap of paper, which I leave on the seat of her car.

THIRTY-FIVE

"Dance with me." Larry and I were getting ready for bed, and I'd put some music on. "C'mon," I said, extending my hand and swaying my hips.

Larry stood as if he were waiting to jaywalk across a busy street, unsure about whether he should move, so I took the towel from his hands and drew it around his waist, then pulled him toward me. "C'mon."

As Prince sang sultrily about pink cashmere, I let the towel drop and, with my arms wrapped around him, pulled him the rest of the way toward me. But as I tried to entice Larry into my rhythm, his hips stayed locked, and something in his eyes was tremulous: it was the unmistakable look of fear.

"It's okay," I said, releasing him. "We don't have to dance."

And I stepped back, and neither of us moved for several long seconds, while Prince wailed passionately and the towel lay strewn, a gash of white, on the floor.

"I'm sorry," he said.

Larry once told me about an experience he'd had as a boy on the playground, shortly after he came to the States from Taiwan. With his clean white shoes, he climbed the ladder to the slide again and again so that the slick metal could send him flying. He was having fun, enjoying those few seconds when he let go of his body and let the force of gravity carry him, until a group of kids surrounded him before he could climb back up another time. They were speaking to him, at first one at a time, then all at once, their voices climbing over one another in their bulbous and unfamiliar language. Larry couldn't tell from their eyes or their postures what they wanted, what they were trying to convey, so he repeated over and over the only sentence he knew: *I don't know, I don't know, I don't know.* Then he ran away from them.

Sometimes I wondered if that's how he felt around me. I wondered if my language, particularly the language of my body, was foreign to him—if my passion was as intimidating, as demanding, as a group of hungry children.

When it was finally time to see the therapist who'd appeared on *Oprah*—let's call him Opther—I was pretty disenchanted with therapists. This one was an inscrutable, mild-mannered man somewhere in his fifties. He had pale, receding hair and large eighties-style glasses. I had to take a winding country road to get there. It was dark already.

Panic drove with me but stayed in the backseat, pecking at me every now and then. *I have no time for you right now,* I told it. *I'm trying to get somewhere.* And like me, it was waiting to see what would come next.

Opther invited me to sit on a couch, where he sat across from me in a chair, behind which was a massage table. I gave him the five-minute rundown of my recent history with panic disorder, followed by the five-minute I-still-think-I-may-have-a-heart-disorder disclaimer, followed by the five-minute snapshot of my childhood. And I concluded with a five-minute explanation of my marriage: "It's like we're both stuck. I used to be the one to come with the stick and yank him from the quicksand, but now we're both sinking. And we rarely have sex."

"Well, you have a lot of reasons to be anxious," Opther said. "And a lack of sexual connection is certainly one. Freud spoke about the link between sex and anxiety."

"What sexual link *didn't* Freud speak about?" I said jokingly, but Opther didn't laugh.

"Your anxiety has been with you a long time," he said. "You've been on high alert since you were a kid. You learned that being in a relaxed state isn't safe, because you had to keep your guard up. Look at your breathing now, for instance. It's shallow. Anxious people aren't deep breathers."

I tried to take a deep breath, but he was right: it was all caught up in my throat. Noticing this made me more anxious.

"My approach to anxiety is to remind the body what it's like to be in a relaxed state—to teach the body that it's not only safe, but a natural state of being. Look at a baby—you throw it up in the air, and it giggles with joy without a thought of falling, but over time our environment degrades that trust. And we have to teach the body to regain it."

I liked Opther. "How do we do that?" I asked.

"We start with breathing. Now remember, that primal part of your brain—"

"The amygdala?"

"Yes, the amygdala. It's been in overdrive for a while now, and that's probably altered the way your brain perceives ordinary stimuli, which is why everything seems dangerous. With a hyperactive amygdala, the world is a terrifying place."

"So I'm not crazy for being scared of the shower?"

"Not at all. In fact, claustrophobia, as well as agoraphobia, is common for people with panic disorder. Checkout lines, exercise, hypoglycemia—these can all be pretty scary things."

"Yes, yes—I'm afraid of all of them!"

Opther smiled. "In the world of anxiety, you're actually pretty normal."

"Do you think medication is the only way to fix my brain?"

"No. Definitely not."

"But if my brain chemistry has changed, what if I can never get it back to how it was before? What if I'm stuck like this forever?" I could feel the panic starting. "I failed CBT, you know."

"That's why we're going to remind your body to relax." He nodded his head, so I nodded mine, too. "Nobody ever has to be stuck this way."

Opther had me lie on my back on his table. It wobbled when I got on, and I was worried it would break and spill me to the floor.

"Are you okay with touch?" he asked.

"Sure," I said, lying very still, unsure what to expect.

He placed his hand on my abdomen. His touch was warm, and I could feel it generating energy there. "Now I want you to breathe into my hand."

I tried to breathe deeply, but the air didn't make it past my top rib.

"Just take your time," he said. "Breathe into my hand."

I tried again, but no dice. How hard it was to simply breathe.

He presided over me like a wizard, his hand sure. "You're safe now. You can relax."

Eventually the breathing came deeper, and I could feel my lungs expanding. At the same time, a terror skittered through me. "I'm scared," I said. And the urgency of my voice scared me more.

"What are you scared of?"

"I'm scared my lungs will explode if I keep breathing like this."

"Impossible. Remember, your body has forgotten what this feels like, so it'll feel strange at first."

"But I really think my lungs might pop."

"No. Your body needs to remember this, so just try to go with it. This is your life force. Let the air come in."

I opened my eyes and gave him the imperative of my gaze. "Do you promise I'm safe?"

He placed his other hand over my sternum. "I promise."

His touch felt like a sun-bright stream. It was moving through me, this soft force. And he kept his hands on me, and the table wobbled a little as I breathed, but I kept breathing, thinking how funny it was that he would have a wobbly table for us anxious types, but I could hear his voice saying I was safe, and it felt like a cocoon around me, and then suddenly I was crying, and he was telling me it was good to cry, and I couldn't believe how many tears there were, how fast and silently they came. And he stood there, and he kept his hands on me, and turned me into a stream.

THIRTY-SIX

I'm going on a date. This tall blond named Bruce saw me hanging around outside the 7-Eleven and asked me if I wanted to go see a movie, so of course I said yes. Dates are something that pretty girls in novels have, but not me. They're the same girls who get walked to the front doors of their houses on lush summer nights and who smell like flowers and shampoo and who get kissed by wide-eyed football players beneath their porch lights. They're the same girls who wear pink puffy ski jackets and drink hot chocolate by fireplaces in ski lodges. They have sweet sixteen parties and straight teeth and confidence. They have homes.

Bruce has very long arms. He wears his Converse sneakers loosely tied and his hair long in the back and spiked on top. I don't mind that he doesn't get us any popcorn or candy, or even that he's chosen the last row. I'm still happy to be sitting in the theater, waiting for the rumble of the big screen: *Back to the Future*, starring Michael J. Fox, the kind of guy who would definitely walk a date to her door. But when the theater goes dark and the previews start, Bruce wants to make out. I let him fish his tongue around in my mouth for a few minutes, but when the previews end, I turn back to the screen. Bruce grabs the back of my head and pulls it toward him again.

I resist. "Can't we watch the movie?"

"Yeah," he says, "sure." But a minute later, he grabs my hand and puts it on his cock, which he's popped out through the fly of his pants. "Go ahead and suck it," he whispers, trying to push my head down.

"I want to watch the movie," I whisper, pulling away.

"Just suck it first."

I look out at the rows of dark heads, all poised forward. Nobody else is pushing anyone else's head down. Shame sears my throat. "I just wanted to watch the movie," I say, my voice louder than I expect. Then I get up and leave.

Near the popcorn, I hear a voice behind my shoulder. "Are you all right?" The voice is sweet, like a child's.

I turn to see a couple standing arm in arm. "We saw you in there with that guy," the woman says. Her eyes are pale blue, concerned.

"I'm okay. He was just a jerk."

"Where do you live?" the woman asks. "Do you need a ride?"

I look down at my jeans. I've been wearing them for weeks, and there's a blotch of pizza sauce on my right thigh. "I'm kind of between places right now."

She gives me a long, considered look, and for a moment I think she sees me—I mean, really sees me. "Bader," she gives her boyfriend's arm a little tug, "I think she should come with us."

His eyes are playful, his smile sweet. They are both like children. And I am going home with them.

The first thing Giselle does when we get to the apartment is heat up a can of New England clam chowder. She sits and watches me for a few minutes until Bader puts on music and starts twirling her around the living room to Madonna's "Lucky Star."

Giselle moved here from France three years ago and works as a translator for a company with letters for a name; Bader is here from Kuwait on a six-month visa, along with several of his friends who all live in the same apartment complex. Some of them work as firefighters, but many, including Bader, are looking for jobs. Bader's apartment is a one-bedroom, so I sleep on the sofa. Giselle spends weekends there, and then she and Bader are always giggling. Neither of them asks me about my life, and Bader never asks me for money or how long I plan on staying. I feel like a stray dog, and I want to nuzzle them both.

At dinner all the friends come over, and we sit around newspaper on the floor and dip pita into hummus and baba ghanoush and couscous. The collection of hands meeting in the center, sharing, is like a heart beating, and sometimes I let myself believe we are one big family. We drink wine and vodka and tequila. Tequila sunrises are Bader's favorite, so I learn to make them for him. The best part is watching the grenadine sink to the bottom.

Without Giselle, I am the only girl. And these men have huge dark eyes and thick lashes and smooth skin and full lips and sleek black hair. I don't have to sleep with any of them, but sometimes I do, mostly with Bader. I like the billowy sounds he makes and the gentle way he kisses. I like the way he holds me afterward. I like the way he shuffles around in his pajamas and slippers. He feels like love.

Giselle feels like love, too. Being with her is like splashing around in a swimming pool. She is fun and sunny and also a bit jumpy. Her auburn hair always looks tousled, and she's always ready to laugh. The strange thing about her is that she never takes off her shoes. She says it's because her feet are too small, and she has to wear children's shoes, and because of this, all I want is to see her feet.

"C'mon, please," I beg. "I bet your feet are so cute."

"Nobody sees these feet. In fact, I was born with shoes on." When she smiles, her chin crinkles.

"What about Bader? I'm sure *he's* seen them."

"Ah, the thing about certainty," she says, tapping the side of her cheek, "is that it's the great illusion."

"But—"

She leans close and whispers into my ear, "Socks." Then she tickles my ribs, and we both fall to the floor laughing.

But she never lets me see her feet.

Sergio is also French. He's a squat, round-bellied man who flings his stubby hands around when he speaks. His peachy brown hair puffs out around his head to match his thick handlebar mustache. I like how he speaks, how he often ends sentences with *yes*. "It's a lovely day, yes?" "You are hungry, yes?" I meet him during an afternoon walk through the neighborhood. A school bus has just unloaded a group of kids who walk slightly slumped under the weight of their backpacks. They must be my age, fourteen. As they disperse and start walking home, I wonder what they're thinking about, what they're carrying home from school, what books, what notes, what daydreams, and as they make their slow parade down the street, I realize I will never be one of them.

And then there's Sergio, also walking. He offers me a hundred dollars, so I sleep with him. When we're finished, he pulls his pants off the floor, removes his wallet, and gives me five twenties, which I stash in the front zipper of my purse for safekeeping. He strolls naked into the kitchen and offers me a drink while I put my clothes back on. There is a kindness about him—in the simple gesture of offering me a drink *after* sex—that I appreciate. I have orange juice.

Bader and two of his friends, Abdullah and Siraj, are taking me to a D.C. nightclub called Numbers. We sing loudly with the radio as we speed down the highway with the windows down, and I think *Yes, this is life, this is my life.* When we get to the club, they go in first, then sneak me in a side door. It's my first time in a nightclub. The music thumps through me and the barstool I'm sitting on. Bader orders me amaretto on the rocks—"You'll like it," he says, "it's sweet"—and I drink it through a skinny straw, watching the people on the dance floor move together, one dynamic entity.

The DJ is playing a funked-up version of Duran Duran's "The Wild Boys," and the drums are big, and I want to dance. Bader takes my hand, and we snake our way onto the dance floor. Strobe lights dart through space, staggering time—a hundred mini-snapshots of Bader's face, each one slightly varied from the last: a slight tilt to the head, angle of the chin, spread in the arms. Beautiful Bader. There are so many people, and soon I am dancing with them, too, and then Abdullah joins us, and I am diving in with all my body to the flashing, beating night.

W hen it's over, I can't find Bader or the others. The club is thinning out, and I keep making tracks around it, looking in every dark corner for a familiar face. I call into the men's bathroom for Bader, but no one answers.

A beefy bouncer lumbers over to me. "Time to go home, sweetie. C'mon back tomorrow, okay?"

"I can't find my friends."

"Well if you go on home, I bet they'll turn up."

I step out of the club feeling lost. How could they have left me here alone? The streets are already desolate, the sky starless. There is nothing else to do but start walking.

"Roxanne!" a voice rings out. I turn to see two dark figures down an alleyway, hunched below a burnt-out streetlight.

"Bader?" I call.

But he doesn't answer. I walk toward the men, and as I get closer I see a third body, lying on the ground.

"Bader?" I try again, more urgently. I start running. I see one of

Bader's shoes turned sideways in the street. And then I see Bader, lying on the sidewalk with Abdullah and Siraj kneeling over him. His blood is spreading over the cool concrete. His throat is cut.

I drop to my knees. An ambulance howls ominously. I pray the way the sisters taught me: *Please, God, let him live. In the name of the Father, Son, and Holy Spirit.* We are all reaching for Bader; we are wearing Bader's blood. The fear in his eyes is our fear.

The hospital gives us five minutes with Bader. They are filling him back up with blood. Sutures line his neck; they remind me of the Scarecrow from *The Wizard of Oz.* Even his eyelashes, sealed shut, look like stitches. His face has turned gray and nearly doubled in size, as if the tubes are inflating him somehow. I'm afraid to get close, so I stand at the foot of his bed and imagine my whisper as a soft wave touching him: *I love you.*

THIRTY-SEVEN

In the waiting room of the cardiology department at Boston Medical Center, I wriggled in my seat like a child hyped up on Pop Rocks and Pepsi. After the session with Opther that brought me back to my body, I'd finally decided to take a look at my heart. "I'm worried the doctor is going to find something bad," I told Larry. He was sitting beside me, flipping through one of the waiting room copies of *Newsweek*.

"It won't be something bad." He put his hand over mine. "You'll see. You're healthy; your heart is healthy."

"It doesn't feel healthy."

"I know. But trust me," he said, giving my hand a squeeze. "I'm a doctor."

We both sort of laughed. But the tentacles of fear I had about my heart ran deep. They took hold when I was eleven and certain I was dying of a heart attack. I woke my father up that morning, my hand over my chest, barely able to utter, "Something's wrong with my heart."

And instantly I knew from the way he glared at me, still half sleeping, that I'd made a mistake. I quickly exited his bedroom and quietly but mightily hoped he'd go back to sleep. But he didn't; he got out of bed and chased me through the dining room and kitchen in a terrifying and seemingly ceaseless loop. As we ran, he threw random things at me. One of them was a brick left over from some remodeling work being done to the kitchen. When it struck the back of my leg, he told me I better never wake him up again, not if I knew what was good for me.

That morning, as I ran from him like some hunted thing, I didn't know what would kill me first—my heart or my father. And in those moments, nothing else existed in the world but that fear.

That's what panic was like: only the fear and the fear and the fear. And now, after all those years, I was finally going to learn the truth about my heart.

When they called me into the exam room, the nurse immediately hooked me up to a cardiac monitor. Dr. Davidoff came in and shook Larry's hand. "Good to see you, Ravin," Larry said. I wondered if Larry was embarrassed to have his panic-stricken wife in a hospital gown in front of one of his colleagues. Dr. Davidoff was tall and handsome, and I tried to pass off a mien of elegance as I shook his hand and ignored the multiple cardiac leads sprawling out of my gown.

"So you've been worried about your heart?" he asked.

I could feel my pulse instantly rise. "Yes," I said. "I started having panic attacks several months ago, but I'm worried I have an underlying heart condition." I had told enough people about panic that it had started to become easier to say, less fraught with shame. "Also, sometimes my heart skips a beat. And it beats very fast, even at rest."

"Yeah," he said, looking at the monitor. "You're at about one forty right now." He said this calmly, without a hint of alarm, and for this I was grateful. "Are you anxious right now?"

"Yes," I said. "I'm afraid of what you're going to tell me."

Dr. Davidoff took a little more of my medical history, then gave me a stress test, whereby I had to run on a treadmill for five minutes. I started running, and about two minutes into it, my heart jumped in my chest. "It just did it!" I huffed, my feet pounding the treadmill gracelessly. "It skipped a beat—did you see it?"

"Everything looks good," he said, "just keep going."

When I finished, I stepped off the treadmill and hunched over like a marathon runner, trying to catch my breath.

"That little skip you felt," Dr. Davidoff began, "was a PVC—premature ventricular contraction. Basically, it's what we call an ectopic beat, or early beat. Everyone gets them, though, and in a structurally sound heart, they're completely benign. I get them myself, in fact."

"You do?" I wanted to know more. I wanted to know every detail of his irregular beats.

But he just nodded.

"You said they're benign in a structurally sound heart, but what if my heart's not structurally sound?" That was the question of my life. I could feel my heart speeding with the asking of it.

Dr. Davidoff smoothed his left hand over his right. "From what I've seen so far, your heart is completely normal. But we'll get you set up for an echocardiogram now, and then we'll have a complete picture."

As we waited in the echo room, I asked Larry, "Do you think they'll find a mitral valve prolapse?"

"I think they'll find a beautiful heart." Larry kissed me on the cheek, and my eyes filled. This was my love. My steadfast, imperfect, surprising love.

The technician who would be performing my echocardiogram was a young, sprightly guy, with a soft sweep of hair across his forehead. "Goooood afternoon," he said, gliding into the room. He was thin and limber in his movements.

He coated my torso with gel, turned off the lights, then slowly pushed a transducer across my chest. The swishing sound of my heartbeat filled the room, wet and percussive, and my heart appeared on the screen—a blob moving in various shades of gray. Finally, here it was, this worried engine of my body, revealed.

I was afraid to ask. "How does it look?"

"It looks like"—the tech pressed the transducer into me firmly— "you have a heart."

I laughed nervously.

"See this here?" he asked, pointing to more gray. "This is your left ventricle. And over here is your right." Then he turned to Larry. "But you've probably seen this tons of times, Dr. Chin."

"No, actually," Larry said. "I look at brains and spines mostly."

"Then between us, we've got the most important stuff covered," the tech said, grinning.

Despite the jovial atmosphere in the room, I kept thinking that at any moment, one turn of his hand would uncover my hidden malady, this abject thing I'd been carrying inside me. "And they look okay?" I asked. "The ventricles?"

"They look like very good ventricles," he said. I smiled, and a part of me began to relax. A man had looked straight through my skin and muscle and bone, and hadn't run screaming from the room. *Very good ventricles*. It was kind of amazing.

The entire exam took almost an hour, during which the tech approached my heart from every angle. When he was finished, I asked him, "What's the verdict?" I braced myself.

He turned the lights back on. "Your heart," he said, "is perfect."

Sometimes a sun rises in a room. Sometimes what we believe for a long time is the wrong thing. Sometimes we get the gift of knowing that, of beginning to believe something new. "Thank you," I said. A rush began to surge through me, warm and electric—the smooth expanse of relief.

"Happy Valentine's Day," the tech said, sashaying out of the room.

It was Valentine's Day? I couldn't believe it. How could I have forgotten? I sat up on the bed and reached for Larry just as he was reaching for me. "Happy Valentine's Day," he said.

THIRTY-EIGHT

Nobody knows who tried to kill Bader, or why, but Abdullah tells me that he's slowly getting better; he's even started breathing on his own. When I ask him about Giselle, he says she's out of town. She might be in France, but all I know for sure is that she and Bader are gone. Bader's friends have decided it's best that I don't come to the hospital, where I might draw unwanted attention, so I stay by myself in the apartment and wait. There is no humming, no dancing, no slippers, no love. It's eerie without them. Even the daylight seems dimmer. It's as if the world has lost an octave.

During the days, I revisit the cupboards for cans of soup and sit around watching game shows and soap operas. When I tire of that, I play music and smoke pot. In the evenings I smoke more pot. I stare at the dark windows and fixate on their black sheen. I keep expecting a head to pop up, and this terrifies me. But I can't look away. When I finally fall asleep, I dream of windows with faces pressed against them.

On a rainy day, one of Bader's friends, Duwahi, shows up and breaks the monotony by asking if I want to make a drug run with him to D.C. He is the only one of the Arabs I don't like, not because he's not beautiful like the others—with his yellowing teeth and frizzy hair and disproportionate nose—but because he doesn't smile, not even when everyone else is smiling. But I'm lonely and bored and almost out of pot.

As we drive in the rain, I watch the slick road through the squeaking swipes of his windshield wipers, the runnels from tires spreading into mini rivers. We aren't even a mile from the apartment when we stop at a red light and a strange feeling overtakes me: something tells me to get out of the car and run. That familiar kick surges through my legs as I peer through my rain-blurred window and instinctively start plotting my path away from the car. I don't know why I'm doing this, only that it feels urgent. But at the same second I put my hand on the door handle, the light turns green, and Duwahi steps on the gas. So I shrug it off and sit back in my seat while the bleak world streaks by.

Duwahi parks the car on Fourteenth Street, among a row of strip clubs. "I'm picking up a friend," he says.

"I'll wait here then."

"No. I don't know how long it's going to take, so you better come in."

Outside the club is a sign that reads, THIS IS IT. Inside there are three naked women on three separate stages. As we approach the bar, one of the dancers comes down the stage toward us, her head up, her large breasts bouncing to the music. I've seen nude women before, but the accessibility of their naked bodies here, only a few steps off the public street, is shocking at first. I sit down next to Duwahi, and order a Tequila sunrise. On the next stage over, a woman is squatting face-level in front of a couple, her knees open. They're having a conversation, the three of them, and I wonder what they're saying as the couple slips dollar bills inside her garter while peering nonchalantly between her legs. Something about it turns me on.

By the time I notice the girl talking to Duwahi, they're deep in conversation, leaning in close, speaking into each other's ears. She's tall and blond, with a bit of an overbite. When she notices me looking at her, she stares back at me hard. "So you must be Roxanne," she states coolly, eyeing me up and down. "Interesting name."

"This is Karen," Duwahi says.

"C'mon, let's go back," she says, motioning toward the back with her head.

I assume two things but am right about only one: Karen is a stripper at the club. But we don't go to the back of the club for the drugs Duwahi promised. Instead, we step into a small room with a mirrored wall and a single chair. An overweight man dressed in black is in the chair, waiting for us. There is no introduction.

"Okay, let's see what you've got," he says, looking at me.

I look at Duwahi, then back at the man. "Excuse me?"

"What are you waiting for—a written invitation?" Karen barks. "Take your clothes off."

"Do I even know you?" I ask.

"Listen, smart-ass, you're going to have to make some money sometime—you can't live off Bader for the rest of your life."

"What do you care about Bader?" I say.

"This is bullshit," says the man in the chair.

"You're a real prima donna," she says.

Somehow I feel my only choice is to do what I'm told, so I catch a glimpse of myself in the mirror as I take off my shirt and pants, then drop my bra to the floor.

The man in black folds his fat arms in front of his chest. "Everything," he says, pointing to my underwear.

I slide those off, too.

"Turn around."

I turn around, while Duwahi and Karen stare blankly at me, then at the man in black.

"When can she start?" he asks, looking at Duwahi.

"Can I get dressed now?" I ask.

"In a few days," Duwahi tells the man.

And all I want right then is to go back to Bader's apartment and wait for him to come home. This time I'll wait as long as it takes.

On our way out of the club, Karen hops up onstage, turns her back to us, and pulls her pants down. She bobs her ass up and down a few times, then jumps off. Buttoning her fly, she tells no one in particular, "When I was young, my body was even better than hers." Then to Duwahi, "I've still got it, don't I, baby?" He nods, and I vow to myself that once I get back to Bader's, I will never go anywhere with Duwahi again.

Duwahi and Karen take me to an apartment in D.C., where Karen lives with a muscular man named A.J. and a woman he calls his bitch, a pretty, dark-skinned woman who shares his bedroom. The apartment has so little furniture that the entire place could be cleared out in minutes. In the center of the living room is an unmade sofa bed. The walls are bare.

"So there's this guy—he's so fucking rich his mattress is probably stuffed with money—and he's a regular at this bar—sits on the same stool each night, knockin' back Black Label and looking for some pussy. That's where you come in." Karen tucks a wad of hair behind her right ear. "What you're gonna do is flirt with him—get him to pick you up. And then, after you've fucked him and he's passed out—and trust me, he'll pass out—take everything you can. And check all his pockets because sometimes guys stash money in different pockets. Oh, and that Rolex he wears. Definitely wanna get my hands on that." Her brown eyes widen.

"Listen," I say, trying to make sense of where I am and why this woman is saying these things to me and why I didn't just jump out of

Duwahi's car when I had the chance, "I thought we were coming here to get some pot. That's what Duwahi told me, and that's the only reason I'm here. I'm sorry if I gave you the wrong idea, but now I need to go home."

Karen bolts up. "Home? You ain't got no home! And life ain't no free ride, girl. What we're giving you is a chance to make some money."

"Bader said I could stay with him, and that's nobody else's business." I turn to Duwahi. "I'll go find a cab."

He speaks in measured strokes, "You heard Karen. And you'll do what she says."

I pick up my purse. "I don't have to do anything." But before I can turn to leave, Duwahi fires his backhand into my cheek, sends me falling backwards onto the bed.

"Shut up! Do you hear me, you fucking bitch? Just shut up!"

Now I'm scared. The side of my face burns, but I say nothing. Duwahi stands over me for several seconds, his hand cocked. Nobody moves. And then slowly, as if at any moment he might change his mind, he withdraws his hand.

"Now let's get you fixed up," Karen says with a rabbity smile.

She piles my hair up on top of my head and gives me a black silk dress that bows down beneath my cleavage, with a small black beaded purse to match. "You can leave that big red thing here," she says, pointing to my purse. "It'll be safe." She pencils Cleopatra-black eyeliner onto my eyelids and lines my lips with burgundy liner. Then she stuffs a spiky pair of too-big patent pumps with cotton balls so that they don't fall off when I walk. But by the time we arrive at the bar, Mr. Rolex is already sitting with a redhead.

"Great, we fucking blew it. Why'd you have to make trouble?" Karen hisses.

We sit down at the bar anyway, and I smoke cigarettes and drink amaretto while Karen prods me and points around the room. "What about that guy? I bet he's got money." By the time a man with sloping shoulders and a drooping shirt approaches me, I'm drunk. I ask him his name and he says Timmy, and I laugh and say he doesn't look like a Timmy, and then Karen and I are following him to his apartment.

"I'll just wait out here," she calls from the car.

His apartment is squalid—crusted plates and empty pizza boxes strewn on every surface, the steady stink of mildew thick in the air.

He leads me to the bedroom, and I do as Karen instructed. "No offense or anything, but I kind of need to get the money up front."

"You're not a cop, are you?"

"No."

"Well how much do you charge?"

"A hundred."

"How about I give you half now and half after?"

"Okay."

I put the money in the small purse Karen gave me, and he asks me to take my dress off. "And whatever you have on underneath. But do it nice and slow, okay?"

I struggle to pull the tight dress over my head, then stumble into a wall as I pull my underwear off. "Oops," I say, "sorry."

"Can I give you a massage?"

"Um, okay."

I lay facedown on his musty bed while he puts a movie into his VCR. He straddles me and starts to rub my back, and the movie begins: a woman stands naked as a man pushes her breasts through a metal vise. With pliers, he begins to twist her nipples. She screams, and blood runs out in jagged lines. I turn my head away.

"You know what?" I say, trying to shimmy out from beneath him. "I really don't feel well—you know, I'm really drunk, and I think I'm going to throw up."

He slides off me. "Well go in the bathroom—don't puke here!"

I quickly pull my dress back on, not bothering with my underwear. And then I'm running through his apartment the way you run in dreams from whoever's about to do you in. All I want is to make it through the door and never think about bleeding nipples again. I fling it open and barrel down the stairs to the car.

When I get in, I'm out of breath. "Let's go!"

"Where's the money?" demands Karen.

I lift up the purse. "It's in here."

"What's *wrong* with you? Why are you shaking like that?"

"Because the guy was a freak, that's why."

"Honey, they're all freaks in one way or another. Get over it." She smirks knowingly, then puts the car in drive.

Duwahi is waiting for us back at the apartment, in bed with a single lamp on. "How'd it go?"

"Miss *Roxanne* here was only able to pull in fifty." She narrows her eyes at me. "Spazzed out."

"She's new," Duwahi says. "Now come to bed."

"Glad to see you're sticking up for her all of a sudden," Karen huffs, throwing her purse on the floor.

"Don't start. Come to bed." Then he looks at me. "Both of you."

I am too exhausted to protest.

W hen I wake up, they are still asleep. I dress quickly and quietly. I grab my purse and start for the door, but Duwahi pops his head up. "Where are you going?"

"Um, I'm going to wash up in the bathroom."

"Wrong direction," he says, pointing toward the bathroom.

I turn around, and he puts his head back on the pillow.

In the bathroom, I start plotting. I have to make a run for it. If I can just get to a pay phone, I can call Gina. I unzip the front pocket of my purse, and a chill runs through me. My money and phone numbers are gone. I quickly open the main zipper to find everything but my makeup is gone. My pocketknife, scraps of paper, unsent letters, old letters from my mother—all of it, gone. I look at myself in the mirror. Last night's eyeliner is smudged around my eyes, and my skin is pale. *Think, think.*

I have to think. I splash handfuls of cold water over my face, and then I make a plan.

I come out of the bathroom and tell Duwahi and Karen about a guy I know who would definitely be good for a hundred bucks—Sergio, the French guy from Bader's apartment complex—but I don't tell them his name. And I don't need to; the lure of a quick hundred hooks them. Duwahi asks how I know he'll be home. (We all know I have no phone numbers left to call.) I tell him the guy works nights and will definitely be there. They agree to take me, and Karen writes a phone number on a piece of paper and hands it to me. "It's the bar where we'll be waiting, so call us when you're finished. And don't fuck around after—don't keep us hanging."

When we arrive, they watch me from the car as I enter the building next to Sergio's. I wait for a long time before coming out, and when I do, I inch out slowly, peeking carefully around the door for any signs of them. When I see they're gone, I sprint to Sergio's building and knock frantically on his door.

"Hey, Roxanne, what a surprise! Come in!" His enthusiasm instantly warms me. "I was just leaving," he says. "Going to Florida for a little business." His accent twirls like his mustache.

For a few seconds, I don't know what to say. I can't go back to Bader's because they'll find me there, and I don't know where I was last night except that it was someplace far, farther than I've ever been, and for the first time I don't see a way forward, but more than anything, I don't want to go back. I don't know how to say any of this to Sergio, so instead I run my hand through my hair. "I was kind of hoping I could hang out here for a little while, with you, but now you're leaving, so—"

Sergio puts his hand on my shoulder. "Say no more. You'll stay here while I'm gone, yes?"

It's as if he knows. I feel like Willy Wonka must have felt in that strange room of halves, when Charlie gives back his everlasting gobstopper. *So shines a good deed in a weary world,* says Willy Wonka, smiling down at the candy. I hug Sergio, and then he and his suitcase are gone.

I take the longest shower of my life. I can't get clean enough. Then I raid Sergio's kitchen, all the while wondering if Duwahi and Karen have figured out that I've ditched them. On the coffee table, a half-smoked joint rests against the rim of a green glass ashtray. I light it, and as I get stoned, the people on the television become hilarious. I laugh until my stomach hurts and wonder when everybody got to be so funny. But the more stoned I get, the less funny things become. I start noticing things I didn't notice before—creaks in the walls, loud footsteps just over my head in the apartment above, darkness licking the windows and closing me in. Suddenly it's as if I can feel all the evil in the world surrounding me, and I have the distinct sense that something terrible is about to happen. I can't bear the thought of being alone any longer, but without my list of phone numbers, the only person I can think to call is my friend Cindy. Though I haven't spoken to her in ages, when she answers the phone it's as if no time has passed at all. I want to thank her a million times, just for being there on the other end. And when she agrees to catch a cab and come over, I know that everything is going to be okay.

When she knocks on the door, I leap up in a rush to open it. But after years of watching my mother check the peephole every time someone knocked, I don't think to do it. And then it's too late. I see everything at once: the glint of the knife blade, Karen's face, Duwahi's rage. He presses the cold metal to my throat, and Karen runs to the back to see if anyone is there. "It's empty," she calls, while Duwahi pushes the blade harder against my neck. "If you make a sound, you won't be as lucky as Bader was," he says, pressing his mouth against my head as he speaks. Karen grabs a bag from the kitchen and starts dumping things into it, and they are Sergio's things, *nice* Sergio, and Duwahi will probably kill me and Sergio will live the rest of his life thinking that I stole from him.

How could I have been so stupid? How could I not have realized I'd written Sergio's address on my phone list?

They push me into the car. Duwahi is yelling, "You fucking bitch! You left us waiting there all day!"

"You're a fucking liar, too," Karen seethes. "We were at Bader's today, and you know who else was there? The police, that's who. Your name's not Roxanne, is it, *Rita*? You're a fourteen-fucking-year-old runaway."

"Please," I say, wishing, for the first time, that the police had found me.

"Shut the fuck up," Duwahi says.

The rest of the drive is silent. I pray for a car crash.

When we get to Karen's apartment, she runs in and out, loading the trunk with stuff. Duwahi stays in the car with me and hits me in the face. "If you ever try to leave us again, I'll kill you. I'll slit your throat and throw you in the Dumpster." His hands won't stop hitting my face.

"I won't, I promise, I won't."

"I'll kill you," he keeps saying.

"I'm sorry," I keep answering.

After Karen loads the car, they drive me to a motel in Virginia Beach. I sleep across the backseat and wake up confused, thinking I'm in the backseat of my mother's car. When I close my eyes again, I pretend that I am, that my sister is beside me, that we're still looking for something.

In the motel room, they keep me stoned and stripped down to my bra and underwear. At night, I have to have sex with them. "Put your fingers inside her," Duwahi orders me. "More. Harder." I hate having to touch her.

They make me sleep between them so I won't try to run in the night. I think of Dawn, my childhood best friend, and how one night we slept in a sleeping bag together on the floor. *Will you be my best friend forever?* I'd asked her. Her skin was warm, and she smelled like popcorn. "Of course," she'd said. *Of course,* I whisper to myself. *Of course.* I feel Karen turn her head toward me in the dark. "Whatever the fuck you're saying, shut up." But she can't stop me from remembering, which is what I do, and how I finally fall asleep.

THIRTY-NINE

The sound was like a car crash, a seizing metallic thud. Claret had just kicked a hole in the wall, the final sharp kick out from behind after several other kicks. Gerta was riding him, and each time she dug her spur into his right side, he launched his foot back. "You're not getting your way with me," Gerta warned, with a quick boot on the right. "You'll fucking turn on the forehand." She kicked, and he kicked, and I watched, stuck.

Though I had found a horse I loved, I soon learned that the ride with Claret, like most things in life, wasn't going to be easy. Besides his erratic behavior on the trail, Claret had begun acting out indoors during his work with Gerta, who suddenly wouldn't take no for an answer. And sometimes, that was Claret's answer. I was surprised by this rigidness in Gerta because when I'd had lessons with her on the mare I rode before Claret, she'd been patient and forgiving. But now, as she became increasingly demanding of Claret, he became increasingly rebellious, which he expressed at first by refusal, then by swishing his tail and backing up, and ultimately by bucking and kicking holes in the walls. Sometimes I had the sense he wasn't ready to do the exercises she was asking him to do, and when I suggested this, she dismissed me. "All I'm asking is for him to turn on the forehand. He can do that."

Whether he could or couldn't, he wouldn't, and that was the problem. He'd say no, and she'd kick him or smack him with the whip, and he'd kick out in an even louder no, and she'd smack him harder, and the two of them would escalate, and eventually he'd give in. Then it would be my turn to ride him, and when I was on him, he rarely kicked or bucked, and Gerta would say, "That's because you don't ask anything of him. You have to get angry. You never get angry." And I'd say, "But I'm not angry," and she'd say that Claret didn't respect me and would never respect me if I didn't get angry. So I'd ride him passionately but not angrily, and after my ride, I'd stand with him in his stall and look up into his eyes and stroke his long neck. Sometimes he'd nuzzle my belly or my neck or the top of my head, and I'd swoon a little, and I'd think *Okay, we're going to be okay.*

But I was worried. Why wasn't Claret happy? Was it true that he was refusing to do something that was easy for him to do? And if so, wasn't that his right? Should he be forced to do anything he didn't want to do? Was it true that Claret didn't respect me?

I began to think so. After a few months, I could no longer catch Claret when it was time to bring him in. Happily holding out his halter, I'd enter his paddock, and he'd walk over to me. But as soon as I'd reach to put the halter on him, he'd step away. I'd try again, and he'd step away again, over and over until I was near tears. If horses could laugh, I was sure he'd be clutching his belly and trying to catch his breath.

One day after a protracted episode in the paddock, Gerta was standing by the crossties as I brought him into the barn. "You're late," she admonished. I explained that it had taken me a while to get his halter on. "That's because he doesn't respect you," she reminded me. Then I tacked him up, and the two of them fought again.

Through all of this, I was still learning. I was learning where Claret's favorite places were to be scratched—his shoulders, alongside his withers, in the creases between his front legs and belly—and what his favorite cookies were—pressed molasses with a peppermint on top. I was learning how to keep him balanced when we turned a corner and how to keep him going in the canter. And I was learning basic things, like how to put his blanket on, how to best clean his bridle, how to apply liniment to his back after a ride. But no matter what I learned, Gerta's words haunted me. Was I so inept at horsemanship that I couldn't gain the basic respect of a horse I so dearly loved?

Again, all signs pointed to yes. There was the day Claret stepped on my foot, and stood there, on my toes, until I cried out and smacked him to get off. (A horse knows when a fly lands on his back, so he surely knows when he's stepping on your foot.) There was the day he bit my arm, just a little bit of skin between his front teeth, hard enough to leave a bruise. There was the day I tried to ride him outside and he backed me into my own car. And then there was the day, after following him all around the paddock before I could catch him, that he spooked as I led him back to the barn, then yanked away from me and got loose. I yelled for Gerta to come help me, and she grabbed him and led him in easily.

"Are you angry now?" she asked.

After that, they fought through another ride, and he kicked another hole in the wall, and I got another bill for it. And the answer was yes, I was starting to get angry.

On what would be another day of recent days that I drove home in tears, I played back the last few months in my mind. I couldn't pinpoint exactly where things had gone wrong, only that they were undeniably going wrong, and getting worse. I chalked some of that up to my inexperience with horses, but there was no doubt that the more Gerta fought with Claret, the worse things got. It seemed then that I had only one choice left: to move Claret to another barn. I had no idea how I would manage him on my own—I didn't know a lot of things, but one thing being a runaway taught me is how to leave a place. And I knew as certainly as I knew anything that things would keep getting worse if we stayed there.

I found a beautiful and quiet barn about twenty minutes from my house—acres of farmland and paddocks sprawling next to a tranquil pond—and I gave Gerta thirty days' notice, and I gave the new barn owner a deposit, and when she asked who my trainer was, I told her I was taking a break from having a trainer for a while. Then I came back to Gerta's barn and told Claret. "I'm sorry that you don't like it here," I said, "but don't worry—I'm going to move you to a new barn. It's got lots of grass and a pond." He nuzzled into my neck then, and I closed my eyes and breathed him.

FORTY

A few days go by, and Duwahi brings a guy back to the motel from the naval base. By now a lot of the swelling on my face has gone down, but I still have a black eye and my left ear is bruised purple and my bottom lip is scabbed and swollen. The young man looks so fresh in his crisp white suit and white cap, with his pink cheeks. He fumbles awkwardly with his pants. My pants are already off.

I fantasize about telling him to call for help, call the police, do anything—but I don't dare. I know they are waiting outside. I know what they are capable of.

"This is my first time, you know, paying," he tells me. It's as if he hasn't noticed the marks on my face. "Because it's not like I *have* to pay or anything." He steps in front of me, and I give him what he wants.

People don't care about other people. This is the hardest lesson I never fully learn.

Duwahi and Karen are talking about moving me, prostituting me across the country while scouting for other girls along the way. But they aren't finished with the naval base yet, and who knows how long that will take. Each time they try making plans, they can never agree on where we should go. Karen wants to go south first, get a tan in Florida and a cowgirl hat in Texas, but Duwahi wants to go to Chicago. They speak as if I'm not there, which is fine by me. But the more they talk, the more tense things become. And the more tense things become, the more I have to have sex with them.

"I know you like fucking her better," Karen huffs. "You think I didn't have a tight little pussy when I was fourteen?"

Duwahi reaches for her shoulder, but she pushes his hand off. "I don't like her better. I like you."

She pushes her hands into his chest. "You're a liar and a bastard! And how come you get to hold all the money?"

"You want to split the money? We'll split it. Just calm down, okay?"

"No, I'm not going to calm down. You're a liar, and you know what else? You're a lame fuck! A lame fuck and a stupid fucking Arab!"

In a flash he knocks her down, and the two of them start rolling on the floor.

I look at the door. The chain is hooked, the dead bolt locked. A lamp crashes down. I look back at the door. At the chain. At the dead bolt. Duwahi and Karen are rolling and flailing and punching. Karen is screaming. Duwahi is grunting. The lampshade comes off. I look at the door.

I run.

I swipe the chain and turn the lock and tear the door open, and then I am running and screaming outside in the live air, passing door after door as fast and loud as my body will go. I keep looking behind me, and for a second I see Duwahi pop out, still naked, then dart back in. I don't stop running and screaming. A man steps out of his motel room. I am wearing nothing but underwear and knee-highs. He is holding the door open. I run into his room and lock his door and close his shades. He is frozen, eyeing me up and down. "Never in my wildest dreams," he keeps saying, slowly shaking his head.

"Please," I say, "you have to be quiet. You don't understand. If they find me, they'll kill me."

"Who?" he wants to know, and I say, "Please don't speak, don't say anything," and so quietly he brings me a T-shirt, and I put it on.

I don't know why, but I want to call my mother. The operator puts the collect call through, and when my mother answers, I have never felt so relieved to hear her voice.

"Mom, it's me!"

"Where are you?"

I hold the phone with both hands, shaking. "I'm okay, Mom. I'm okay. I got away."

"Got away from what?"

"These people. They kidnapped me, but I got away. Can I come home now? I just want to come home."

"Tell me where you are."

"And you'll let me come home?"

"Rita, you know you can't."

I stand for a minute in this oversize T-shirt in this strange man's room in this seedy motel in this place called Virginia Beach, where I have never seen the beach, and I let my mother's words sink in, really sink in. My mother is not mine. Her love is not mine. Her home is not mine. I hang up the phone.

And, thanks to the bored motel operator who was eavesdropping on my call, the police show up. I surrender, and they retrieve my clothes and purse from the motel room, where they place both Duwahi and Karen under arrest.

The last time I see them is under the blaring lights of the police station: Karen is led in first, with Duwahi behind her. They are handcuffed.

Karen has an open cut across her nose. Duwahi's left eye is swollen. Though they walk right past me, neither of them looks at me. I'm sitting at a police officer's desk, eating a muffin that he gave me. Later that night, the same officer takes me to a shelter, where from my room I can hear the women huddled together on the porch, speaking in hushed tones about me and my bruises and the story on the news. I pull the blanket over my head, and for a minute, I hear them faintly—that old sound, that familiar herd, the horses.

Back at Montrose, I turn fifteen as quietly as I turned fourteen. I feel the dark mornings grow cooler, then cold. From behind the bars I watch the leaves turn and fall, then scatter across the grass. When Duwahi and Karen's court date comes, I fly back with my mother to Virginia Beach and sit outside the courtroom waiting to testify, but they plea-bargain, so I never get called. Karen gets probation, and Duwahi gets deported back to Kuwait. But even with him gone, I still have nightmares of him finding me, folding me up, breaking my bones.

Meanwhile, in these cold stone buildings, the rumors haven't stopped—the ones about the ghost of a girl who never made it out. Even though this time the prisoners are different, the rumor has stayed the same.

FORTY-ONE

Sometimes when we change what we believe, we change who we are. I had always believed I was weakhearted. "You're so gentle," my grandmother used to tell me. "You're not like the rest of the family." And I took that to mean fragile. I didn't trust my own body, and that mistrust held me back from many things and caused me to settle for many more.

I had often felt nostalgic for my days as a runaway, a fact I'd struggled to understand. Why would I miss the callousness of the streets? The people who treated me as if I were nothing? The bad drug trips, the hunger, the childlike hope that people kept stepping on? It wasn't until after that Valentine's Day, when a stranger gave me my heart back, that I began to understand: it wasn't the streets that I missed; it was myself. Nostalgia, after all, is in part a longing for ourselves through time; it's a way of looking back and saying, *Hey, I remember you. You're not gone from me.* It's a way of saying, *That was some crazy shit we got into back then*. I longed for that girl who ran away, because she wasn't fragile. She was spirited and strong and fueled by hope. She was compelled by fairness and the stubborn existence of beauty. She was a fighter.

We are many things. Depending on how we balance our lives, we can live some aspects of ourselves more fully than others. And sometimes the voices in our minds want to tell us two completely contradictory things at once. For example, by the time I was eleven and had first run away, blazing through our front door at the outer edge of dusk, a part of me knew that my parents were damaging me and that I could save myself if I got away. But that same year, another part of me believed that the problem lay within me. *You're defective*, it said. *Your heart is defective.*

And that voice—the voice that told me I was dying when I was eleven—was the same voice that told me I was dying when I called 911 at thirty-five. It told me I wasn't safe, and I began to live the life of an unsafe person. The voice became so powerful that it even changed the way my brain functioned. I imagined my enlarged amygdala, agitated and unbalanced, perceiving everything as dangerous. *I don't know*, it was saying, *that marshmallow looks pretty sketchy to me.*

Panic had sent me running for my life, by running *from* my life. But panic, it turns out, wasn't the bully I thought it was. It wasn't a virus or an erratic black bird. Though it felt like all of those things. It felt bigger than everything. But in the end, panic was *me*. And it wasn't even all of me; it was one small part of me, grown wild. Realizing this, I suddenly felt like Grover in *The Monster at the End of This Book*: I'd been building brick walls to hide from *myself*.

If I wanted my life back, I finally had to accept that the only way to get it was to move toward panic, toward myself. I would have to reach for what scared me. I would, as the wise social worker I once knew said, have to suffer my suffering. Though running away from home nearly killed me more than once, it also saved my life. I had taken control in a situation that was out of control. I rejected the imbalance of my parents and sought solid footing. I didn't always make the right choices, but what mattered was that I was *making* choices, that my intention for love and health and balance *was* a kind of love and health and balance. And that intention was the same intention that I carried to the therapists and the practitioners, to the clay classes and cooking lessons, to the underlined passages of Rilke. It was what gave me one whole day without panic. Of fight-flight, it was the fight.

I had asked a question—what can I learn from panic?—and already I was learning a lot. There is a momentum that builds in the asking that carries you forward.

W hen we got home after seeing the cardiologist that day, Larry gave me a gift. "Happy Valentine's Day," he said, handing me a piece of sketch paper, on which he'd drawn a picture of me. The picture was based on a photograph of me taking a photograph of a field. In it, I'm looking through the lens of my camera, while a tree arches over my head and purple and yellow clouds float by. He titled the drawing *The Observer*.

"It's beautiful," I said, wrapping my arms around his neck. "I love it."

I looked at it again. "It must have taken you ages. But I don't have anything for you." Shame moved through me, slimy and cool. "I'm sorry."

"Don't be sorry," he said, kissing my cheek. "You give me gifts every day."

I hung my drawing over my desk and went upstairs to take a shower. Since I'd started panicking, I'd always left the shower door partially open—just in case—even with Larry in the room. But on that evening, Larry wasn't in the room. And I closed the door all the way. Now that I was sure nothing was wrong with my heart, I had no excuse. And then midway through my shower, I realized something: even with the door closed, I wasn't alone. I stepped out of the water's spray and stood beside it, dripping in the mist. *Hi*, I said. *I'm here*. In the reverb of the shower, the words seemed to travel, to move in every direction at once—all the directions I'd ever run in, reversed. They resounded, small but powerful as a heart. I realized then that I'd never really been alone— I had been with myself from the beginning and would be so until the end. I knew then that wherever life took me, I could count on myself. I would abide. And the water roared. And my skin was red and alive. And I could feel how palpable this gift was—this gift of presence within us, which no one can ever take away.

FORTY-TWO

On the morning of my court hearing for violating my probation, I know I'm in trouble. Since my mother pressed those fake charges against me, I've lost track of how many times I've violated my probation by running away. If I hadn't called her when I got away from Karen and Duwahi, I might still be on the run. But now that I'm back at Montrose, it's almost certain I'll be committed here indefinitely. So when a grumpy staff member gives me a razor to shave my legs, I run it across both of my wrists instead.

I don't intend to kill myself. But I don't know any other way to get the judge's attention. What I've learned is that the courts already have an opinion of us before we even get there, that standing before the judge is little more than a formality that usually lands me in handcuffs. And I've learned that the juvenile justice system has nothing to do with justice. I don't cut too deep—just deep enough to draw blood, and to keep stinging after.

The best possible thing I can hope for is to be sent to a drug rehab. Everyone in lockup knows these are the most coveted placements when you can't go home and, for some, even when you can. Though my father's out of prison, I haven't heard from him in a long time; I'm not even sure where he is. As for my mother, I've learned to stop asking. So when I stand before the judge, whose white hair and flushed cheeks make him look a little like Santa, I tell him that I never committed that crime against my mother, that it had always been the other way around—me on the end of her blows, of my father's. I tell him that I ran away to find a better home, that I got myself into trouble with sex and drugs instead. And I tell him that I still want that life, the one I ran away to find.

I have sworn to tell the truth, and I am telling it. "Your Honor, if you commit me to Montrose, I will not live. I can survive a lot of things, but I don't believe years at Montrose are one of them."

Though I'd planned to show him my wrists, I don't have to, because he shows me mercy. "You seem like a very bright girl," he says, "and I agree: you don't belong in Montrose."

The Jackson Unit is a coed adolescent drug rehab in a psychiatric hospital called the Finan Center, sprawled out amid the Appalachian Mountains in Cumberland, Maryland, and when I arrive, I am sure I have never seen a place more spectacular. I fall instantly in love with the mountains all around, jutting into the clouds. I fall in love with the space and the open doors and the people who work there— their smiles and their knowing eyes and their kindness. For the first time in years, I don't want to run.

In the mornings they take us for long walks while the sun is still low in the sky. It angles through the trees in a mosaic of light so that when you least expect it, a burst flashes warm on your face. The birds sing lazily, as if they, too, are just waking. Everywhere, the green shines. Sometimes from the vastness, a butterfly quivers its loopy course across the small road we walk on. Sometimes a grasshopper leaps out of the grass, the whole of life bound in its springy legs. Sometimes the sound of someone laughing rises tall into air.

In the main sitting room a large corkboard hangs on the wall. "Warm Fuzzy Board" it's called: a board to leave "warm fuzzies" for each other: notes of affection and encouragement: things like *Great job in group today! I know how hard it was for you.* Or *Don't ever forget what a beautiful person you are.* Seeing my name up there is like getting a Valentine: *Welcome, Rita. We're glad you're here.* "That's what the world's missing," says my therapist, "warm fuzzies."

He's a sprightly, bearded guy named Buck Ware. He rides a motorcycle and has spiky hair and is so direct that it throws me a little off balance at first. Five minutes into our first meeting, he sits forward in his office chair and tells me, "When I was a boy, I was abused." His eyes are like talons; they won't let go. "See, now I've trusted you with something. And maybe you'll start to trust me."

I laugh. I don't mean to, but it comes out, a kind of nervous reflex. No adult has ever talked to me that way, and it seems like a lot of responsibility to receive that kind of information from someone you just met. "I'm sorry," I say. "I didn't mean to laugh. It's not funny, what you said." But then, in spite of myself, I laugh again.

"It's okay," he reassures. "That was a nervous laugh. And just below the laughter, my friend, are the tears."

During the week, we sit at small round tables scattered throughout the room, and a teacher comes and gives us easy schoolwork. I always finish mine before lunch, then spend most of the day flirting with Dallas, a boy whose dark, inquisitive eyes and ready smile make me feel shy. I want to give him presents. On his notebook he writes my name inside a heart, and then I can't stop thinking about him. Everything about him—his dimples, the sound of his laugh, the sheen of his black hair—is exciting to me.

In those rare moments when I'm not imagining Dallas's kiss, I've taken to reading Emerson, mainly because the book is thick and I don't understand half of it. Mr. Ware gave it to me. "You have to challenge yourself," he said. As I turn the pages, I know I'm reading something important. "You've been looking in the wrong places for love," he told me, "when it's been all around you the whole time. It's like nature—it's always there." Sometimes a line from the book echoes in my mind for days, the way the scent of sunlight can linger in your hair: *Nature is loved by what is best in us.*

Randomly I yank a word from the book and start using it, completely unaware of its meaning. My favorite is *hobgoblin*. I love the sound of it. I start calling everyone hobgoblin, just because. "You're one crazy girl," Taby says with a laugh. But I know she likes it.

I'd met Taby once before, at Noyes, a detention center slightly less menacing than Montrose, and we became friends immediately. She was short and bouncy, the kind of girl who was always ready for an adventure. In that way, she made the time at Noyes easier, because she filled the room with sparks of possibility. So when she arrived here at the Jackson Unit, we tackled each other to the ground in a hug. We're family; we share a life most people know nothing about.

She and I go outside and throw horseshoes together as the sun is setting. "I'm really glad you're here, Rita," Taby says to me. She's looking out at the mountains. Her eyes are blue as wildflowers.

"I'm glad you're here, too." I look out beside her, and the light begins to smolder.

Ms. Hanlin is a night counselor on the unit. She's a large woman, and her spider black hair, regardless of the weather, is invariably frizzy and unkempt. Her skin is sallow and pocked, but at night, when I lie in bed and look up at her face, just before she bends down to hug me and turn out the lights for the night, she is as beautiful as anything.

I share a room with a perky but capricious girl named Tina. She is someone who would always be described as cute, but never beautiful. She has freckles and a bob haircut and an upturned nose that gets pink in the sun. At night, we lie awake and tell secrets in the dark until our voices get tired from whispering.

One night she asks me if I've ever kissed a girl.

I pause for a moment, deciding whether or not to tell the truth. "Yes," I confess, "but it was never a girl I wanted to kiss."

"Is there a girl that you *have* wanted to kiss?" Her question makes my body stir.

"I don't know yet," I say. "What about you?"

Now she pauses. "I don't know yet, either."

Then we both shift in our beds for a long time, without saying a word.

FORTY-THREE

After I spoke to myself that afternoon in the shower, I was never afraid to shower again. And I stopped being afraid of staircases, though it took a little while for my brain to believe it. My heart would still speed up, and I'd think, *Silly heart, you're okay*. And I'd climb the stairs, and my heart would be racing, and my amygdala would say, *Panic?*, and I'd say, *I don't know, maybe*. But then, I'd gather myself like pages starting to scatter in a wind, and I'd say, *No*. I began to go to the grocery store alone again, too, though for a while I kept to the twelve-items-or-less lane, and even then sometimes I had to put down my basket at the end of an aisle and flee to my car, where I would sit and breathe and try to ground myself by focusing on things around me— the sky, the people coming and going, the scent of the air. Then I'd go back inside and make it through with my twelve items or less. My night terrors still came, though less frequently. And I stopped wearing my panic button, but usually kept it nearby. I liked knowing it was there.

I still couldn't drive on the highway.

Sometimes I panicked for no reason at all, which was always discouraging because I worried that maybe I would never be free from it. But I was also learning that healing is a jagged trajectory, a dance of forward and back, like most things. I was relearning the basics of life—like a routine I'd known and forgotten—and it would take time.

"Now you can work out again," Larry said. He had just put on his running shoes and was heading downstairs to the treadmill. "Do you want to come?"

My first reaction was to say, *Ask me again next year.* But I knew that this was exactly the kind of thing I had to push myself to do. It was a chance to suffer my suffering! So I put on my running shoes.

"I'm only going to do it for a few minutes," I informed him. It's true that I was scared, but I also knew that I needed to set small attainable goals for myself and build on those goals, in order to slowly start breaking the association in my brain between ordinary things and danger. If I panicked on the treadmill, it would only reinforce a belief that treadmills were dangerous things. Get on, get off—that was my plan.

But the same second I got on, I wanted to get off, and I realized that voluntary suffering is really hard. And I hadn't even started the machine yet. "I don't know," I said. "I don't think I'm ready."

"Of course you're ready," Larry said. "I'm right here."

So I started the treadmill and began to walk at a very slow speed. Everything in me was screaming, *Noooooo,* and *ruuuuuuun,* and *fuuuuuuuck,* and my heart was already rocketing off, and my face felt cold and tingly, and I said, "I really don't think I'm ready."

And Larry said, "C'mon, you can do this."

"Look," I said, holding out my hand, "I'm shaking."

"But I'm right here. Nothing bad is going to happen to you. I'm *right here.*" He was exasperated, which was completely understandable. There is nothing logical about panic.

Unfortunately, it was too late. I was already panicking. "I'm just not ready," I said, getting off. I paced rapidly for a minute or two, then sat down on the edge of a chair and began to rock myself in small movements, waiting for the panic to subside, all while Larry watched me from across the room. He just stood there looking, the way you focus on a thing moving in the woods, trying to understand what it is.

B ack at Opther's, I asked him, "Are you afraid of death?"

He had his hand over my sternum, and I was relaxing into my breathing, into the ethereal music playing softly, into his hand.

"No," he said. "I actually look forward to it."

"You look forward to death?" I was astonished. "Why?"

"Because it's peaceful. I like the idea of finally being able to drift into nothingness—no more pressure, no more struggle."

I wanted to ask him if his life felt like a lot of pressure, because it seemed a strange impulse to look forward to death, but I kept breathing instead. He placed his hand on my abdomen, and I breathed, and then on my low abdomen, and I breathed, and I thought about death. *Light as a feather, stiff as a board*, we used to chant as children, lifting each other up. How exciting those nights were, when we played at the netherworld, when we closed our eyes and let ourselves be lifted to the heavens.

T he next day, I put my running shoes back on. Larry was napping on the sofa, his book and mouth open. I slipped down to the basement and started my music. I eyed the treadmill, its unassuming gray scale of steadiness. *Hi*, I said. I remembered reading a Tom Robbins book in which inanimate objects had secret animate lives, and I thought better to make friends, just in case.

One group I can recommend for anyone seeking the inspiration to step onto a treadmill is the Black Eyed Peas, which is exactly how I got myself walking a grand three miles per hour on mine. My goal was small—five minutes—and it had one rule: I could not stop, no matter what. Of course, the first thing my body wanted to do was stop. I felt that swoosh of panic in my head and that jittery burst in my legs. But then there was the song, that steady beat, and my legs kept going. About three minutes in, I even dared to increase the speed for exactly five seconds before pressing the down arrow. At around the 4:40 minute mark, I realized I might make it, and I started to walk with real purpose, counting down to my five-minute finish line. I even went an extra two seconds, just because I could.

I called my poet friend Meg to brag about my victory.

"Great," she said. "But how's your writing?"

"You know how it is. I write to you."

"That's not what I mean. I mean your writing *life*."

"Did you hear what I said? I walked on the treadmill. For five minutes!"

"Just think about it. You're part of a community—you just have to connect to it."

After Meg told me to write to her about panic, we started writing things to each other daily—lists, mostly, of things we encountered each day. "No ideas but in things," said the great poet William Carlos Williams, so I wandered around with my notebook as I did when I was a child, observing my little world: Larry floating on his back in the pool and wearing perhaps a little too much paste-white sunscreen on his face, the lulling sounds of splashing water, the jeweled body of a dragonfly, bits of conversation overheard at a gas station, the sagging roof of an abandoned building, a woman falling and breaking her hip in a bookstore, the first five minutes of the local news. And as I filled the pages of my notebook, two things were happening: I was beginning to reconnect to the world I'd grown so devastatingly afraid of, and I was writing again.

So when Meg said it was time to connect to a writing community, I took her advice. That day I called a nonprofit writing center in Boston and scheduled an interview for a teaching position. But on the day of my interview, I was terrified. Larry generously came to support me by waiting in the lobby, only we discovered upon arriving that there was no lobby—just the one small room in the middle of the writing center, which turned out to be the interview room. When the director, a handsome man with soulful eyes, came out, I was already in the middle of one long panic attack, like a cresting wave that wouldn't end. I shook his hand, and introduced him to Larry, and we sat down. I wondered if he could hear the fear in my voice when I laughed and tried to explain that I thought there would be a waiting room.

Chris nodded thoughtfully. "It's such a struggle, space."

I'd never been able to fully keep my composure during a panic attack, but I was determined not to blow it for myself. So I pretended to sit calmly by crossing my legs and folding my hands in my lap, while my heart, small fist that it is, was knocking furiously on the inside of my chest. "I really loved your poems," Chris said, looking down at my file in his lap. "Especially the one about the circus freaks."

"Ah, yes, the circus freaks. Thank you."

Chris launched ahead into the interview, asking me various questions about my teaching style and about the poets who've inspired me. And as we talked about writers, my heart started to slow—as if I were singing it a lullaby: *Rilke, Bishop, Neruda, Oliver*—and I was able to calm down and have a real conversation with this man who was smart and self-deprecating and impossible not to like. But then I did a risky thing: I confessed I'd been suffering from panic disorder. "I'm coming through it now," I said. "But I'm not totally out of the woods."

Chris looked at me compassionately.

"Also, I want you to know that if you hire me, I won't bring my husband to every class I teach."

We all laughed, and Chris shared that he, too, had struggled with panic attacks in the past. Then he hired me.

Mostly, life to me feels like a lot of stumbling, punctuated by rare moments of grace—those moments when everything is exactly right, when the heart wants nothing. That's what I found in Chris, this kind man who was holding my poems and telling me, in his way, *You are more than your panic. And you and I are members of the same tribe.*

That night, I curled up on the sofa next to Larry, nestling like a puppy into the side of him. "Thank you," I said.

Larry glanced down at me. "For what?"

"For leaving work early to come with me today."

He shrugged his shoulders as if it were nothing. "Of course."

"Do you remember when we were first dating, and you talked about life being like a boat—a smallish boat—and that you wanted me in yours?"

He nodded. "Yeah, I remember that."

"I'm glad we're sharing a boat."

With two fingers, he swept a few strands of hair off my forehead. "So am I."

Around that same time, I filled out an application for a waiter scholarship to the Bread Loaf Writers' Conference. This was the conference of conferences, and the waiter scholarships are part of a long-standing tradition whereby the recipients—budding writers who are chosen based on the merit of their writing samples—serve meals to the rest of the conference goers in exchange for their own meals, lodging, and tuition. I had always wanted to go, but when Larry read an article in *The New Yorker* that referred to it as "Bed Loaf," he said, "I hope you never go there," so I never applied. But now more than ever I knew Meg was right: I needed to be a part of a writing community again, not only as a teacher but as a student. I also knew that these waiter scholarships were competitive—only twenty-five were given each year—which made me feel somewhat relieved because I was unlikely to get one. Still, I was challenging myself to do things that were outside my sphere of comfort, and going away to the mountains for eleven days with a bunch of strangers certainly fell into that outer region. When I dropped my application in the mail, I told myself that if they accepted me, I'd be ready.

My life was starting to take on a rhythm. I had my clay class every Friday, and I was amassing a multiseasonal collection of floppy-eared dog plates. My plate-dog frolicked in the snow, swam in the ocean, stood under a rainbow, stared out from a bed of flowers, contemplated the stars. In the mornings, I started showing up at my computer and attempting to write seriously again, even if that meant writing one sentence, even if it meant deleting that one sentence and then writing and deleting fifty more. But I didn't think it was fair to teach writing classes if I wasn't writing myself.

In the evenings I started making jewelry again, and it felt like a homecoming to hold all those stones in my hands. I cooked, I sang hymns (badly), I walked on the treadmill a little longer each day. But even as my days began to coalesce back into something that felt like a life, that life was still held under the jurisdiction of fear. When I wasn't panicking—when my hands were full of clay or stones or pages—I was thinking about the fact that I wasn't panicking. It was as if everything I did was measured on the scale of fear, so that even when I had days completely free from panic, I still wasn't free from panic. This left me feeling like a pale version of my former self—injured somehow—as if I were walking with a limp nobody could see.

While I'd appreciated my sessions with Opther, my breathing exercises had reached a plateau, so I thanked him and his wobbly table and never went back. But I still longed for someone to talk to, so I decided to try one last therapist.

Norm was a shine-eyed man who spoke in the most soothing voice I'd ever heard. "Right this way," he said, offering a smile, which I returned as I followed him. His office was in a tall yellow Victorian that overlooked a quiet expanse of land. It was a cheery house, and his office had windowed French doors that opened to a garden and spilled in the airy light. Spring was on its way, and the day had a frenetic feel to it—everything waking up at once.

I told Norm about my panic attacks, about all the therapies I'd tried, how CBT left me almost catatonic. Norm nodded his head, and in that nod I found a universe of understanding.

Because it was a first session, we'd booked extra time, during which

I worked my way back to my earliest days, recounting the places where fear began for me. ". . . So my father ordered my mother to close all the windows, and I knew then that I was really in for it, that he didn't want the neighbors to hear. He picked me up by my ankles and began to whip me with the buckle of his belt. He was hitting me everywhere, and I was crying and screaming at first, but then I started to black out, and the next sound was my sister wailing. She was only three then, but she'd lunged at him to stop him, and the belt buckle accidentally split her lip open. That's what stopped him. He'd never hit her, not once, and never would, and yet suddenly he had made her bleed."

Norm looked aghast. "Why did he only hit you? Why never your sister?"

"Because when she was a baby, she almost died. I think he always felt guilty about that—that they hadn't noticed how sick she was until it was almost too late. She was bleeding internally, though no one ever knew why."

"It's just all so sad."

"And after he dropped me and the belt to the floor, I remember being so grateful to be alive, to be able to sit in the corner of our living room and gaze at a picture book of butterflies. Blue morpho was my favorite." There was a lot to tell, and it would take years to tell it, but this was a start.

Norm grabbed a tissue and wiped his eyes. "It's not your fault," he said.

I wasn't expecting those words. Easy as they were, no one had ever said them to me before, so simply.

"I'm sorry," I said, feeling terrible for making him cry. "People have it a lot worse."

"You had no one." Norm blew his nose.

"I had myself," I said.

"Yes, well, you have this extraordinary spirit. That's how you survived. You got beaten, and then you looked at butterflies. You more than survived."

"Do you think I'll survive panic?"

Norm looked at me squarely. "You already are."

That day Norm explained that when we panic, we revert to a child-like state. "Everyone does it," he said. "Suddenly the world seems big and scary because we feel small and helpless. Different things can trigger the child state in people—for some it's being in a hospital gown, for others it's an unexpected life event, for me it's the holidays—and some people are just naturally more sensitive to it than others. But when we're in a child state, we all tend to go home. For you, home is a very scary place."

"So do all people who panic have difficult childhoods?"

He shook his head. "Not at all. Some people really do panic without any obvious cause. Though there are studies that suggest that some people are more biologically prone to it."

We kept talking, and the sound of Norm's voice was like a calm sea. "Your first panic attack wasn't a few months ago. It was when you were eleven and thought you were having a heart attack."

"That was a *panic attack*?" I asked in disbelief. How had I never realized that?

"You betcha. But when you ran away and had to take care of yourself, there was no room for you to slip into that child state. You couldn't afford to. But now you've moved to a new place and you're isolated—just weak enough to find yourself in a child state."

"But if I had my first panic attack so young, what if I'm one of those people who are biologically prone to it?"

"It doesn't matter. The approach is the same for everyone who panics, regardless of the cause."

"What's the approach?" I asked.

"Number one, it's compassion."

"Compassion," I repeated.

"We have to have compassion for that child place in ourselves. A lot of people tend to beat themselves up for panicking. They think, *What the hell is wrong with me? Why am I afraid of such silly things?* But when a child is trembling from a nightmare or convinced there's a monster in the closet, we don't say, 'What the hell is wrong with you? Why are you afraid of such silly things?' Instead, we comfort the child. We have compassion. Then we open the closet door to show there's nothing there. Of course, sometimes we have to be firm with kids—we can't let them run the show. We have to step in as adults who are in control, but we have to do it with our hearts. That's why CBT didn't work for you—it's a great system that helps many, but it's got no heart."

And when he said that, I knew I'd finally found someone I could talk to. "You have heart," I said.

"So do you, kiddo."

FORTY-FOUR

Afraid, I had spent so much energy hoping for some magical mother or therapist or guru to appear and unfurl a scroll of answers into my hand—ones that would tell me which steps to take and how to feel better, less afraid—or for my own husband to sweep me up as if into the arms of God, as if in a single motion he could undo a lifetime of motion. I had no idea then that the voice that would come to me would be my own, or that what I really wanted, more than I wanted someone to give me answers, was for someone to listen.

I wrote about Claret to Meg:

In the night when I can't sleep, I trespass into the stable. My trainer lives in the apartment next door, so I'm careful not to wake her. The door is roped, the lights off, but I want to feed Claret a purple carrot. I step through cautiously, the way you walk through the narrow hall of a haunted house, but soon my eyes adjust to the darkness. The moon is big and frames the windows in blue light. There are quiet sounds: small snuffles, shifts, and sighs from the stalls. I find Claret in the back, already eating. Most of his body is swallowed by the darkness of his stall. A shaft of moonlight exposes the side of his face and makes his globe eye shine. Hay pokes out of his mouth like makeshift whiskers. I break the carrot in half and feed it to him through the bars. He takes it from my hand soft as a kiss. His chewing is the sound of walking through snow. It is the sound of taking, of contentment. After the carrot, he returns to his hay, disappearing entirely as he bends to take a bite. In between he pops back up to watch me. His eye is a night lake.

FORTY-FIVE

After I'd had a few more sessions with Norm, he introduced me to a type of therapy called EMDR (Eye Movement Desensitization and Reprocessing). Because he'd diagnosed me not only with panic disorder but also with PTSD (post-traumatic stress disorder), he thought this approach would be especially useful. Many people who suffer from panic disorder without any prior trauma can suffer from PTSD, because panic attacks themselves are a type of trauma. EMDR addresses that trauma by helping patients reprocess the scary residue of panic—or any event—until it's no longer scary. Here's essentially how it works: the patient is asked to recall a traumatic memory. While she is doing so, the therapist moves a pencil or other object back and forth in front of the patient's eyes, and the patient follows the movement while recalling the memory, and continues to do this until the memory stops being frightening. Though the science isn't conclusive regarding *how* EMDR actually works, many people believe that it works via synchronization between the two hemispheres of the brain, while other people attribute its success to relaxation or distraction.

In my case, we started by focusing on the core negative belief: *I'm not safe.* The first memory I chose was my first panic attack.

Norm was holding a pencil in his hand. "Okay, now I want you to remember that first panic attack and tell me what feelings or words come up for you. Just follow my hand with your eyes."

As Norm waved the pencil back and forth, I found myself unable to concentrate on the memory. The eye movements made me uncomfortable, and I started getting anxious. "I don't like moving my eyes like that," I told him.

"Good. That's good you told me. I have something else for you then. We can do this another way." Norm opened a drawer and pulled out a pair of earphones. "Try this," he said. "You'll hear alternating beeps on each side."

I put on the earphones and the beeps began. They reminded me of those hearing tests that make you raise your left and right hands. I closed my eyes and started with the memory of my first panic attack, but my mind quickly took me elsewhere. It took me to a dream. I opened my eyes. "I switched memories."

"That's okay. What did you remember?"

"It was a dream I used to have as a kid."

"Tell me."

"My parents are taking me to this place, and I don't know why. All I know is that something is very wrong with me. When we walk into the building, they're holding my hands, but not in a sweet way—in a way that says *you can't escape.* The room is steely, steeped in blue light, and is full of people. It's some kind of hospital, but worse. And they're all looking at me—they've been waiting for me—because they've never seen anything like this before—anything so wrong with a person. Some of them are even crying because of it. And I'm really scared. And there's nothing I can do about it."

"Okay, let's go back to the same memory and see what comes up for you. Just follow your mind where it wants to take you."

This time when the beeping started and I closed my eyes, I could see the dream more vividly, as if I were dreaming it again. I watched my parents leading me and could feel the light on my face, cold and metallic, like their hands. I saw the people crying, all of them gathering around, and I was tiny compared to them. My wrists poked out from my old blue coat, bony and pale, and the faux fur around the hood was matted and dirty. But then the dream changed, started happening in real time: I enter the dream as my adult self. I see the girl; I see her parents; I see all of the people. And I run to her. She looks up at me, and her face is pale, and I say, "C'mon, you're going with me. I'm getting you the hell out of here." And I wrestle her away from them. Then I hold a sign up to everyone in the room: WE'RE OKAY. And I carry her into the sunlight, and we start walking down the sidewalk together, holding hands, free.

When I told Norm, my eyes teared up. "I just carried her right out."

"That's amazing," said Norm. "It's exactly how you have to approach yourself when you panic, by separating the child from the adult. Then you can have compassion for little Rita, and you can help her feel safe."

On my way home, I stopped at Walden Pond. I'd been passing it for weeks before and after my sessions with Norm, and each time I had the urge to walk down to it. Everything was thawing: the ice in the pond had been melting, breaking apart into small white islands. I was aware of how fast life is—how one minute we're children with all our strange dreams, and the next minute we're reaching back, like a person pulled out to sea by a tide. You never expect all that distance. You never expect to get so far so fast.

I'd learned a lot in the past months—about panic and about myself—but I'd also lost a lot. I'd lost the summer, fall, and winter. I'd lost months of work. I'd lost my confidence. But every day was a chance to reclaim my footing in the world. Thoreau writes, *There is no ill which may not be dissipated like the dark, if you let in a stronger light upon it.* I could either be someone who kept driving past Walden Pond, or I could be someone who actually stopped and walked down the big hill to the water.

When I got there, the pond's melting ice was making a gentle hissing sound. I dipped my hands into the water, a cold bite, then started to walk. Snow and ice still lined large portions of the path, so I had to be careful not to slip, and as I ventured farther in, I felt a moment of unease over being alone. Only weeks earlier I had been anxious about walking to the edge of the azalea bushes in our yard; now I was going to walk almost two miles, on ice, in the middle of the woods, by myself. But I could hear the words of Emerson, as if he were right there speaking them to me: *Trust thyself: Every heart vibrates to that iron string.* So I walked, and the lake whispered, and my feet crunched through the snow, and everything around me seemed perfectly impermanent, and I realized how all we ever get—the only guarantee we really have—is this moment. So I surrendered to it. I kept walking.

When I arrived home that afternoon, I began cleaning. I put new sheets on the bed and fluffed the pillows mightily, then misted them with rose water. I scrubbed the floors and polished every faucet. I swept the front steps and the walk. I threw away old magazines and placed a cobalt bowl filled with lemons on the kitchen counter. I burned sage, winding the smoke through each room in the house. Then I walked into my office with purpose and stopped at my desk. There, beside a notebook with a lotus flower on the cover, lay my panic button, its chain streaming out beside it like a wavy flag. I scooped it up and took it back to the drawer where I found it. "Thank you," I said.

FORTY-SIX

I'm learning that boys, like men, are always watching girls. But it's different with boys—sweeter. So I flirt with all of them, and soon my name shows up inside hearts on several more notebooks. John, Dallas's brainy friend, writes *Lovely Rita* on his. For years, my parents called me terrible names. But now, in black ink, I am lovely. "I don't care," Dallas says smiling, pointing to John's notebook and tousling his hair—"He can write whatever he wants. I know you love me." And I do. At fifteen, this is the most normal my life has ever felt. And every time Dallas smiles at me, I heal a little.

I cheer for Dallas on the baseball field, and he claps for me when I bowl a strike (or more often, a gutter ball) during one of our unit's weekly outings. We gaze at each other across the room. We draw each other's names in bubble letters and hang them on our walls. We take Polaroids of ourselves and give them to each other, as if we're giving ourselves. *Here,* we keep saying, *I'm yours.*

Mr. Ware stares at me intently, leaning forward with his hands cupping his knees. A month has passed since I first arrived at the Jackson Unit. "So, you really like getting that attention from the boys, don't you?" he asks, though it's more of a statement.

"I don't know." I feel myself blush and look away.

"Bullshit, Rita. You know exactly what I mean." He pulls his chair closer to me. "I mean, c'mon, anyone can see how you play them. And it works—you've got them all drooling. So now the question is why?"

I tap my foot nervously. "I don't know." Here, for the first time, someone is exposing me, and I don't like it—not even from Mr. Ware.

"C'mon, you're smarter than that. What do you think?"

"Maybe because I just want to feel pretty."

"Maybe it's because you're afraid of what's underneath. You present this façade—as if who you are without the makeup and the tight Harley shirt won't be good enough."

I chew on the tip of my finger. "What if I don't know who I am?"

"That's what we're going to find out. We're going to start focusing on the inside. You think Dallas loves you? Dallas doesn't know you—and how can he if you don't know yourself? What Dallas loves is an idea of you. And that's not bad. It's just not love."

"What if nobody loves me?" I barely whisper.

"I do." He pulls a book from the shelves and swings his chair around beside me. The book is white. On it is a pencil drawing of a little circle with an eye and a pie-shaped mouth. He opens the book and begins to read: "It was a missing piece. And it was not happy . . ."

In the dark, Tina and I keep whispering. She tells me about her family, about drugs, about things I promise to keep secret. "Tell me more about what it was like to be a runaway," she says.

I turn over on my stomach and lean on my elbows, resting my face in my hands. I've never talked to anyone like this. "What do you want to know?"

"Where did you go?"

"Different places. I just met people, and they let me stay with them sometimes." I don't tell her about Duwahi and Karen, though sometimes they still find me in my dreams.

"What did you do when you didn't have a place to stay?"

"I slept on staircases. And sometimes in empty cars. And once on a bus. And once I snuck into my father's yard when he was in prison and slept on a lounge chair."

"What was it like? Out there at night?"

I close my eyes and think. "It's strange, but it stopped being scary. I mean, when I was with my parents, I was always afraid, especially at night. I had a lot of nightmares, and even when I woke up, it felt like I was still in them. But when I was on the run, it changed. *People* were scary sometimes, but nighttime, it was—I don't know—*possible*." I turn over again to lie on my back. "Kind of like now."

"Yes," she says. "Like now."

"You know, the stars—I think they listen."

"Do you think they're listening now?"

"I think they're always listening."

We're quiet for several minutes, and I wonder if Tina has fallen asleep. Then I hear her get out of bed. Without a word, she comes across the room in the dark and sits down next to me. Her hip presses against mine. She leans forward, so close I can feel her breath on my lips, and at that moment, the thing I want most in the world is for her to kiss me.

But she doesn't. Instead, she lingers there, then gets up and goes back to her bed. In the silence, we breathe darkness. It's as if she and I own it, the darkness, together.

We have some free time before an N.A. meeting, so I go outside. Dallas is leaving tomorrow; he's going home. Right now I'm the only one out here. The sun has slipped behind a mountain and lit the sky in mauve, tangerine, sienna—a warm blanket lowering itself into every crevice. I sit on the grass in the middle of a hill and watch the sky drop in layers. At the top, a sapphire sheet deepens, starts spreading down. The buzz of insects is as steady as stillness. The air is electric, a charge to my skin. In this moment there is nothing but mountains and the swirling atmosphere and the invisible stars poised behind it all. There is no distinction between the air and the buzz and the mountains and me: we all flow into each other.

The next morning, before Dallas leaves, the staff finally lets us have the embrace we've been waiting two months for. His hug is softer than I expected, and he smells like soap and sun and salt. Everyone has crowded around us, as if they're rooting for us. We're like the rehab version of prom king and queen. "When you get out, I'm comin' for you," he whispers in my ear. I am crying, in part because I'm going to miss him, and in part because I've already learned the mileage of these kinds of vows.

"So, how are you going to keep yourself clean when you're home, and your mother's pissing you off, let's say, and the thought of getting high starts to sound pretty damn good all of a sudden?"

Behind Mr. Ware's head hangs a picture I made for him: a road starting in a dark slug-ridden pit and ending in a rainbow that arches right off the page. I wanted it to represent my journey—how the road before had been mostly dark, and how coming there, to him, to the Jackson Unit, to the mountains, to myself, I'd found light. It isn't a particularly good drawing, but it was the best I could do.

I give the answers I've been taught, and though I love Mr. Ware, it's something of a performance: "Well, for one, I'm not going to engage in magical thinking, and if things get tough, I'm going to keep myself off the pity pot. I'm going to pray and definitely avoid people who use drugs. I'll go to an N.A. meeting every day, and I'll get a sponsor I can call for support. I'll think before I speak or do something I might regret, and I'll find hobbies and fill my time with things like writing and going on picnics and taking walks." It's not so much that I'm being dishonest as it is that I don't really understand what I'm saying. These words have been repeated so much that they've lost their meaning. They're flat. But even if they had a shape, I wouldn't know how to fit them into the mystery of my future. I haven't lived with my mother since I was nine, and I haven't lived freely for years. I don't know my sister anymore, aside from the occasional letters we send each other, and I don't know where my father is. So a picnic with my family is a fantasy. Each time I think of it, all I can see is the ground, and a blanket, empty.

FORTY-SEVEN

At Norm's, we were working on my fear of highways. "They're too fast," I explained. "And too big, and too hard."

"Too hard?"

"Yes. Too much concrete and metal. And tunnels and bridges—they're just evil."

"But you used to drive on the highway fine?"

"I used to drive on any highway, anywhere—and usually in the fast lane."

By then, Norm had changed his EMDR approach and was doing something called RDI (Resource Development and Installation) with me. Instead of remembering trauma, I was supposed to remember positive things, because, as Norm said, "there's just too much trauma."

We'd switched from the earphones to a pair of sponge-covered clickers that took turns buzzing in my hands. I found the tactile aspect more relaxing than the visual and audio options. Norm handed me the device and instructed me to remember a time I drove on the highway and liked it. The memory that sprung into focus was from my early twenties. I was on my way to Ocean City, Maryland, and I was alone, driving my boyfriend's black convertible, blasting reggae down the road. As I crossed the Bay Bridge, I started steering with my knees as I took my hands off the wheel and shot them up into the air, the way you do on roller coasters, because I felt like I was flying in that wind, so high up, free.

Norm was writing on a pad. " 'Free.' What other words would you use to describe how you felt?"

"Happy. Strong. Alive."

"Good," he said. "Now let's go back and remember some more."

That day I didn't drive home on the highway. Instead, I took the usual country roads, except for one extra turn: I stopped at a barn. I'd passed it once when I'd accidentally taken a wrong turn, and I couldn't stop thinking about it after. The barn was painted white and had its own built-in silo, and the paddocks sprawled from the edge of the road to a distant line of pines. When I pulled in, a girl was riding a black horse, her spine straight. All my life I'd dreamed of riding a horse, but I didn't know if I ever would. I'd never forgotten my friend Jennifer's horse, who filled me with such untouchable desire that I could no longer be Jennifer's friend, but eventually the years had faded that desire, and what was left had turned to fear.

Now I was determined to blast through that fear and give myself something my parents never could. Now I would finally step through that door between the horses and me.

Inside the barn, country music trickled from a small radio on a ledge. The horses stood quietly in their stalls, periodically swatting at flies with their tails. Sunlight sliced through the windows, dropped bright squares on the floor. A lone guitar shaped a sad tune. "Hello?" I called. The air smelled of hay and wood and horse sweat, sweetly musky.

And that's where I first met Applesauce, the horse that started it all. The girls referred to him as "a fat gray sofa," and my first thought when I saw him was *He's big.* My second thought was *He's big.* It's difficult to understand just how big a horse is until you're standing next to one, until you lose your balance by staring into one of his eyes. But it didn't take long before I was accustomed to Applesauce's size, as I groomed him the way the instructor showed me, using the currycomb to massage him in small circles along the sand dune of his back, then sweeping away the dust with quick flicks of the brush.

The instructor took me outside to a small sand-filled ring, and as the sun beat down on my shoulders, I climbed up the mounting block and, for the first time in my life, I mounted a horse. And when I felt him move beneath me, I was happy.

As I made my way home that day, all I could do was think about horses. *I ride horses now,* I was thinking. *I'm an* equestrian. All those years I gazed from the roadside at horses in fields, until they seemed farther and farther, until they were specks on the horizon and the sound of them in my mind felt like the most I would ever get of them. But now I had finally touched a horse. I'd groomed him. I'd climbed onto his back. And for a few short minutes as he walked lazily around, I'd ridden him.

And then, an already perfect day got more perfect: Larry came home with the mail.

"Guess what! I rode a horse today!" The words tumbled out before he'd managed to close the front door.

"A horse? Really? Where?" He put the mail down on the side table, and I kissed him.

"Yes, because I'm an *equestrian* now. I found this barn and rode a horse named Applesauce!"

"Wow, just like that? Your very first horse! Good for you, sweetie!" He leaned forward and hugged me. "I'm proud of you." Then as he sorted through the mail, he pulled out a large envelope. "This is for you."

It was a letter from Middlebury College in Vermont. I had gotten the scholarship to Bread Loaf.

A few weeks later, on my way to my first real riding lesson with Tommy and Shaddad, I stopped at a tack shop and told the lady behind the counter that I'd just started riding horses. "Wonderful! Where do you ride?"

I looked at the shelves of boots on the wall, then back at her. "Actually, I've only ridden a horse once. And I didn't exactly ride it—I more like sat on it. But I have a lesson today with someone new."

"I see." She nodded.

"Don't I need some special clothes?" I asked.

"Do you have half chaps or breeches?"

I wasn't entirely sure what those things were, but I was sure I didn't have them. Within a half hour I'd purchased a helmet, a pair of tan breeches, brown paddock boots, and brown suede half chaps. When the lady caught me eyeing the tall black boots displayed on the wall, she told me, "Those are for after you've been riding for a while." I wondered how that would happen—that one day when I would say, *It's finally a while—now I can get those tall black boots!* I changed into my new ensemble in the dressing room, then paid for my merchandise, proud as a kid who wears her new shoes straight out of the shoe store.

Over the next year, I would ride many different horses, with many different instructors, before I would meet Claret. But no matter where I went, each horse would teach me something new. One of the most important things I came to understand is that horses are prey animals—they live on the edge of panic, always ready to flee—and they require us, as riders, to help them feel safe. One horse I rode spooked at wind, another at doors, and another at just about anything that moved. And always, they needed me to be brave. If I got scared as we neared a door, the horse knew instantly and turned away. But when I steeled my core and kept my legs on firmly—when I looked ahead with determination at the object of fear—the horse moved with me, toward it. This, I learned, is how you move past fear.

One particular afternoon, I was trying to come to terms with the whole idea of falling off a horse. Would it happen? Would it hurt? Would something break? Would I die? "If I fall," I asked the instructor, "will it be very painful?"

"It's not exactly going to feel *good*," she said. "But, it's not a matter of *if*; it's a matter of *when*."

That's a strange feeling, that moment when you know, *I'm going to fall off a horse*. Most people don't know what accidents await them in their futures, but I knew at least one of mine. At first this knowledge was difficult to reconcile. It was like an equation I wanted to recalculate until the numbers came up differently. *Maybe I'll be the lucky one. Maybe I'll become such a good rider that it will be as if my behind is glued to the saddle. Maybe I'll stop riding.* I knew right then that I had to make a choice: I had to either go after my passion or give it up. There is no halfway with horses. Either you're present or you're gone. And I realized that if I let fear stop me from doing something I was passionate about, I was only one small step away from being back on my couch, afraid to even stand up. There's risk in everything, from the moment we're born, but, as Dylan says, *He not busy being born is busy dying*.

So I kept riding, kept seeking the horses, kept stepping each day a little farther from my fear. And all of those steps—and pauses and lurches and swerves—would lead me to a barn in New Hampshire, where a copper-colored, bright-eyed horse was waiting for me.

I sent my confirmation letter back to Bread Loaf, and started driving on the highway again. At first I'd merge on and whip right off at the next exit, my palms clammy, my heart knocking. But then I'd get back on again. I'd play music and look at the clouds and hang in the right lane, close to the shoulder so that I always had a way off. After a few tries, I began to feel comfortable with it again. *Highways are good*, I thought. *They get you places.* Sometimes the child voice would say, *Oh my God, you need to get off RIGHT NOW. These cars are going TOO FAST.* And I'd say, *It's okay. I've got it under control. Just stick with me, kiddo.*

When it was time for me to leave for Vermont, Larry loaded my things into my car. A consummate gentleman, he'd always rushed to open every door, to carry my heavy suitcases, to fill up his arms with grocery bags. It was August, the light a miasma hovering over the grass, the chatty birds dipping through it, these last warm mornings of the year, and Larry was standing in the middle of it with a gift he held out in front of him with both hands, the way he'd once held chocolate at my doorstep when we were dating: a box wrapped in metallic paper with sunbursts on it. On the top he'd written in black marker: RITA'S BREAD LOAF BOX. "They're letters," he said, "one for you to open each day you're there." He kissed me softly on the mouth. "Now go have a good time, and come home to me."

Larry pushed my car door closed, and I drove away. I drove on one highway, and then another, and another. I passed trees and jutting rock walls and mountains. I passed a fading sign on the roadside that said, PACKING PEANUTS WANTED. I passed little huts selling firecrackers. It was the farthest I'd driven in more than a year, and I wasn't scared for one moment of it. Instead I felt like a kid on her first day of school, eager and nervous and ready to learn.

Bread Loaf—which was held on a gorgeous sprawling campus on a mountain with no cell phone coverage and a single pay phone surrounded by sunflowers out in the grass—was a whirlwind in another world. We waiters didn't stop—whether it was working our shifts or attending workshops or craft classes or talks or readings or late night parties where we danced in living rooms in our socks. We were a tribe of motion and mutual love. Just keeping up took all of my energy—I barely had time to eat or sleep let alone think of panic—and I was smitten and aroused by every minute, by this chance to be so completely thrown into a world of kindred spirits, with the mountains rising and falling all around us and the Milky Way floating above us like snow suspended in the black sky.

The entirety of my eleven days there was like that sky—a swath of dazzling fragments: Ilya Kaminsky singing his poems until there was no one left in the room who wasn't crying; a woman in a classroom with the chalk in her hand—*ut pictura poesis (as is painting so is poetry)*; snippets of conversation overhead between girls while I showered—"I felt so stupid in my tsunami dream"; Steve Orlen, my workshop leader, offering the etymology of my maiden name: "descended from martyrs"; sitting on steps with a beautiful girl who had a Snoopy shirt that matched mine, who stood at a podium in a red halter dress and transfixed me utterly as she read to us about the ways we hold on to things; the tremble and passion in my heart when it was my turn to stand at the podium and read a poem about a two-fingered boy; watching the sun set over the mountains from a bench on a porch beside a lovely woman, the last light holding her face as we looked at each other and out at the sky, which was changing—one moment, the protracted swipe of a flamingo's wing, the next, the exhalation of a toy dragon—while the waxing moon appeared low over the hills, ready to drop.

In quick stolen minutes at my bed, I opened Larry's letters. Each envelope was dated and had a small gift tucked inside—rocket stickers, Albert Einstein stickers, a miniature pen-drawn self-portrait of Larry waving, a sushi-shaped eraser, a blue button with a green bird and the word *rare*—and in each card, Larry inscribed a quotation from a famous writer. On the first day's letter, he quoted T. S. Eliot:

> *We shall not cease from exploration*
> *And the end of all our exploring*
> *Will be to arrive where we started*
> *And know the place for the first time.*

In one card was a button with a picture of a tree and the word *hugger* below it. *The world's tallest tree is a redwood in California measuring over 360 feet,* Larry wrote. *The oldest trees are the 4600-year-old bristlecone pines.* In another note he invited me to the sky: *The moon phase tonight is a waxing crescent. Meet me in orbit around Luna. Let's be astronauts!* He asked if I was eating and sleeping, he told me to be brave and to shine, he said he loved me and missed me, and he reminded me that he was always a phone call away. Larry's box of letters was the most magical, thoughtful, loving present anyone had ever given me. It gave me hope that things could change for us, that we could be closer, and that when I came home, maybe I would know the place for the first time.

FORTY-EIGHT

Since Tina and I have seniority, we get our own private rooms as new girls come in and take our old room. On my orange wall I tape a picture Dallas drew for me—a field of flowers with bubble letters above it that read *Dallas loves Rita*. Next to it I put a picture of him grinning widely, looking at me. But in my new room, I miss my late nights with Tina. As if to make up for the new separation, we've started showering together in the evenings, giggling most of the time while we wash each other's hair, scrub each other's backs, and soap each other's breasts. Hers feel so perfectly full in my hands, as if nothing has ever truly filled my hands before. Sometimes I can't wait for dinner to be over just so I can feel connected to her body again.

One night before "lights out," Tina steps into my doorway. This time she isn't giggling. She picks her left foot up and places it on my night table, just for a second, just long enough for me to see under her long T-shirt. She isn't wearing underwear.

It happens quickly, and then she walks away. "Wait, come back!" I call, but Ms. Hanlin quickly replaces Tina's spot in my doorway. "Good night, you little rascal," she says, bending down to hug me.

In the dark, I'm overcome with desire. I roll over and press my hands to the wall that separates our rooms. "Come back," I whisper into the darkness. And then, as if to answer, she does.

My heart is pounding. She sits on the bed, and I sit up to meet her. This time there is no pause, just her lips against mine, warm and open—softer than any man's. She kisses my neck, my collarbone, my breasts, and her hands on my body make me realize how loud breath can be. I want her as I have never wanted anyone. I want every part of her. We pull into each other, over and over, and I am born in her hands, into desire.

W hen it's finally time for me to go home, Tina won't come out of her room, and I can't bring myself to knock. We don't know how to say goodbye to each other.

I'm wearing Taby's dress, long and black with a low strappy back.

"You have my dress, so now you *have* to see me again," she says, smiling.

"I can't wait," I say, squeezing her hard.

"Love ya like a sister!" she calls as I lug my suitcase to the door. Everyone is crowding around to give last hugs, and as I turn to wave, I catch the sunlight coming through the windows and glittering in her hair.

Though I know my mother doesn't want me, this time she doesn't have a choice. I am almost sixteen, and the system is finally ejecting me. "Let's just hope you're ready," she said the week before.

"I've *been* ready," I told her.

When I see her coming down the hall toward me with Joanne following behind, it's Joanne who stops me flat. She's twelve now, and in the year since I've seen her, her face has lost some of its roundness, and her body has started to change. She stands with her hands straight down by her sides, and I can tell she's unsure about where she is, and about what comes next, and that she's biting her lower lip because she doesn't want to cry.

Many of the memories I have of my sister are of her behind a window: waiting for me at the balcony door to come home from school; pounding her fists on the back window of my mother's car as my mother drove away without me; crying behind my father's patio door as I bolted away from her; sitting inside a kitchen on a cloudy day, the day I flew toward her, breaking the glass, running.

And now I'm walking toward her, and there is no glass between us—only the years we've lived apart. "I'm glad you're coming home, Rita," she says, and then she starts crying. I wrap her in my arms, but for me there are no tears, because for the first time I feel truly free.

It's windy when Mr. Ware walks us out to the car and hands me a cassette. "This song will always remind me of you, and when you hear it, I want it to remind you of me, and of everything you learned here." His eyes go red and watery. "And of everything that you are." The song is Cat Stevens's "Wild World."

We hug goodbye one last time under a low gray sky, and before we part, Mr. Ware speaks into my hair, which tangles in the wind. "I'll always remember you like a child, girl."

FORTY-NINE

When I arrived home from Bread Loaf, I found the truth in T. S. Eliot's words. I experienced those first tingling moments of recognition that come when you've been away for a while, when everything is at once familiar and new. This was our town—with its steeples at the center, its quiet porch lights glowing through the trees, its two-lane roads winding like stories—but it could have been any town. This was our black mailbox, our driveway, our windows hazed with light—but it could have been any house. For a moment I considered that maybe time had warped, that I was coming back to a town too late, to a house that was no longer mine. But then I saw my dogs sitting alert at the door, as if they knew I was coming, and then Larry appeared behind them, and they all came out to greet me, and Larry brought my suitcases back in, and within a few minutes the chimera disappeared and the sweetness of being home set in.

One of the first things I did was sit down at my desk to write. Really write—take those snippets in my notebook, and make something with them. Larry came to my door and stood without saying anything.

"Yes?" I said, smiling. "Can I help you?" He did that sometimes, just looked at me as if he were on the verge of speaking, as if all his words were collecting there, just behind the dam of his throat.

"I'm glad you're home," he said.

"You know, there was a moment, up on the mountain at Bread Loaf, when I got overwhelmed. It was all so intense, and parts of it reminded me of being in those institutions when I was younger, all crammed in with strangers, and suddenly I had this urge to leave. I felt like a runaway all over again." I laughed. "But you know what kept me there, in that moment? Why I stayed?"

Larry looked at me tenderly. "Why?"

"Because I had your letters to open."

I had a dream that Larry and I were going on a bicycle ride. At first I was having some difficulty with my bike—the shocks were too stiff and the seat was too high and the gear shifters were sticking—so we pulled into a parking lot where, by our good fortune, we happened upon a bike repair crew. They took out their wrenches and screwdrivers and went assiduously to work. "Here, try it now," they said. I sat down in the seat, and the bike fit my body like the hug of an old friend. I bounced up and down, the shocks yielding. "It's perfect," I declared. Larry was beside me on his, waiting. "I'm ready," I said, excited for the adventure we were about embark upon together. We were going to take the road for all it was worth, he and I. We were going to coast down hills and feel the wind fluttering past. We were going to slow down sometimes and talk, just the two of us against a scrim of fog with the scent of the ocean in the distance. We began to pedal, and suddenly Larry started going very fast. He thought it was a race. It was the fastest anyone had ridden a bicycle in the history of bicycles—so fast that he lifted off the ground. And suddenly we were in this very tall building, in a room one hundred feet to the top, and Larry kept ascending, almost to the ceiling by then in a magnificent arc, and I couldn't believe what he was doing—he was heading straight for the windows. "What the *fuck!*" I yelled. Larry shattered the windows. I watched the impact hurt him—I could see the force of it temporarily stop him, the glass lacerating his face—but he kept going. He was in the air, at the apex now, so high up, flying over the grass, which turned out to be our own yard. He was coming down the arc's other side, heading toward the neighbors' property. I couldn't reach him; I couldn't stop it. I felt my organs seize as he came down and crashed into the fence.

"We have to talk."

Larry was on the couch, reviewing a legal case for which he would serve as a medical expert. He was surrounded by pages and pages of medical records.

I'd seen him on the witness stand once, when one of his cases had gone to trial. "No," he was saying, "it is not below standard of care because this is an expected complication. It is well known than an intracerebral hemorrhage can occur from placement of an ICP monitor." As he calmly and eloquently answered each question, I knew that he held the patient's entire medical history in his mind.

He took a stack of pages off the couch and placed them down on the floor, then looked up at me expectantly. I sat down beside him and told him about my dream.

"That's weird," he said.

"I know. But I can't stop thinking about it."

He took my hand. "It was just a dream."

"But it feels real." I wrapped both of my hands around his.

"How?"

"It doesn't feel like we're pedaling together."

"What do you mean?"

"In life."

Larry adjusted his glasses with his free hand. "I think we're pedaling together."

And I realized then that the unspoken deal we'd made in the beginning of our relationship would not hold. I couldn't go on pretending that I was only certain parts of myself, though for years that's exactly what I'd done. I'd willingly tried to erase any part of my life I thought Larry might find unsavory or intimidating—in the name of innocence I did this, so that we could both clutch it for our own—but we are all of our lives, and I was beginning to understand that if innocence truly exists, then it can never really be lost.

"You don't know me."

"Of course I know you."

"You don't know about my past."

"I know you now. You're beautiful."

"Who I am now is because of my past. And if I can't tell you my story, how can you really know me?"

"I think that's a fundamental difference between us. You want to know things. And I don't."

"But that's not true. You want to know everything. You know more than anyone I've ever met."

"Bad things, I mean. I admit, your past scares me."

I let his hand go. "Sometimes we have to be more than our fears."

One evening while I was watching a fire climb the back of our fireplace, I was thinking about how lucky I was to have the life I had. If you would have asked me as a runaway what I was running for, I would have said *this, this life, this kind and steady man, these sweet dogs, this house, this fire.* There wasn't a day of my life that I didn't feel grateful, if for nothing else than to simply be alive. And as I was thinking about these things—about how I finally had love, had a safe life, the kind of life I used to imagine the people in L.L. Bean Christmas catalogs had—I heard a voice ring clearly in my mind: *Too bad you will leave him.* The clarity and unexpectedness of that voice, and the words it spoke, jarred me for days. No, I wanted to argue with it, I will never leave him.

Thoreau writes, "I have met with but one or two persons in the course of my life who understood the art of Walking, that is, of taking walks, who had a genius, so to speak, for *sauntering;* which word is beautifully derived 'from idle people who roved about the country, in the middle ages, and asked charity, under pretence of going *à la sainte terre'*—to the holy land, till the children exclaimed, 'There goes a *sainte-terrer,'* a saunterer—a holy-lander. . . . Some, however, would derive the word from *sans terre,* without land or a home, which, therefore, in the good sense, will mean, having no particular home, but equally at home everywhere."

Safety is largely an illusion, and panic knows this. Panic disorder happens when this knowledge becomes unbalanced, when we apply all of our grit and muscle to railing against our own inexorable lack of control. I had always rejected my mother's saying, "Man plans, God laughs," but I was starting to see a wisdom in it. On the run, I'd never had the luxury of planning. Sometimes there were beautiful moments, and sometimes ugly ones. And after each, I moved forward with a kind of wonder over it all, wanting to know what would happen next. Life was a series of small choices, one by one—which street to walk down, which car to get into, which candy to buy with the change at the bottom of my purse—and without a map of my future, it was relatively easy to shake off the days when the road didn't lead where I hoped it would. Panic, I'd found, had been like that; it was only when I surrendered to it that I started to become free.

So after days of railing against that matter-of-fact voice that told me I would leave my husband, I neither rejected nor accepted it. I simply shrunk the scale: each day I would make a choice. And I would be grateful for my home, knowing also that there was a truth to Thoreau's words, that in some ways, when we are present, when we abide by ourselves and our own lives, we can be equally at home anywhere.

FIFTY

Though things went steadily and unforeseeably downhill during our time at Gerta's barn, at the end of our time there, after I decided to leave, my relationship with Claret deepened. And we began again.

I was grateful to the horses I'd known before Claret for what they gave me, but it was Claret who whinnied for me when he recognized the sound of my car pulling up; it was Claret who nickered for me every time I walked through the barn doors, every time he heard my voice. While all the other horses stood quietly in their stalls, it was always Claret shifting around to see me, to call out to me. And it was Claret who taught me that we could trust each other during the afternoons I spent walking with him through the pastures as he grazed, working the currycomb into his neck and back, feeding him peppermints and letting him lick the sugar off my palms. He taught me balance and strength through hours of training my body to follow his movements.

He taught me focus as I repeatedly refined my communication during the different exercises I did with him. And he taught me, when I finally did fall off, how to brush the dirt away and get back on again: as I sat up on the ground after a sudden and hard landing on my back, Claret walked over to me. I was crying by then at the shock of it, quick silent tears despite my will not to cry, and Claret, who had originally spooked at the sound of ice falling off the roof and sent us both flying in different directions, gently put his nose down on the top of my helmet. He stood there quietly for a minute, and I felt his warm breath on my face, and I stopped crying, and I righted myself, and I climbed up onto his back again.

By demanding my full presence, Claret taught me a calm and strength that panic had no part of.

In the month before I moved Claret to his new barn near the pond, spring came, and sometimes I stood beside him in the paddock and looked up at the pine trees. He seemed to be looking, too, both of us standing so still. Sometimes a breeze would flutter his mane, and I'd think, *You wild, wild thing.*

While I was spending days with Claret, Larry was, in his free time, learning to become a pilot. "What's it like up there? Is it scary?" I asked over sushi.

Larry rested his chopsticks on his tray. "No, it's not scary, because there are all kinds of things you're thinking about, like your speed, your altitude, where you're going next."

"That sounds a lot like riding," I said.

"They're very similar, I think."

"Does it feel different in such a small plane? Does it feel like you're actually flying up there? Like in dreams?"

"In the plane, when it's smooth, you don't feel like you're flying so much. It's like being on the ground, only the view is different. It's only when there's a little bit of turbulence that you feel like you're bobbing a little, and that feels like flying." Larry held his hand out flat, imitating a plane. "Not that it's pleasant to hit turbulence. But if you're moving through something, like a cloud, you can feel that speed—when there's some kind of acceleration or deceleration. That's when you really feel connected with the plane, when you're making movements. And of course, when you're taking off and landing. That's when it can get scary, as you're coming in for the landing and you're getting closer and closer. That to me is the most interesting part."

FIFTY-ONE

Now that I was driving on highways, I decided to take a trip to Baltimore to visit my sister, Joanne, and her daughter, Kiana, as well as some friends. On the way, I was going to stop in Brooklyn to hear one of my best friends—the fellow Bread Loaf waiter who had a Snoopy shirt that matched mine and whose writing struck bone—give a reading. But on my way to the reading, I missed the exit. My plan was to get off on the next exit, but that turned out to be very far away, and in the meantime I'd hit a giant traffic jam, and I was watching the minutes on my car clock inch closer and closer to the reading time, and I still hadn't arrived at the next exit, and then it was too late. I'd missed the reading. So I rerouted my navigation for Baltimore, and eventually the traffic got moving again, and suddenly I found my highway merging with another highway to form the biggest highway I'd ever seen. I saw it happening, saw that I was in the center of this megahighway, so I pulled over on the shoulder just before the merge point, and I began to panic. My heart was racing, and I couldn't see straight, and everything suddenly got very, very loud, and the traffic was zooming past me, rattling my car, and I knew that if I didn't move, I would probably get smashed by an eighteen-wheeler, but I was too terrified to move. I thought that if I could just talk to someone, maybe I could get through it, so I called Larry, and he didn't answer, and I called every friend I could think of, and they didn't answer, and I started calling random acquaintances, and nobody would answer.

I had to drive. I was stuck in the middle of the Biggest Highway in the Universe, and all I wanted was to disappear—to be magically airlifted and delivered safely home, with my dogs at my side. But I had to drive. I tried to remember all the things I'd learned about panic along the way, but somehow all I could come up with was the word *fuck*. So I went with that. "Fuck!" I yelled. I gripped the steering wheel and sat up tall. "I can do this! I can fucking do this!" I turned my radio up so that it was pouring over the traffic. "I can drive on the fucking highway!" I looked in my rearview, and when it was clear, I gunned it and merged back into the traffic. "You're doing this," I said. "You're doing it." But I was still terrified, so I started singing with the music—*I just have to be louder than the fear*, I thought. I sang so loudly that I was almost embarrassing myself, and that got me smiling, and since it's hard to panic when you're smiling, that's how I soothed myself to Baltimore, singing loudly, off-key.

I had about five more panic attacks on the way: as long as I could be next to a shoulder, I was okay, but whenever the shoulder disappeared, my adrenaline lit flames just under my skin and my breath came choppy. I suppose there are many of us who feel better knowing the shoulder is there on the side of the road—that there's a way out, just in case. But eventually, there's always a way out. *Just wait*, I kept telling myself when the shoulder disappeared and I was suddenly speeding alongside a concrete wall in a panic. *The shoulder will come back*. And the shoulder always reappeared.

When I arrived in Baltimore, I recognized the air. I stood outside in the parking lot of my hotel for a while and looked at the fat orange moon, while cars came and went. Having lived in Maryland for over twenty years, I knew there were certain warm nights, like this night, when the wind came in cool fluttery laps through the balmy dark and wanted to seduce you—they were the kinds of nights when, as a kid, I knew it was time to run again—because the air seemed to be promising something, and the invitation—the possibility—was irresistible.

The next day I went with Joanne and Kiana to the mall across from my hotel. Unlike me, Joanne had maintained relationships with our parents. She lived one street away from my mother and saw my father from time to time on weekends. Family meant everything to her—a single mother, she lived for her daughter, a brilliant and beautiful dancer, and was determined to give her everything we never had. I admired her for that, for her selflessness and generosity when she had been given so little.

I gave up contact with my mother about a year before Larry and I moved to Massachusetts, but before that I'd spent years trying to be close to her. I listened to her problems and gave her advice, as I'd done during that brief time in my childhood when she'd let me be her friend. I cleaned her house, listened to her stories of her past, wrote her letters of encouragement, brought her fresh vegetables and books and her favorite perfumes, invited her to come stay with me so that I could feed her healthy foods and take walks with her and help her quit drugs and cigarettes—but nothing made a difference, and for me our relationship was often painful and one-sided. When I met the wise social worker—the one who told me that sometimes it is necessary to suffer—I could feel myself reaching an end.

"She's never going to be a mother to you," the social worker told me. "You can prop her up a million different ways, but that won't make her a mother." Though he wasn't smiling, his eyes were smiling, as sages' eyes do. "So, you can either let her go and grieve her, or you can spend your life chasing a phantom."

That evening I took a walk through my neighborhood. It was dusk, and though the streets and trees and houses were dimming, the sky still held the light, like a window lit from inside. *A person can lose things*, I thought, *and still have this*. I realized then that the social worker was right, that what I'd been trying to give my mother were all the things she'd never given me—and never would. So I let her go; I let the hope for her go. And I grieved her. And I suffered. And the sky kept glowing, in its generous, impenetrable vastness.

I let my father go, too. Our relationship through most of my life had been spotty at best. In the years after I was sent to Montrose, I saw him once, when he came to visit me. I was fourteen then, and it would be almost another two years before I'd see him again. There are photographs marking the event: in the first one, the two of us are sitting beside each other, leg to leg, on a couch in an institutional visiting room. I'm wearing a shirt with palm trees on it; he's wearing one that says NEW YORK. He has his arm around me, and he's gazing at me with an expression that could probably be read numerous ways—is it longing in his face? love? curiosity?—while I sit beside him, looking at the camera. In the second picture, he's touching my hand to his short beard, and we're laughing. And in the last picture, I'm hugging him. It was two unsteady and strangely intimate hours of our lives, during which his girlfriend took pictures of us and suggested that I wear slightly less eye makeup. Still, the photographs, if nothing else, demonstrate something warm between us. And it was that warmth that nurtured my hope that one day he would finally be the father he promised he'd be; it nurtured my own child-blind love for him. But there came a time—a day many years later when I was hospitalized with viral meningitis and my father came to visit me—that I understood the irrefutable truth: my father wasn't going to change. It was summer, and I'd been admitted to the hospital in sandals, and it was cold in the room. Despite the blankets they gave me, my feet were icy and I was shivering, so I asked my father, who was wearing a sweat suit and sneakers, if I could have his socks. He said no. I thought he was joking at first, but when I pushed it, he quickly became indignant. "No," he repeated, "I'm not giving you my socks." After he left, I lay there wondering what my life would have been like if I'd had a father who thought I was worth a pair of socks. But those things are futile to wonder, so I stopped. A nurse brought me hospital socks, and I began to let my father go.

At the mall, I took my niece to buy some clothes while my sister got a pedicure in the nail salon. Kiana was thirteen and in her bliss as she stepped from the dressing room modeling one outfit after another, twirling around under the glaring store lights. We'd just made our first purchase when my sister called, upset. I told her we'd be right over, and when we arrived, she was in the waiting area in the front of the nail salon, her face flushed. "What's wrong?" we asked.

"That girl over there"—she nodded with her head—"did a terrible job. She rushed through everything, barely did my cuticles, and massaged me for like three seconds, like this." She demonstrated by hastily and sloppily rubbing my hand. "And it's streaked!" Her voice was raised and unsteady, and I could see she was near tears.

I looked down at her feet. She'd chosen a coral polish, and I thought it looked okay, but I'd never had a pedicure and didn't know what to expect. "I'm sorry," I said. "Let's just get out of here."

"No. I want my money back." She approached the counter. "This is ridiculous."

The manager came up, and Joanne repeated what she told us, and he said, "No refunds. It says here on the sign."

My sister's response to that was to get louder. "I don't care what it says on your stupid sign. I didn't get what I paid for, and Miss Thing over there has an attitude problem. What, is she too good to massage my feet?"

By then some customers in the store had begun to notice. I touched my hand to Joanne's arm and said, "C'mon, they're not worth it. Let's just go."

Her daughter stood behind me. "Yeah, Mom, let's just go."

But instead of going, Joanne walked further into the store and yelled, "I'm not leaving until I get my money back!"

And the manicurist, who was still sitting at her little station, yelled back, "No money back!"

By then everyone in the store had gone silent. Immediately to our right was a wall of women up high with their feet in tubs, sort of like an audience in bleacher stands.

"C'mon, bitch, let's take this outside!" yelled my little sister.

The manicurist responded with something unintelligible, to which Joanne responded by pulling the purple foam toe separators out of her toes and throwing them at her. Only she missed, and hit a customer in the back of the head. The customer hunched forward and put her hands over her head, and I pulled my sister out of the store.

I felt sad for Joanne. She was a single mother who'd put herself through school and worked hard to make a living as a nurse, and she rarely treated herself to anything. She spent all of her time as a care-taker, both at work and at home, and she'd always done this alone—she'd never believed in herself enough to date a man who was good to her, so no man she ever dated was good to her. And this one special thing she was giving herself didn't end up being special at all. The lady had rushed her. She'd made her feel small. And I saw then a fundamental difference between my sister and me. I'd gotten away from our childhood home— I'd had the shoulder on the side of the road—and she was left there alone, with no choice but to fight. She'd been fighting since she was three and stood in between my father's belt and me. And she was still fighting. What a struggle it was to know when to fight and when to flee.

After we left the nail salon, I took my sister and niece shopping, and we laughed and held hands and made things better. Then

I drove back to Massachusetts from Baltimore, fighting through several more panic attacks on the way, taking circuitous detours on back roads to avoid the highway when I could.

Once I was home, I stopped driving on highways completely. I was defeated. It had been more than a year since my last panic attack, and I'd thought I was cured. Then one drive changed everything. *When we're in a child place,* Norm had told me, *we go home.* I couldn't stop thinking about my sister, how I'd gotten away from our parents but she hadn't. The way I'd always assuaged my guilt for leaving her was to remind myself that she never got it from my parents like I did, that I was the first-born, the target, and she was the round angelic baby who almost died but didn't. In my heart, she was still that baby, and I was wrapping her in sparkling things from a jewelry box with a twirling ballerina inside. But I was aware of my helplessness, the vastness of it, and how the past keeps happening, though it remains so firmly out of our reach.

"The potential is always there," Norm said, as I sat pouting across from him on the big white couch, "for any of us to revert back to a child state. We all have the capacity for panic, so there is no *cure*, per se. But as long as you can continue to separate the child from the adult, panic will never rule you again."

Norm suggested that we do some EMDR to process what had happened on that Brooklyn highway, but I wasn't ready to go back there. And my inability to drive on highways simply became a fact of my life.

"Be careful," said Norm. "Avoidance is what panic eats for breakfast."

FIFTY-TWO

Things at the new pond-side barn started out promising. When I went to bring Claret in from the paddocks, he came to me. Where I led him, he followed me. What I asked of him, he gave to me. And though we weren't piaffing and passaging around the arena, I rode him on my own, and we did okay. But I was aware that I still needed help. There was so much I didn't know, and in the school of dressage, I was a toddler. So I tried a few lessons with Laura, the barn owner, and she seemed mellow and knowledgeable, and Claret seemed happy, so I agreed to let her train us.

Laura had grown up on the property, and her father built the barn for her when she was a girl. If life were an experiment, she would have been my opposite: a girl whose parents wanted to give her everything. I wondered what it had been like for her, growing up with that unshakable haven, knowing that wherever she went in the world, she had that to come home to. I wanted to ask her what Christmases were like, what any ordinary morning was like, when the day shone ahead like a big fat jewel.

One day after a lesson, I was giving Claret a bath in the wash stall and he began to spook. I don't know if it was the closed space of the stall or the birds flying in just over his head to a nest in the corner or the snake of a hose near his feet on the ground, but he started taking little hoppy steps as his head shot up and his lip quivered. I could see he felt trapped. As he tried to flee, he lunged forward, but the crossties stopped him and he fell backwards, his hind legs buckling beneath him. Now he was at the apex of panic, the adrenaline bulging out the veins in his neck, his hooves scrambling as he launched himself up and this time broke the crossties.

Fortunately, Sal, the equine massage therapist who worked on some of the horses there, happened to be standing nearby and helped me get ahold of him. "There, there," he said in a gentle melodic voice that seemed incongruous with his hulking stature and rolled up sleeves bearing his muscles and tattoos. As he helped me lead Claret back to his stall, I thanked him and booked Claret's very first massage. "He's sure going to need one after that," I said.

The next time Claret started to spook in the wash stall, I quickly unhooked the crossties while he hopped around, and I patted his neck. He was breathing hard, and I knew he wanted to flee again. "You're okay," I said, keeping my hand against him. "You're okay." And after a few seconds he was standing still again. When he turned to put his nose against my arm, I reached into my pocket and gave him a cookie, and with each chew, I could see him relax a little more. After another cookie, he began to lick my palm in a slow rhythm that seemed to be calming us both.

Just then, Laura walked over to me. "Enough babying," she said. "He needs to learn to deal."

She took Claret from me abruptly and tied him back into the wash stall, and I could see the tension returning to his face, his eyes darting nervously at me and the door and the hose on the floor. I went to soothe him, but Laura told me to get out of the way. She turned on the hose, and as he started to spook again, she yelled, "Cut it out!" But he couldn't cut it out. I knew; I had lived it. He was panicking, and I was watching the fear escalate, watching him try to get away. When he scooted over in Laura's direction, she smacked him. "Don't you crowd my space!" she yelled. Then she turned to me. "He's too big a horse to be losing his shit like this. Believe me, you don't want him smashing you into the wall. He needs to learn to stand still and respect your space." She had a point. But even though I was a novice who had little more than a thimbleful of knowledge about horses, I knew what it was to be a flight animal. And I knew that the way to Claret's heart would never be with a hard hand.

It didn't take long before I learned that the kind of lesson we would have depended on Laura's mood. Sometimes she sat in her chair in the doorway and taught the entire lesson without moving. Other times, she was up, yelling, chasing us around the arena. "Toes *in*, hands *down*, *look* where you're going!" As I focused on my hands, I'd lose the position of my feet, and when I focused on my feet, I'd tilt my head down, and it seemed that I couldn't get the independence I needed in my various body parts, or the synchronization.

On one very hot day, Claret and I had been circling the arena for over an hour. We were drenched in sweat, and I couldn't seem to get it right, and a storm was coming. Through the little windows I could see the clouds rolling in, so dense I could almost feel their weight pressing on the roof. "I think he's had enough," I said meekly. I had come to accept that the cost of learning to ride a horse was to have someone yelling at you three days a week, so I rarely spoke up at all. "He's fine," she said. "Now hands *down*, feet *in* . . ." I was trying to get Claret to canter. I hadn't cantered him in weeks, since Laura had started us on her training program. Everything I'd learned and read taught that you ask a horse to canter with the outside leg back, but Laura was insisting I ask with my inside leg. And I could not pick up the canter.

At one point, Laura's helper poked her head into the arena. "Hey guys, there's a tornado coming. Just heard it on the radio. One touched down five miles from here."

By then the rain and wind were already starting to whip against the windows and batter the roof. "Okay," Laura said. "Try it again."

"We're going to die," I said.

"No, you're going to canter."

So in a moment when she'd looked out at the crumbling heavens, I snuck my outside leg back and asked him to canter. And he cantered. I stroked his neck. "Good boy!"

"Now you're finished," Laura said.

I led Claret back to his stall and wondered how long it would take for a tornado to travel five miles. I gave him a cookie and buried my nose into his neck while he licked my open palm. I didn't care that we were both sweaty—I took in the musk of him, and it grounded me. I began to massage Claret's back, which I thought might be tight after our lesson, and he whipped his head around to massage mine with his lips, the way horses do to each other in the fields. "Thank you," I said. The wind picked up, and we both stopped to look out the window. The trees were starting to bend, and the charcoal sky was beginning to boil. I considered trying to find better shelter but quickly decided against it. We were two wild things, he and I, and I would not leave him. Let the tornado come.

FIFTY-THREE

Twenty years later, the corn still grows along the road. The old stone buildings still stand, some making a crooked ascent toward the sky. And the grounds are still beautiful—hilly, green. A few years after I left the Montrose detention center for the last time, it was condemned and shut down, and the Army National Guard bought the land. I walk from building to building alongside Major Kohler, a tall, affable veteran with eyelashes most women dream about. He's wearing fatigues and a black beret, which suits his dark hair and handsome features well. Though he's supposed to be escorting me, he lets me give the tour. "Here's where I stayed," I tell him, pointing to a mansion-size stone building that, even in the daylight, looms dark. Ivy spindles across its stone face, obscuring more than half of it.

Major Kohler sweeps his eyes over me. "It's hard to believe *you* were in a detention center." I'm wearing a flared skirt, a lacy camisole, sandals, and a necklace I made out of kyanite, labradorite, and Roman glass. "What did you do wrong, anyway?" he wants to know.

I consider his question and find I have no good answer. "I ran away."

The military has already renovated most of the buildings, many for office space, some for barracks, but a few are still in disarray. We walk through one that's been gutted. Scraps of wood and nails are strewn across the subfloor. "Be careful," Major Kohler says, holding the door for me. The dirt from the rubble turns my toes black.

The grounds are vacant as we stroll from building to building. There's something intimate about sharing this quiet time with him, this late afternoon, these steps through the grass with this stranger who's willing to let me go back, open doors, climb steps, crest hills. I can still see the girls piled into the bathroom, elbowing each other for water. I can see us on our knees, scrubbing the floors with steel wool pads. I can see us jammed together in that one big room with nothing to do but stare again and again at the same sullen faces, playing Spades over and over and poring over magazines until we memorized every recipe for pie, dreaming of a different life.

Major Kohler asks why I ran away, and again, I don't know how to answer. How do I tell a stranger an answer like that? But then I realize the answer is simple. "I ran away because I believed there was something better out there."

"Did you find it?" he asks.

I look around at the land and remember how I once gazed at it from inside the barred windows, how I longed for this, here, now—this very moment. A groundhog skitters by, all fat with summer. "Yes," I tell him, "I did." And something about the way Major Kohler slowly nods his head makes me believe he understands.

As we start to head back toward my car, we come upon a spider in her web in the corner of a building. The light pressing against it has created a brilliant rainbow, and we stare silently for a moment at the luminous silk. "It's kind of like your life in a way," says Major Kohler, "finding a rainbow in a spiderweb."

A place inside me turns quiet. *Some of us didn't make it through.* A phantasm comes into focus, taps against me from inside. Taby. Her blue eyes. Her laugh. Her hair in the sun. Sometimes I think I can feel the impact of the car crash that killed her only two years after she left the Jackson Unit. I imagine the volume of it, the force. I imagine her laughing in her last seconds, probably with a beer in her hand, tilting her head to feel the wind rush through her open window.

And Dallas. On a summer night three years after he wrote our names in bubble letters, he blew his head off with a shotgun. His last moments are harder for me to picture. I get as far as his hands shaking at the barrel, its large hole of a mouth pointed at the center of his face. His face—that's where, each time, I'm sent back to the mountains, to his inquisitive and playful eyes. I keep seeing that ready smile, those dimples. And I hear his voice—*I'm comin' for you.* I can't let him pull the trigger.

I almost didn't make it through, either. When they released me from the Jackson Unit, things between my mother and me didn't change: it wasn't the happy ending I'd hoped for that day when Mr. Ware put a Cat Stevens cassette tape into my hand and I drove off suddenly reunited with my family. I will never know why, exactly, my mother had so much hatred for me, but I think part of it was displaced hatred for herself. Part of it may have also been the demands I brought to her young life, and the divorce battle with my father, when I told the judge I no longer wanted to live with her, and a raw jealousy that was born the moment I started to become a woman—but knowing these things didn't change them. So I spent a few months in her apartment before moving out: I ran away from her for the last time by driving off with the first guy who was reasonably nice to me. He was a construction worker with long hair and freckles and a habit of putting his cigarettes out on the heels of his cowboy boots. I had just turned sixteen. He was twenty-four. Our life was threadbare.

After years of bouncing back and forth between institutions and the streets, I'd finally come to a halt, and I didn't know what to do with myself in the stillness. I didn't know who I was. I didn't know how to live in anything other than the present tense. What I did know—what I felt late at night when I was the only one awake—was a nameless desire pulsing in me so insistently, so powerfully, that I thought it would crack me open.

I got a job as a hostess in a restaurant and started drinking after my shifts, whenever the bartender felt like sneaking me shots. I didn't love the man I lived with, and when I started coming home at four in the morning with the scent of other men's cologne on my neck, he left. Weeks later I let a man I barely knew slip a needle into the tender part of my arm, and for the first time, my desire was sated. That was all it took—that one rush, that one moment that rose up from my life like a hydrogen bomb. *Here*, it was saying, *is your present tense*. In the months that followed, there was nothing else. I shot cocaine into my arms until the track marks became scabs, which I kept poking through with more needles. It was summer, and unlike the other junkies, I didn't try to hide my arms—I wore those dark red lines proudly wherever I went. Some might say my flagrant display of what should have been my wicked secret was, in fact, a cry for help, but I think it was more a kind of testimony, as was the blood left on the sheets after I'd lost my virginity: *I have endured.*

I went days without sleeping or eating. I weighed eighty-five pounds. I was shrinking; I was being consumed. And it felt right, as if this were the destruction my life had been heading toward all along. So I pledged myself to cocaine, gave all the love I had to it. I worked as a stripper on the Block in Baltimore for it. I hocked almost everything in my apartment for it. I scammed for it. I unsuccessfully tried to break into a neighbor's apartment with a butter knife for it. I slept with men I wouldn't want to admit to knowing for it. And even after accidentally overdosing—after falling unconscious into a fit of seizures on my kitchen floor—I woke still wanting it.

I was nearly dead when I finally put the needle down. I'd lost my apartment and was living with a fellow junkie named Kevin in a rodent-infested house in the middle of nowhere. We slept on a bed without any sheets, and at night I could hear the mice scratching in the nightstand next to my head. One day it had started to rain. Kevin had taken a mouthful of pills and had systematically and inexplicably begun to move what few belongings I had left out onto the lawn. Raindrops were beading up on my stereo, which I struggled to lug back toward the house. I begged him to stop, but by then even my voice was weak. The rain picked up, made a rustling sound like a forest of old leaves waking to wind. Kevin didn't speak. And he didn't stop. His eyes looked past me, disconnected, inhuman.

Seeing that look in his eyes, I knew then that I'd become exactly like the people in those N.A. meetings I'd attended when I was at the Jackson Unit, the people whose lives I couldn't fathom back when I was flirting with Dallas and watching the sun set over the mountains. I remembered what they'd said about addicts having to "hit rock bottom" in order to stop getting high, and how for many addicts that bottom is death. Maybe it was the ghostly way Kevin was standing there, almost transparent, pulling out the last little scraps of my life into the rain. Maybe it was the rain, its impenetrable gray, the way it was collecting on my stereo. Maybe it was how Kevin was holding my box of record albums, tilting them forward, aiming them for the grave.

Maybe it was that for the first time in my life, I was too weak to run.

What I knew was that I was as low as I was going to get. Any lower would have been in the ground.

Knowing this, I managed to summon one last flicker from my spirit—the same spirit that first sent me running out the door of my father's house with an answer I would later forget that I had: *No*. No, I had not wanted my parents' violence. No, I had not wanted to spend my teenage years institutionalized for a crime I didn't commit. No, I did not want to have loveless sex, and I did not want to mistake sex for love. No, I did not want this corpse of a man killing my music. I did not want death.

I corralled what traces of strength I had left and pulled my box of records from Kevin's hands. He resisted at first, and his eyes, for a second, flared, but then like a monster that pops out of a 3-D movie, he quickly receded, and I left him standing there in that overgrown grass in the rain. I called a friend, and we filled her car with what we could and left the rest to the rodents.

After I drove away from Kevin's that day—after I dropped to my knees and cried every kind of cry I could cry and begged any God who would listen to let me keep my life in exchange for a vow I would keep all of the years after: I would never get high again—I asked my grandparents for three hundred bucks and got a tiny apartment on the top floor of an old Victorian. And slowly, slowly, I began to heal.

I didn't have much in the way of internal reserves—there hadn't been a lot of love in my life, and my confidence was as creaky as my living room floor—but I had a belief stubborn enough to weather any bomb: the belief that there was beauty to be had in this world. There was love. And thanks to the Jackson Unit, my sanctuary in the mountains, I'd been given enough love to carry me through the darkness still to come. So I took that love, that wonder, into my new days. I noticed things like dandelions sprouting up in sidewalk cracks, and the way it felt to go for a walk and know I had a place to come home to, and stars. Sometimes life felt vast and unknowable, and sometimes a terror fished through my heart so intensely that I was left gasping. But I kept walking, kept looking, kept writing in notebooks about what I saw. And the pages added up—the days added up—to something.

Ultimately, there was no one thing that lifted me from the muck of my past. But there was my first real boyfriend, who was free-spirited and funny, who gave me crystals he'd mined in Arkansas and who taught me that sex with a man could actually feel good. There was a beautiful friend—a fairy with long red hair—who brought me chocolate cake and poems, who sang to me, who was compassionate and generous and true. There was an older man who rode a Harley and who introduced me to the ocean and Joni Mitchell and beurre blanc sauce, who gave me a haven for five years in which I could heal. During that time, there were hikes deep into the woods, explorations into unmarked caves, sublime moments swimming with stingrays in the sea. There were the books I devoured, the ones I should have read in high school— Steinbeck, Salinger, Plath. There was the poetry of Mary Oliver, who put into words a peace I carry with me still. There was the day I walked into a room that seemed as big as a baseball field, holding two No. 2 pencils and that same stubborn hope—the one that almost killed me, the one that saved my life—that I could keep moving forward. There was the day I learned that I'd passed my high school equivalency test. And there was the day I went to my first college class—on a campus where I would later teach—ready to learn.

I was one of the lucky ones.

Major Kohler and I run into two other guardsmen who greet him with a salute. I know they're curious about me and why I'm there, walking around with Major Kohler. In the parking lot, we lean up against Major Kohler's pickup, and I tell them briefly about my time there. They listen, while the sun drops and swells and the air begins to cool.

One of them says he's heard ghost stories about Montrose.

"Really?" I ask. "Like what?"

He shoots a glance at Major Kohler, then at his friend, then finally to me. "A lot of guys here say they've heard a girl crying." He turns his head and points. "Word is she hung herself right back there in that building."

The officer beside him nods slowly. "I've never seen her before, myself, but one of my buddies swears he actually saw her one night. Looked right at her!" He motions with his hand by gliding it forward in my direction. "Probably wasn't any farther than you are from me."

I'm jolted by the memory of that story and how even now, twenty years later, it still lives.

FIFTY-FOUR

The tornado ended up skirting the edge of the pastures, far enough not to damage us, close enough to roar. Claret pushed his nose into my hand, and I held his head and stroked his neck and spoke to him, such soft things, and it wasn't long until the rain stopped, and the clouds dissipated, and I walked Claret out to the wet grass so he could eat, while a cluster of starlings rushed up from a fence rail and dove down all around us. Claret and I shared a bond I'd felt building all my life, from my earliest memories, from the earliest sounds of hoofbeats storming through me, and I knew he was not happy.

One of the ways he'd begun to express his unhappiness was through what had become a regular habit of headshaking. Sometimes he'd randomly start tossing his head up and down violently while he was being ridden, as if a bee had flown into his nose. Because there was no way to predict when he might do this, it almost always startled me. Then the two of us would flail in unison as I struggled, and usually failed, to hang on to the reins.

"I think his body is uncomfortable," I told Laura one day while she was on him.

"I think it's his mind that's the problem," she said. And then he bucked her.

I had a vet come out to examine him anyway. "Yup," he said, "horses don't lie." He diagnosed Claret with chronic allergic rhinitis and put him on antihistamines, but the headshaking only got worse. And so did Laura's frustration with it. Meanwhile, Claret, who I was coming to believe was all heart, had changed his attitude toward Laura after she bullied him in the wash stall. He'd become defensive, less willing to do what she asked, which made her ask more forcefully, which made him say no more forcefully, until they'd firmly entered a pattern I recognized well. Within weeks, their relationship deteriorated to pure combat: whenever she attempted to ride him, he bucked, kicked, backed into things, or simply refused to move. I could see the anger reddening her cheeks. *It's because he doesn't trust her,* I thought.

That trust was further tested when Laura left Claret tied alone in the wash stall for two hours. She did it when I wasn't there, but I found out about it later when I asked her how his halter had gotten broken. That's when she explained that she was trying to teach him "to deal" by leaving him alone in the wash stall until he could get past his fear and relax, but eventually, instead of relaxing, he broke the crossties again, and this time his halter, too. Hearing this, I had a sinking, queasy feeling. I understood what she was doing—it wasn't much different from CBT, from the running in place I'd done over and over to the measure of a doctor's stopwatch—but I knew by then that Claret, like me, needed something more, something with a little heart.

After that, it was nearly impossible to take Claret into the wash stall. And he continued to become more and more anxious, until I could no longer predict what would cause him to jump—a bird, a flower bending in a breeze, a person in the distance, a trash can, a chair. It seemed there was nothing that couldn't potentially terrify him.

My horse, simply put, was panicking.

Then one day Claret decided that he wasn't going down to the far end of the arena at all. It turned out that in addition to all the other things he was afraid of, Claret was also afraid of cows, and through the windows at that end he could see the two new cows that had come to live across the farm. Every time Laura asked him to venture toward them, Claret refused vehemently. She put her leg on him, and he kicked out sharply from behind with his own. She tugged on the reins, and he spun around madly. She smacked him on his flank, and he backed her into the wall with a bang. No matter what Laura did, she could not get him to walk to the other end. He must have backed her into the wall five times before she finally got off and "ground-schooled" him right there in the middle of the ring. She raised the whip to him, and he reared up, away from her, his eyes bulging, his mouth peeled back in a kind of grimace. But she had his reins and wasn't letting go. "When I touch you," she told him, "you move away. You fucking move away!" She smacked him on his flank with the whip, and he darted away.

I had been told many times by many riders that there is nothing we can do to a horse that can compare to the roughness with which they treat each other in the herd: it's perfectly normal for horses to bite and kick each other to establish their position in the hierarchy, and I had to remind myself of this as I watched. Laura was merely establishing her position as alpha mare, which was a natural thing to do, and crucial to our safety as riders. But the more I watched, the more my heart disagreed. Sometimes when a thing feels wrong, no amount of logic can make it right.

After about five minutes of ground school, Claret began to submit, and Laura got back on him. He was marginally calmer, but she still could not make him go down to that far end. This was a rider who had climbed far up the ranks of dressage, who had taught many riders and ridden countless horses over the years, who commanded the respect of all the other horses at the barn, and yet she could not make my horse walk from one end of an arena he'd been in a hundred times to the other. Claret had spirit, and despite the trauma of his ground schooling, I was proud that he'd come through with his spirit intact, as if to say, "What part of *no* don't you understand?"

When she was finished with him, the fur over his eyes and under his ears had darkened with his sweat. I walked him back into his stall and put some hay down for him. "You're a good boy," I told him, and he answered by touching his nose to my hand. I unbuckled his girth, then scratched the wet fur beneath it. Once his saddle and bridle were off, I sponged him down with a cool bucket of water (I wasn't about to take him back to the wash stall again). And when I came around to sponge his right side, what I saw sucked my breath away. He was bleeding. One of Laura's strikes with the whip had left an inch-long slice in his flank.

I bit back tears and kissed him gently, just next to the cut. "I'm so sorry." I kissed him again. "I'm so sorry." I said it over and over, until it became a kind of mantra. Claret arched his head around so that I was embraced between his shoulder and his neck, and I kissed his face, then wrapped my arms around him, and we stood there for a period of time that felt nothing like time.

"I'm thinking of sending him to a horse whisperer," I told Laura the next day.

"Don't waste your money," she said. "All they do is run the horses around all day until they're tired."

I looked at her and thought about the good life she'd had. And yet, it hadn't made her a better person. It hadn't filled her with love. Sometimes I think we're born with all our love already in our hearts, the way we're born with a certain amount of intelligence or eyelashes or the ability to dance.

It takes a certain kind of power to lead a horse, and after three trainers, I could see how sometimes that power grows malignant, like the blackish things Larry pulls out of people's brains. There is no question that horses can transform us, but only those of us whose hearts are open.

"Listen," she said, "he's the wrong horse for you. He's too dangerous. You got duped when you bought him."

"He wasn't always like this," I said. "He wasn't like this when I brought him here. I think he's just really sensitive."

"He's an asshole," she said. "He's like a bad boyfriend, and I, for one, am finished with him. You should sell him for a dollar and move on with your life."

She spoke these words with such certainty that I began to wonder if they were true. I was an amateur rider after all, and Claret did kick, did buck, did back into things. By then I'd stopped riding him altogether. "Maybe next week," Laura had been saying. "Maybe then he'll get his shit together and be safe enough to ride." But now Claret and I were two trainers to the wind, and he was a lot of horse, and he was out of control, and I didn't know how to help him.

All that was true, yet still I believed in Claret—as I'd once believed in a better life, as I believed I could reach the other side of panic. I believed in my first moments with him—the way he frisked my pockets the day we met, the way he followed me eagerly on the day I brought him home, then shared those breaths with me as I stood with a child's trust in his stall—moments that felt truer than almost anything else I knew. I believed in his trust in me, in his gentle gaze, in the love I felt when I stood facing him and he reached his head over my shoulder and pressed me to his chest with the underside of his face. And I believed in his physical ability, that when he was feeling good, he enjoyed teaching me to ride. So after Laura walked away from me disgusted and I stood dazed in the doorway for enough minutes to lose count of, I slipped into Claret's stall and wept quietly into his neck. And he stood quietly in return, allowing me to soak and sniffle into his fur, until I faced what I already knew: though my horse was out of control and I had no immediate answers, I was going to stand by him.

How I would do this was much less clear, but I decided to start by leading him to his scariest places, as I'd done for myself when I'd been afraid to leave the house but left anyway. I thought back to his eagerness on that day I brought him home, as I led him from thing to thing and, with curiosity and willingness, he put his nose on it all. *Let it be like that,* I thought.

Our first destination was the wash stall. As I led him in, I walked confidently, my back straight, and I spoke to him. "We're just going in and out. You'll be fine." I kept my voice soft but firm, my hand steady on his lead rope, and he followed me in. "Good boy," I told him, handing him a cookie. "This is your wash stall." We stood there while he ate his cookie, and when he was finished I walked him back out. We repeated this until it became a kind of game and he followed me into the wash stall happily, ready for his cookie. With slow but steady steps, I walked him to the big yellow snowplow on the ground, the one he always tried to dart away from, and when we got there, he leaned down and put his nose on it. "Good boy!" I squealed. And we went like that from thing to thing—"this is your white plastic chair that sometimes blows over in the wind," "this is your potted plant," "this is your bench piled with stuff in the corner"—and after a few days, he seemed to look forward to putting his nose on the scary things, and to the cookies that came after.

The one place I didn't lead him was to the far end of the arena.

In trusting my instincts, I'd begun to help Claret, but I knew I still couldn't do it all alone. Fortunately, there are people who are kind, who are willing to take a few steps alongside us when the road gets rough. One of those people was Sal, the massage therapist who massaged some of the most fancy horses in the world and who always seemed to be around at exactly the right moment. "I know you love Claret," he said, "and I know he's a good horse." He put his arm around me and told me he knew someone who could help me. Then he gave me the phone number of a well-known Grand Prix dressage trainer—an Olympic hopeful—who competed internationally and had a reputation for being fearless. She would ride anything. And she was going to come ride Claret.

When Jane Hannigan arrived, I was expecting a strapping hulk of a lady, not the thin, fine-featured woman who was standing in front of me with a bouncy blond ponytail. "So this is Claret," she said, giving his forehead a rub. Claret and I checked her out. She wore tall boots and a sea-colored silk scarf. She was gorgeous.

She led him into the indoor arena, where a crowd of people, including Laura, had gathered in the corner, waiting for the big showdown: Claret against Jane. "You might not want to watch this," said one of the women, smirking. This was the same woman who'd once said to me, apropos of nothing, that her horse hated my horse, to which I responded that only people hate. But this time I ignored her and the rest of them, and Jane ignored them, too, as she began to walk Claret around the indoor. "He's scared to go to the far end," I said.

"He'll be all right," said Jane, steadily leading him away. When they got near the far end, he tried to turn around, but she stood with him and coaxed him on, and he went with her. I could see in his eyes that he was nervous, but one thing I knew about him was that he wouldn't do anything he didn't want to do. She walked around once each way, while everybody watched, and then she stuck a foot in his stirrup and hoisted herself over him from the ground—a feat most people can't do. "Uh-oh," someone said.

When Jane asked Claret to trot, he went forward without shaking his head. But when they approached the far end, Claret started to spin. Jane was fast. She sat into the saddle and spun him the other way, then patted his neck and told him he was a good boy. And he went forward. It had been so long since I'd seen him truly move that I'd forgotten how lithe and lovely his trot was. Laura muttered to one of the women beside her, "She rides balls-to-the-wall. I could ride like that, too, if I wanted."

Jane rode Claret perfectly, her ponytail swinging jubilantly behind her. She asked him to canter, and he cantered as if he were in the middle of a show ring. I wondered if some part of him was aware of the crowd that had gathered, if maybe he was showing off just a little. I looked at his eyes, and this time they were shining.

Without acknowledging the crowd to my right, Jane rode up to me. "He's actually a really nice mover. But do you want to know what the problem is with your horse?"

I nodded. "Yes."

"He's a righty—stiff to the right and hollow to the left. Imagine you're on a mountain, and you feel someone starting to pull you off. You're going to resist and pull the other way. That's what happens to Claret when you pull on the right rein, which is where his imbalance is. He thinks you're pulling him down the mountain, so he pulls back. And when he feels he can't get away, he starts to fight."

I nodded again. "That makes a lot of sense."

"I know there's a lot more going on than that," she said, "but from a training perspective, that's something I can help with. That's why we do dressage—to help the horses, and riders, be balanced."

I wanted to sprinkle yeses all over Jane like confetti. Yes to balance. Yes to that kickass ponytail. Yes to Claret.

After that, Jane rode him around some more, and with nothing but a happy horse to watch, the crowd trickled out. I didn't see Laura leave, but I was grateful to look over and find her gone.

Jane came back a few days later and gave me a lesson. It had been a while since I'd ridden, but she made me feel brave. "Look how happy he looks. He likes when you ride him." I sat up a little taller.

"That's it," she said. "Now be aware of his right rein—instead of pulling on it, just lightly sponge it with your hand. Let him know you're connected to him. You're communicating with your hand but giving him room to move at the same time."

I squeezed the rein in my right hand like Jane told me, and Claret's neck softened.

"Good. Now let him feel your legs around him. Give him a little tap with your inside leg when he starts falling in, and balance that with the outside rein."

Again, I did as she instructed, and Claret responded by balancing himself. "It's like a constant conversation, riding—isn't it?" I said.

"That's exactly what it is," she said, smiling. "Yeah, I think you two are going to be just fine. Now give him a pat and tell him he's a good boy."

Now it was my turn to smile. I reached forward and stroked his neck with my hand. "Good boy!"

Jane came up and patted his neck, too. "You can ride him alone, too, you know."

"Really? Everyone's been saying how dangerous he is."

Jane shook her head. "I've seen dangerous horses, and yours isn't one of them. You can do it," she said. "I know you can."

The day after Jane came, I walked into the arena. Three people were riding—including the woman who told me her horse hated my horse—and Laura was giving a lesson to one of them. Her voice was shrill, but I didn't look at her. I looked at Claret. "You just listen to me, okay?" I said, stroking the side of his face. As I walked him to the mounting block, I could feel everyone's eyes on me. I hadn't ridden Claret on my own in ages, and I knew they all thought I was crazy. But I didn't care. I took a deep breath and mounted my horse. "We can do this," I said, reaching forward to give him a pat on the neck. We started off by heading down the long side. "That's it, that's a good boy." I didn't stop reassuring him, which was, in part, a way of reassuring myself. Claret's ears turned back toward me as I spoke. "Okay, so we're heading to the far end now, and I know this has been scary for you, but you can do it. I'm with you." *Avoidance is what panic eats for breakfast,* Norm had said, and I didn't want to keep avoiding things. I gave Claret another pat and made sure not to pull too hard on his right rein. Then I did what Laura, a lifetime horsewoman and trainer and competitor hadn't been able do: I rode Claret to the far end.

That's what panic taught me.

I thought about Gerta and Laura and even the woman who tried to ride Claret on the trail—how, despite their experience and their will, and my deference to that experience and will, Claret said no to each of them. It turns out that what he'd been asking for all along was for me to take the lead—for me to trust myself.

It was as if Claret knew. He didn't shake his head or kick or spin or buck or back up. He just kept going. *We* kept going, two wild things.

FIFTY-FIVE

Larry's coworker was hosting a backyard barbecue, an ordinary thing that from the start didn't feel ordinary. It happened in increments, all the ways that day felt familiar. It started with the thick summer heat, a wall of it. It started with the tall grasses past the yard beginning to bend, with the new ledge of cool air arriving at our table like an announcement. "There's a storm blowing in," someone said. But the gray sky, which seemed to keep hovering lower and lower, did nothing to stop the din of the party, the rhythms of voices, people carrying heaped plates to their tables, the kids springing up in the bouncy castle pitched on the other side of the yard.

Larry and I left our table to get dessert, and as we stood on the line, a fair-skinned girl walked past us, skinny and slightly pigeon-toed. Though I had never seen her before, I recognized her. (I have always been pigeon-toed, a trait my mother tried unsuccessfully to rid me of when I was young by making me stand with my spine straight against a wall, my toes turned ballerina-style outward while balancing the Baltimore yellow pages on my head.) I recognized this waifish and awkward girl as kin.

Across her nose was a cut, which appeared to be recent, and in the few seconds it took for her to walk past me, I thought so many things, the loudest of which was *be careful*. I had once thought the same thing while sitting on my front step in the grip of panic, but this felt different—this girl worried me for a reason I couldn't quite place. She touched something visceral in me. And then she was off in the yard somewhere, and the new cool wind started lapping at us, and I asked Larry if he was really going to eat the two pieces of cake and piece of pie he'd loaded onto his plate, and he said, "It's a party," and I smiled, and he smiled.

He hadn't even made it through the first piece of cake when his coworker's wife came to the table and put her hand on Larry's shoulder. "A girl fell out of the castle," she said. "On her arm. I think she might be hurt."

I knew instantly who it was. Larry got up, and I followed him, and we both saw her at the same time, the cut across her nose, her pale face now bleached, and her forearm misshapen, bent the wrong way. As we approached this young girl, I wasn't sure what would happen. Despite Larry's many years of medical training and practice, he had a phobia of one common medical problem: broken limbs. They terrified him. If we were watching a movie and he thought someone was about to break an arm or leg, he'd run out of the room, then call to me from afar, "Did it break? Could you hear it? Could you actually see it?" You couldn't even talk to Larry about a broken limb without him shuddering. We looked at each other briefly, as if to say, *Here it is, that scary thing*. But he didn't pause: he went right up to her.

She was whimpering lightly, and her lips had a blue cast from the shock. "I'm Larry," he said, "and I'm a doctor. What's your name?"

"Alyssa Mayberry," she said.

"So you fell, huh?"

She nodded.

"I'm going to take a look at your arm, okay?"

She nodded again, and Larry gently took her arm into his hands. You could see the dip where it had broken in half. Larry asked if she could move her fingers, and she wiggled them. He asked her to squeeze his fingers, and she did, quite hard, and I said, "You're strong," and she smiled a little.

The aunt who had brought Alyssa to the party said she would call the doctor, and I said, "Her arm is broken. You need to call an ambulance." And I could still hear my mother's voice from all those years ago, after I'd run through the glass door: *Call a fucking ambulance!* So they went to call an ambulance, and Larry kept hold of her arm, one hand on either piece, as if he were willing it to fuse back together, as if his hands could make it so. At one point, Alyssa reached her other hand out and took mine. She just held my hand like that. There was no fear. There was a child who was counting on us to be calm, so we were calm. We spoke to her in such quiet voices. And there was a weighty stillness among the three of us as we all held on—a stillness that made everyone else stay back and watch from a distance. And soon Alyssa stopped whimpering, and the blue hue of her lips began to fade. An occasional drop of rain touched one of our faces while we waited for the ambulance, but none of us moved for what seemed like a very long time, until finally we could hear the howl of sirens approaching.

Things moved quickly then. The EMTs asked Alyssa her name and her age, which was nine—the same age I was when I broke the glass and my mother tended my own injuries. When they wrapped Alyssa's arm in an air cast, I saw then how broken things can be held together, how they can heal. I saw how the bad things we fear might happen do happen and, with courage, sometimes we can be the ones to make them okay. I watched Alyssa be brave, and I watched Larry be brave, and I knew that when it came time again for me to be brave, I would think of her—the child who needed us to be calm, the child who let me hold her hand—and I would be brave. When the EMT asked if she was ready to go, she stood up from her chair and walked, in between the two men, to the ambulance. "At least it wasn't my leg!" she told them in a chipper voice, and her gratitude traveled back to us, covered the distance she was making, and would make, and does still.

FIFTY-SIX

On an icy morning, Jane came to get Claret and move him to her barn. I must have looked nervous, because she smiled at me and told me everything would be okay. And in that moment, I trusted her, in part because I trusted myself, and because I'd stayed true to Claret and believed she'd seen in him what I'd seen: a horse that, in the right environment, could flourish. He could be brave. His body could become strong. He could be happy. And I believed Jane could teach us, and that Claret and I could teach each other.

Unlike the first time I tried getting him on a trailer, this time Jane walked him on easily. He and I were both ready to leave. Laura stayed out of sight, and as I drove away from her barn for the last time, I remembered those words that had rung through me with such velocity: *I know what I need.* As soon as we arrived at Jane's barn and unloaded Claret, I took his lead rope and stood with him on the gravel road outside the barn. He was alert—his eyes intently scanning, his ears pricked forward—but he seemed relaxed, as if he knew he was someplace good. He pressed his nose into my hand, and I gave it a little squeeze. "I'm here," I told him. Then I showed him around the barn, and he put his nose on everything.

As Jane began riding Claret, it was as if he'd forgotten the great ride they'd had together when she'd first come out to Laura's barn to meet him. Now he was consistently defensive, and this worried me. He still kicked and bucked and backed up. But Jane was unfazed. "He just needs to learn I'm not going to fight with him. He's a sensitive horse, and he needs time to understand that he's safe and that he's not in trouble. And I have to be clear about what I ask, which, right now, is to simply go forward."

What I learned quickly about Jane was that she rode each horse differently. She considered the whole horse, each as its own individual with its own physical and mental characteristics, and Claret was the only one she took her spurs off to ride. "He doesn't need them," she said. And no matter what he did, she stayed calm. If he backed her into a wall, she waited until he went forward, then patted his neck and told him he was a good boy. There were no miracles, but Jane was patient and fair, and slowly, Claret began to respond. Instead of kicking five times during a ride, sometimes he would kick only once, and eventually sometimes not at all.

Jane was kind to Claret. If he got nervous on the crossties, she didn't yell at him or leave him there alone. Instead, she joined me in feeding him treats until he forgot about being nervous. Jelly Bean Therapy we called it.

Usually we could figure out what he was spooking at—a towel on the floor, a beam of light from the window, a barn worker carrying a ladder—but one day while he was on the crossties, he started eyeing the empty mat below him, cocking his head and snorting and jittering about. "There's nothing there!" I said, nonplussed.

Jane laughed. "He sees his shadow. He's spooking at his own shadow."

"I know how you feel," I said, patting the side of his face. "I know exactly how you feel."

Soon I developed a routine with Claret—little things we could count on that brought us both comfort. Every time I entered the barn, he whinnied, then nickered, then poked his face through his stall window. "C-Monster!" I'd exclaim, leaning forward to kiss his nose before feeding him a carrot. After I put his bridle on, I patted his forehead. And at the end of a ride, I breathlessly flung my body over his neck and told him he was a good boy. In his stall, I gave him his favorite cookie with the peppermint on top, and he wrapped me against his body with his long neck. Then there were the things I whispered to him each day before I left. One of those things was always *thank you*.

After a while, Claret stopped kicking and bucking and backing up and started to become fit and more confident in his work. But Claret's headshaking didn't stop, and that still made him difficult to ride. We worried that his bit was bothering him, so we tried different bits and then a bitless bridle, but nothing seemed to make a difference. Then someone suggested it might be neurological. I had three different vets come out to examine him, but they found nothing. Upon their advice, I tried him on different allergy medications and steroids, but none of them helped. And then I came to the heart-wrenching conclusion that I might have to send him to a field in Florida where he could retire.

When I discussed all of this with Jane, she convinced me to try one last thing: a complete workup at Tufts animal hospital. "Then you'll know for sure what you're dealing with."

FIFTY-SEVEN

As we pull into Hanscom Field, a small airport about twenty minutes from our house, I want to beg Larry to turn around and go home. Instead, I tell him I'm cold, and he parks the car and takes off his leather bomber that he bought from a pilot magazine, and hands it to me. For a long time, he's been asking me to go up with him in the Warrior, a small single-engine plane that he sometimes rents, and today I said yes. Since he started taking lessons, he's earned not only a pilot's license but his instrument rating as well, and now he's talking about going for a commercial license. "What, in case you can't find a job as a brain surgeon?" I teased. But I know the reason: ambition, pure and simple. If there's more to learn, Larry wants to learn it, and flying is no different.

I, on the other hand, had been steadily rejecting his invitations for the past two years to take to the sky with him and learn a little something for myself. "One day," I'd always say. "Soon." Planes in general scared me. Small planes terrified me. And every time Larry asked me to go with him, it felt like he was asking me to die.

But I once told Larry that he had to be more than his fears. And each time I said no to flying with him, I was not more than my fears, and I was missing another chance to know him—which is why I do not ask him, when we pull into the parking lot at the small airport, to turn around.

Before we arrived, I asked him a plethora of what-ifs—what if the engine stalls, what if we get a bird strike, what if lightning strikes the wing, what if we hit wake turbulence, what if I throw up?—to which Larry steadfastly reassured me that all will be fine, that he can land the plane even if the engine fails, that he has checked and rechecked the weather and there is nothing but clear skies, that a bird strike simply won't happen, and even if it did, he could still land the plane, that we won't get close enough to another plane to hit wake turbulence, and finally, that the plane is equipped with two paper bags, should I decide to throw up.

When we arrive at the plane in the lot, it appears smaller than I'd even imagined. "I think there are some birds bigger than this," I say, but Larry is already focusing on his preflight routine, examining the wings, checking to see there are no deformities in the flaps and that the ailerons move up and down; checking the gas tank, and taking a fuel sample to confirm it's the right kind of fuel and that there's no water contamination; examining the wheels, the lights, the rudder and elevator of the tail, and, of course, the engine. Larry helps me climb up onto the wing to get in, and when he shuts the door, I am once again reminded of how small this plane is. My stomach is doing a wobbly jig, and I keep catching myself holding my breath, while Larry starts the plane and begins checking gauges. He turns on the radio and hands me a headset so that we can hear each other once we get going. For a moment, my nervousness abates as I watch him, the shine in his eyes, the knowledge, the quiet pride. When Larry was a year old, he was sent away from his parents on a plane. Since then, he's never asked for much from anyone; he never wanted to scare anyone away. And though I'd been saying no to him for two years, he never got mad or even let his disappointment show; he simply kept asking, the way a boy might ask, earnestly, with hope. Larry turns to look at me, and his voice fills my headset. "Are you ready?"

I gulp. "Yes."

Larry pushes the button on the radio, and I can tell he's still a little shy to speak to the people on the other end. "Hanscom Ground, Warrior Two Six Three November Delta, ready to taxi with Bravo."

Their response comes through my headset, too. "Warrior Two Six Three November Delta, Hanscom Ground, taxi to Runway Two Niner via Juliet Echo."

"Roger. Juliet Echo for Runway Two Niner, Two Six Three November Delta."

As we taxi to the runway, I take a breath and let myself be excited. Norm once told me that anxiety is a form of constricted excitement, and I can feel the truth in his words. On the adjacent runway, a plane takes off and another lands while Larry has returned to checking his various gauges. He turns the wheel back and forth and revs the throttle, then calls the air traffic control tower for clearance. "Hanscom Tower, Warrior Two Six Three November Delta, holding short, Runway Two Niner, request closed traffic for pattern work."

"Warrior Two Six Three November Delta, Hanscom Tower, clear for takeoff. Make left closed traffic."

"Roger. Clear for takeoff."

Larry begins to accelerate, and pretty soon we're racing down the runway in the heart of the plane's loud growl. Larry is focused ahead, touching different instruments, and then suddenly we're off the ground, hovering over the runway. As we ascend, my stomach wavers, and I close my eyes. I can feel the pull of gravity, the fight in my bones. *Surrender*, I tell myself, and when I open my eyes, we're already high over the trees.

As we crest our projected altitude, Larry banks the plane, and I watch the sun fatten to an orange globe while the moon presides over the darker half of the sky, a silver-white disk. I feel like a child, like we are both children, like Larry took a toy and made it airborne, and we are at the start of an adventure.

"Do you like it?" Larry asks.

When I agreed to come with Larry, I never expected to like it. But as I watch him doing this thing he loves, as I watch the earth and sky—so much of it at once—I learn something I thought I already knew: that the only way to truly trust someone is to risk what you think you can't risk. "I love it," I say.

But we agreed to take it slowly, so after a few minutes, Larry calls in for the landing. As we descend, I feel like we're taking a piece of sky back with us. And when we touch down, it's smooth all the way.

B̲ack at home, I retire to my office to write about our flight. I want to remember always how swift Larry was with his knowledge, how graceful. I want to remember the moon, how it hung over the airport, how even after we landed, I couldn't stop staring at it. I want to remember the feeling of elation I had as we tied the plane back down: the feeling of moving toward another fear, as if into a headwind.

FIFTY-EIGHT

On the day of Claret's trip to Tufts animal hospital, I drove to the barn wondering if Jane's mother, an experienced horse-woman who helped Jane at the barn and who was going to drive the trailer to the hospital, was going to talk the whole way or if she'd let the rain speak instead. Quieted with my own anxiety, I was hoping for the latter. But I didn't have to wonder for long.

"My mom will take Claret in the trailer, and you'll meet her there," Jane announced, walking briskly down the aisle just as I was reaching my hand into Claret's stall for a first hello. "We'll pick him up from the hospital later."

Though I knew the answer, I asked the next question anyway. "How do I get there?"

When Jane confirmed that I'd have to take the highway, my first thought was to tell her that was impossible. But as I heard the words in my head—*I can't drive on the highway*—I knew I couldn't say them out loud. I couldn't let myself be that helpless.

I admired Jane. She was a cowboy at heart. She was kind to horses—she always considered what the horses were thinking and feeling, which was so different from the ways Gerta and Laura had treated Claret—but this kindness was balanced by a calm refusal to back down. "They're prey animals," she reminded me once, "and I make sure they know they're *my* prey." It was her fearlessness and strength that kept her on every spinning, bucking, rearing horse that dared to challenge her. It kept her safe. And every day that I trained with her, I swallowed a little of that strength as my own. "Show me you're going to stay on," she'd tell me as Claret and I trotted around the indoor. "Make me believe that if he spooks right now, you're not going to fall off." It was a matter of intensity then: a focused mind, firm but quiet hands, a strong core, steady contact between my legs and Claret's body. It was a matter of trust. *I trust that I will stay on, that I will lead this horse, that he will trust me as we go.*

Not wanting to admit my highway fear to Jane, I quickly sifted through my other options—calling a taxi and being late to the hospital or driving with Jane's mother and being stranded there without a car—and realized they weren't options at all. Claret needed me. I needed to be there, for him and for myself. It was a matter of trust. So I got into my car, took a sip of water, and started down the road.

As far as I can remember, I have always yearned for the road. Since I was four and my father drove us through Times Square, I fell in love with the world of driving, with the changing snapshots of movement, the lights, the buzz, the luminous earth going by mere feet, and sometimes inches, outside the window. It is hard to think of my life in any significant way without thinking of being in cars. When I was a child, the car represented safety, a place for music, a place to be closer to my family than most other times. When we were in the car, my parents never hit me. I could watch the sides of their faces without reproach. I could pretend that every song was being sung to me or that the happy songs belonged to me. I could memorize every word. Sometimes I wanted us to never get out, even if that meant that my mother and sister and I would drive around forever looking for my father's car. Sometimes even now, I'm still there, on one of those damp summer nights, breathing in that air. Sometimes even now I am a runaway, a girl for whom the road, simply, represented hope. Back then I always sensed there would be a turn that would be the right turn, a street that would be the right street, one where a house would be, where a mother would be, where the life I so desperately wanted would be. As long as I was on the road, I could carry that hope. Even when I was afraid of the highway, I never stopped carrying it.

And as I drove down the road toward the highway, with this chestnut horse I loved in a trailer in front of me, I realized that just as I had climbed out of my childhood, pried the vines from around my ankles, and emerged into the light, I had to take my last steps through panic. When I'd quit drugs, I put on the one dress I had, powder blue with buttons down the front, and I walked several miles up the road to apply for a job selling carpet. I was still recovering from the ways my addiction had ravaged me, and I had to stop along the road several times to steady myself. When I got to the carpet store, the manager liked me—I could tell by the way he kept touching the end of his pen to his lips as he pondered the answers I gave his questions—but because I didn't have a high school degree, he couldn't hire me. But when I'd set out that day, I was determined to get a job. And I did. When he said no, I walked across the street and got a job as a waitress instead. Then I went home and slept for a long time. When I woke, I played music. I cooked French toast the way my grandmother had, crisp on the outside and soft in the middle. I went about each small step of living believing in the next step. That was it. One step and then the next. It was the kind of present-time I'd been accustomed to, and it served me well. Right now we are here. All we can do is try and take our next step the best we can. For me, driving was the last thing panic still had of mine, and I was ready to take it back. Here was my next step.

The highway ramp came quickly but not too quickly. As I merged onto the 495, I was grateful for the steady spring rain, which seemed to soften everything. My heart was hammering, but I kept my eye on the trailer up ahead. Inside of it was Claret, and we were two wild things. *I am with you*, I told him as the rain scattered over my windshield, and as I said it I knew I wasn't saying it to him alone.

A team of doctors and interns greeted us at the entrance to the hospital, and Claret was besotted with the attention, looking everyone in the eye, poking his nose out to look for treats. Tufts animal hospital was a strange place, with huge long corridors and vast rooms with abandoned medical equipment lurking in the shadows. It was in one such room that we were waiting for a doctor to come examine Claret's sinuses with an endoscope. While we waited, I walked Claret around and let him sniff things. Then we stood in the center of the room while a crew of eight interns gathered off to the side and observed us. Claret started to fidget, so I pressed my hands into his back. I massaged along his spine, and he turned his head around and began to massage mine. I heard a small murmur among the interns and looked to see them smiling. "We've never seen *that* before," one said. "That's some bond you two have."

As they sedated Claret, I stood beside him, my hand firmly at the base of his neck, and remembered his prepurchase exam a year and half earlier, when I'd held the weight of his head in my hands and knew that, whatever his tests showed, I was already his. Now, in this strange large room, I watched the doctor, an elegant woman who spoke with her eyes, insert the scope and gently glide it up Claret's left nostril, then the right, while he stood calmly, occasionally swaying a little on his feet, his eyes closed, as if deep in a dream. I didn't take my hand off of him, and in a few moments of wooziness, I realized I needed him to steady me at least as much as he needed me.

The doctor's findings confirmed what the first vet had diagnosed him with: allergic rhinitis. Claret's chronic allergies had caused scarring to the inside of his nose. She explained that this scarring could cause his nose to feel funny—itching, tingling, pressure—and could be the reason for his headshaking.

The next day, they put him under general anesthesia for a CT scan. I wasn't allowed to be there for that, so I came in the evening when it was over, and the same doctor reported that the results of the CT were normal: there was nothing neurologically wrong with Claret. "We've just brought him out of Recovery, so he's still a little shaky," she warned. As I walked into the wing of stalls, I called to Claret, and I heard the faintest nicker in response. When I saw him, my knees stuttered, and I had to grab on to the door of his stall to right myself. His eyes were swollen almost shut, there were small trails of blood seeping from his nose, and he was shivering. I immediately opened the door to his stall, but one of the techs stopped me. "He's too unsteady right now. It's not safe to go in there yet." But as soon as the tech was out of sight, I went in.

"Hey there," I said, gently reaching my hand to Claret. He was wobbly on his feet, and making gentle snorting sounds when he breathed. Small rectangles of fur had been shaven off his neck and face where they'd injected the contrast dye. He put his nose in my hand, and I kissed his face, which smelled of alcohol and iodine. "You're coming home tomorrow," I whispered.

Claret turned away from me and started shuddering more forcefully. I poked my head out of his stall and called for the tech. Though he'd warned me not to go into the stall, neither of us mentioned it when he returned. "He needs his blanket," I said. And without questioning me, he left to find it.

In the meantime, I began vigorously rubbing Claret's body all over, trying to generate some warmth. Even after we put his blanket on, I didn't stop warming him. I would be strong for him. I would touch him back to me. And as his shivering slowly abated, I knew he would be okay.

Despite the high dose of steroids prescribed to Claret after his hospital stay, the headshaking persisted. So I stopped his medication and called one last doctor, a flamboyant woman who was reputed to be very smart, if a bit kooky, and who didn't bother with the niceties of polite conversation. She took one look at him and said, "He's catabolic. Something in him is breaking down."

"Catabolic?" I asked. "Don't you want to see him under saddle?"

She waved her hand to dismiss me. "I don't need to see him under saddle. I see him right here, in front of me."

After more of an examination, she told me she believed he had an inflammatory problem, that it would take a lot of tests and trial and error to figure it out, but she would figure it out. I thanked her, but I was finished with trial and error. Instead, I drove home that day planning out Claret's retirement and wondering how many times a year I'd be able to visit him if I sent him to Florida. I cried openly, even at traffic lights, without caring who was looking. I was losing him, this creature who had changed my life, who had taught me the kind of courage that can only come from love.

But when I got home, I realized something: I wasn't ready to give up. I thought about how many times I'd run away, how no matter what happened on the streets, I kept running, unwilling to give up my search for something better than what I had. I thought about all the things I'd tried when I panicked, how many therapists I went careening away from, how many books I'd opened and closed, how many exercises I'd attempted, how many strangers I'd reached for. There had been an answer—I knew that—I just had to figure out what the question was: what can panic teach me?

Why should Claret be any different? For him, the question was simple: how can I help him heal? The way I trusted myself with my own life, I would have to trust myself with his. So I sat down at my computer and started researching inflammation in horses. I researched allergies. I researched headshaking, which, according to every vet I'd spoken to and everything I read, was one of the most difficult conditions to treat in horses. I spent hours printing out articles, taking notes, making phone calls, and then I made a plan. I ordered a bunch of supplements—including MSM, chondroitin, glucosamine, and spirulina—from a well-established company, and I started Claret on a new regimen.

About a week later, Jane called me. "I just had the most perfect ride on your boy." The next day, I rode him, and he didn't shake his head once. In fact, he felt more fluid in his body than I could remember him ever feeling. "Do you think it's the supplements?" I asked.

"I don't know. But you better knock wood, just in case."

That day Jane and I gave him a shower in the wash stall, his first since our time at Laura's. I talked to him, touching him steadily and feeding him carrots while Jane gently showered him off. "You can do this," I told him. I was talking to him calmly but firmly, the way I'd talked to that child part of myself, who, like Claret, was once afraid of the shower, who was once afraid of her own shadow, and I could feel him responding, lowering his head, relaxing. In between carrots, Claret turned and licked the side of my face.

The next day, I gave him a shower by myself. And over time, he began to enjoy his time in the wash stall. He took jelly beans and carrots from my hand, and he licked me, and I talked to him, and we played with the water: I'd arc a gentle spray in front of his face, and he'd poke his mouth in and out while I laughed.

I think Jane and I knocked on every plank of wood in that barn over the next weeks, as Claret moved around the ring like a new horse. People who'd been watching him for months suddenly didn't recognize him. "Who's *that*?" they asked, and one woman remarked about how transformed he was. "I bet you could sell him for a lot now."

I shrugged. It didn't matter to me if Claret was fancy or not; it mattered only that he was mine, and that he was happy. "I wouldn't sell him for anything," I told her and smiled. And we trotted on.

FIFTY-NINE

As we move deeper into the woods, I feel Claret's back and neck start to relax. I reach forward and run my hand along his coppery mane, and he exhales a long breath. The morning light cuts through the grand old pines in glorious shafts, while the sound of our moving is a steady sound, and the shadows around us are deep. I like to pretend we're in a secret forest, that each nook has its own story, its own particular magic. *Listen*, I want to say, *it's all around us*. But Jane, who is beside me on her horse, is already listening. With each step, we are departing and arriving at once: there to our left is a marsh; now the reeds are thinning out, segueing into ferns; now we are entering another cool pocket of air left over from last night; now we are warm again.

On a straightaway, we pick up a trot, and everything comes faster: an outcropping of massive rocks to our right, cardinals and jays and finches darting between branches, a small stand of dead trees poking up from the silty ground, all the little bits of life in this particular second of their trajectory. In the distance something moves, and I imagine it's Pan, the half-man half-goat Greek god of the wild, slipping rhythmically between the trees. A musical and virile god, he was often seen dancing with the woodland nymphs. But he was also responsible for arousing sudden irrational fear in those who passed through his forests, and thus the word *panic* was born. If he emerged, I would turn to him now and say, *Thank you. I am of these woods.*

And then, the forest lets us go. We break into a meadow, to which I can see no end. Jane and I both halt to let our horses adjust to the expanse, to the full gleaming sun pouring over it all. I wrap my legs around Claret a little more firmly to remind him that, while he is carrying me, I am also carrying him. I'm wearing tall black boots, like the pair I'd once seen in a shop, the kind of boots I was told would come later, after I'd been riding for a while. In response to the light pressure of my legs, Claret turns his head around to the left and watches me with his left eye. I smile. We don't have to say anything. We are already saying everything.

"Okay," Jane says, "gather your reins."

As I do, Claret turns his head forward again, and Jane picks up a canter. We follow behind, easing onto the path that slices between the fields. I let my hips move with Claret, back and forth in the three beats of his swing, and as we gather distance, still I see no end.

When I was ten, I won a bike-a-thon to raise money for cystic fibrosis. I don't remember what made me decide to do it, but I remember knocking on door after door in my neighborhood and outlying neighborhoods, asking people in my shy voice to sponsor me. That year, I rode my bike whenever I could. It was the year before I ran away for the first time, though I thought about running away on those days when I would ride so far that I'd get lost. *What if I never went home?* I'd wonder. *What if I kept on going?*

On the day of the bike-a-thon, I climbed onto my blue Ross three-speed, and I rode. Over and over, through morning light and noon light and late afternoon light, I rode the same two-mile course through the neighborhoods, getting my card stamped with each loop. At one point in the day, I noticed that a group of kids were cheating—they were taking a shortcut that knocked out a good chunk of the circuit. I couldn't understand why they would do that, maybe because winning hadn't even crossed my mind. I was simply riding my bike, and everything in me felt like it could keep on going. That day I rode forty-eight miles and raised more money than anyone else who'd participated. My prize was a new ten-speed, which I lost, along with most of my belongings, when my father abruptly moved us back to Maryland a year later. But what I never lost was that feeling.

And that's the feeling I have now—on this fourteen-hundred-pound chestnut horse, this wild thing, this friend, this beautiful and mischievous and huge-hearted creature—as we move together: like he and I could keep on going.

Since I can remember, I'd been hearing the sound—the galloping hoofbeats, the fracas of wild forceful motion. But now the herd of horses in my mind has gone quiet. Now he has finally come.

ACKNOWLEDGMENTS

Once I realized panic wasn't a bad word, and I began to use it, friends and strangers came forward and shared their fears with me. There were a lot more panicky souls out there than I realized, and to those brave people I am grateful.

I am forever grateful to Larry Chin, my harbor, for his unwavering love and support; to Cathy Chung, for her light, and her Snoopy shirt, and for shepherding this book even when it was a shaky thought: my road always leads to you; to Chris Knutsen, who helped immeasurably in shaping and championing these pages; and to Dawn Eareckson, for her steady presence and insights through several drafts.

Thank you to Clarinda Harriss and David Bergman, my earliest professors, who urged me to keep writing, and to Stanley Plumly, David Wyatt, and especially Michael Collier, a mentor of the highest order.

To the Bread Loaf Writers Conference, thank you. There's no mountain in the world like that one.

Thanks to David Kuhn, Becky Sweren, and the awesome team at Kuhn Projects for their care and expertise in taking my book in hand.

ACKNOWLEDGMENTS

I am deeply grateful to my editor, Millicent Bennett, for her keen eye and creativity, and for making it fun; and to Ed Winstead, Erin Reback, Dana Trocker, and the rest of the talented team at Simon & Schuster for ushering this book into the world.

I am indebted to Alessandra Bastagli, Dominick Anfuso, Sharon Guskin, Meakin Armstrong, Rebecca Donner, Jennifer Miller, Youmna Chlala, Ken Chen, Paul Yoon, Vaddey Ratner, Lauren Alleyne, Miriam Altshuler, Chris Castellani, Kim Adrian, and Dr. Ysaye M. Barnwell for the varied and important ways they've supported me.

Thanks to Pat Ciliberto, Peggy Murphy, and Bill Vivyan, for shining.

Thanks to the delightful kitchen staff at Debra's for the food and cheer that sustained me while I wrote this book.

I tip my riding helmet to Jane Hannigan, the world's best trainer and my dear friend, for taking a chance on us: I wouldn't have been able to tell this story without you. Thanks also to Sibley Hannigan and Jenn Raffi for the help and encouragement.

So much gratitude goes to Joanne Zaks, Kiana Logan, Karen Thompson, Daren Chentow, Heather Holland, and Norm Ephraim for their love and encouragement; and to my parents, for answering some of the difficult questions.

And I am forever grateful to C. E. Courtney, for the match.

RITA ZOEY CHIN was born into a world that roared: a Queens apartment near Kennedy Airport, where planes were a constant storm. But a move to Maryland four years later introduced her to quiet and creeks and the sounds of cows in the distance, and when she saw horses for the first time, she discovered the most primal source of her wonder embodied in their movement across the field. An award-winning poet, Rita holds an MFA from the University of Maryland. She now lives in the Boston area, where she teaches memoir classes for Grub Street, mentors troubled teenage girls, and rides her mischievous horse.